A Guide to British Military History

A Guide to British Military History

The Subject and the Sources

Ian F.W. Beckett

Pen & Sword
MILITARY

First published in Great Britain in 2016 by
Pen & Sword Military
an imprint of
Pen & Sword Books Ltd
47 Church Street
Barnsley
South Yorkshire
S70 2AS

ISBN (Number to be inserted)

A CIP catalogue record for this book is available from the British Library

Typeset in 11/13 Ehrhardt
by Imprint Digital

Printed and bound in India by
Imprint Digital

Pen & Sword Books Ltd incorporates the imprints of Pen & Sword
Archaeology, Atlas, Aviation, Battleground, Discovery, Family History, History,
Maritime, Military, Naval, Politics, Railways, Select, Social History, Transport,
True Crime, and Claymore Press, Frontline Books, Leo Cooper, Praetorian
Press, Remember When, Seaforth Publishing and Wharncliffe.

For a complete list of Pen & Sword titles please contact
PEN & SWORD BOOKS LIMITED
47 Church Street, Barnsley, South Yorkshire, S70 2AS, England
E-mail: enquiries@pen-and-sword.co.uk
Website: www.pen-and-sword.co.uk

Contents

Abbreviations

BIHR	*Bulletin of the Institute of Historical Research*
BJMH	*British Journal for Military History*
EHQ	*European History Quarterly*
EHR	*English Historical Review*
HJ	*Historical Journal*
HR	*Historical Research*
IHR	*International History Review*
INS	*Intelligence and National Security*
JAH	*Journal of African History*
JBS	*Journal of British Studies*
JCH	*Journal of Contemporary History*
JICH	*Journal of Imperial and Commonwealth History*
JMH	*Journal of Military History*
JRUSI	*Journal of the Royal United Services Institute for Defence Studies*
JSAHR	*Journal of the Society for Army Historical Research*
JSS	*Journal of Strategic Studies*
MAS	*Modern Asian Studies*
P&P	*Past and Present*
SOTQ	*Soldiers of the Queen*
SWI	*Small Wars and Insurgencies*
VS	*Victorian Studies*
W&S	*War and Society*
WH	*War in History*
WMQ	*William and Mary Quarterly*

Introduction

What exactly is military history? Forty years ago this would have been a straight-forward question. Just as warfare for many centuries prior to the mid-nineteenth century had been governed by the unchanging factors of the speed of man, the speed of horse and the availability of fodder, so military history had meant only battles, campaigns, great commanders, drums and trumpets. That approach arose from the way in which military history originally developed as being largely the preserve of military professionals, who studied it because they believed that it taught practical lessons for use on the battlefield. Indeed, it is probably the last form of history that is thought to be directly applicable for the learning of lessons: it is still used in military academies to draw out lessons that may inform decisions by future commanders on the battlefield, or decisions that will be taken by future commanders at the strategic level. Beyond its use by military professionals, military history was also used in the past to support national history and nationalism, as part of the heroic national story of the 'Deeds That Won the Empire' kind.

Asking that question now is much more difficult for the study of war has been transformed by the application of new methodologies since the 1970s, not least by the development of the 'war and society' approach to conflict, with its emphasis upon the study of the impact of war upon states, societies, institutions and individuals. In more recent years, further methodologies have begun to be applied to the study of war and armed forces, with examination of such issues as identity, memory and gender. Similarly, a traditional Euro-centric emphasis within military history has now also been extensively corrected with the growth of a more global perspective. Certainly, it is now more generally recognised by those previously hostile to military history within academe that war and conflict must be integrated into the wider narrative of historical development. To recall Trotsky's nostrum, war is the 'locomotive of history'.

This guide seeks to introduce prospective research students to the debates, issues and resources within the field of military history. While the wider European and global perspectives are not neglected, as will be apparent from the discussion of contexts in Part I, there is an emphasis upon the British experience of war in the early modern, modern and contemporary periods in Part II, the periodisation corresponding approximately to the existence of a standing army in Britain from the seventeenth century onwards, and its origins in the sixteenth century. Nonetheless, an effort has been made to relate the debates on the nature of British military history since 1500 to wider issues connected to other armies. Indeed, one increasing area for study is comparison between the British and other experiences of war. Part III is concerned with sources for the study of British military history, though not just in Britain.

Military history is the subject of great popular interest and has been populated by non-academic historians and writers whose work often borders on what might be characterised as military pornography. Indeed, in the media, 'military historian' is a much abused, and all too easily applied term. Popular military history is characterised by often being narrative in structure rather than analytical, and invariably follows a simply explanatory path, is often enamoured of equipment and technology, and tends to place combat centre stage. Such writing is not referenced in this volume. By contrast, academically rigorous military history is characterised by being firmly based on archival/primary source research, on having a firm line of argument or overarching interpretation, on having a wide perspective, and having some comparison with other works in the field. What follows in this volume, therefore, is the integration of the military narrative within the wider political, socio-economic and cultural context. Like any other form of academic history, there can be significant divergence of interpretations between historians, and this will also become apparent, be it the nature of the 'military revolution' in Europe in the sixteenth, seventeenth and eighteenth centuries; the 'learning curve' on the Western Front during the First World War, or the nature of 'total war'.

It needs to be stated that naval history and emergent air force or air power history are the subject of other volumes in this series and, therefore, the Royal Navy and the Royal Air Force will not be a primary concern in this. Of course, it has also not been possible to mention every monograph, chapter, journal article or doctoral thesis on British military history since 1500, and a high degree of selectivity has had to be employed to represent the rich tapestry of academic research available.

PART I
Contexts

Chapter 1

The Historiographical Context

It is usually suggested that modern military historical writing in Europe was a product of the eighteenth-century Enlightenment, and of the new quest to discover underlying universal principles of war.[1] It might equally be argued that it began with the dissemination of classical works on the warfare of antiquity – such as those of the early fifth-century Roman author, Flavius Vegetius Renatus – in new vernacular editions in the sixteenth century. Machiavelli's *Art of War* in 1521 particularly drew upon classical examples to inform the conduct of war. Ironically, it was a moment when warfare was changing dramatically as a result of the gunpowder revolution. It has also been argued that few if any of the leading condottieri in the Italian Wars relied on anything other than their own hard-won experience to guide their military decisions.[2] To be sure, many of the military texts of the sixteenth century might best be characterised as simply military manuals. In *Of the Knowledge and Conducte of Warres* (1578), for example, Thomas Proctor extolled the virtues of Vegetius's writings, these having been translated into English by John Sadler in 1572.[3] Yet, in one other respect, they drew upon the pattern of antiquity in combining a degree of narrative with didactic military analysis. That pattern is glimpsed in the work of the very first acknowledged military historian in the western world – and also one of the first recognised historians – namely Thucydides, whose *History of the Peloponnesian War* was unfinished at his death in about 400 BC. He was an Athenian general and, until the nineteenth and twentieth centuries, it was nearly always soldiers who wrote military history.

---

1 Azar Gat, *The Origins of Military Thought: From the Enlightenment to Clausewitz* (Oxford: Clarendon Press, 1989), pp. 26–9.
2 F. J. Taylor, *The Art of War in Italy, 1494–1529* (Cambridge: Cambridge University Press, 1921), p. 9. See also Christopher Allmand, *The De Re Militari of Vegetius: The Reception, Transmission and Legacy of a Roman Text in the Middle Ages* (Cambridge: Cambridge University Press, 2011).
3 Roger Manning, *An Apprenticeship in Arms: The Origins of the British Army, 1585–1702* (Oxford: Clarendon Press, 2006), p. 129.

The narrative ended abruptly in 411 BC, covering only the first 20 years of the 27-year long conflict between Athens and Sparta but Thucydides set out to record events as accurately as he could in order that his text should be a 'possession for ever'. This did not mean that he did not have a particular historical agenda, not least in recounting the unsuccessful expedition to relieve the Spartan siege of Amphipolis in 424 BC, which led to his own 20-year exile from Athens. Indeed, Thucydides has been characterised as a 'revisionist' historian.[4] Nonetheless, the narrative was framed consciously in the belief that lessons were to be deduced from such a momentous war. Much the same might be said for the six volumes of the Earl of Clarendon's *The History of the Great Rebellion and Civil Wars in England*, which the then Sir Edward Hyde had begun in 1646: the first volume was not published until 1702, 28 years after his death. Clarendon claimed there was no 'untruth nor partiality towards persons or sides' in his narrative.[5] But he had been a key member of King Charles I's Council, and his history was intended as a vindication of Royalist principles.

Some narratives intended simply as memoir also emerged from the conflict that engulfed Britain and Ireland in the mid-seventeenth century. Such memoirs became more marked during the War of Spanish Succession (1702–14), with the publication of works by those who had campaigned with the Duke of Marlborough such as Sergeant John Millner (1733), Corporal Matthew Bishop (1744), Brigadier Richard Kane (1745) and Captain Robert Parker (1747). Much more significant, however, was the first truly modern analytical military history by a British soldier, Major General Henry Lloyd. Ironically, the Welsh-born Lloyd never served in the British army but in those of Austria, France, Prussia and Russia. Indeed, he was among the French soldiers accompanying the ill-fated Jacobite invasion of Scotland in 1745–6. *The History of the Late War in Germany between the King of Prussia and the Empress of Germany and her Allies* was published in 1766. Asserting that even soldiers had not yet fully managed to explain the dynamics of warfare, Lloyd sought to identify scientific principles of war through an exhaustive analysis of the campaigns in Germany in 1756 and 1757. A further volume published in 1781 covered the years 1758 and 1759.[6]

---

4 Donald Kagan, *Thucydides: The Reinvention of History* (New York: Viking, 2009), pp. 23–34, 223–34.

5 The Earl of Clarendon, *The History of the Rebellion and Civil Wars in England Re-edited from a fresh collation of the original MS with marginal dates and occasional notes*, ed. Rev. W. Dunn Macray, 6 vols. (Oxford: Clarendon Press, 1888), I, p. xiii.

6 See Patrick J. Speelman, *Henry Lloyd and the Military Enlightenment of Eighteenth-Century Europe* (Westport, CT: Greenwood Press, 2002).

Lloyd's rigidly mechanical approach to identifying universal principles was to characterise the work of the continental military theorists such as the Prussian, Adam Heinrich von Bülow, whose *Geist des neuren Kriegssystems* appeared in 1799. Most notably, the Swiss-born interpreter of Napoleonic warfare, Baron Antoine-Henri Jomini, adopted a similarly rigid anaylsis of the campaigns of both Frederick the Great and Napoleon in *Traité des grandes opérations militaires*, published between 1804 and 1811, and above all, in *Précis de l'art de la guerre* in 1838. In turn, Jomini was influential in shaping the work of Lloyd's effective military heirs in Britain such as Sir Patrick MacDougall, whose *The Theory of War* was published in 1856, and Sir Edward Hamley, whose *The Operations of War* appeared in 1866. Both again looked back to the campaigns of Frederick the Great and Napoleon, though Hamley also included more recent conflicts such as the American Civil War. MacDougall was the first commandant of the Staff College at Camberley from 1858 to 1861, and Hamley was the fourth between 1870 and 1877. Hamley's work remained required reading at the Staff College until 1894. In recounting examples from history, Hamley's preferred method was to present the facts of a representative case study as a means of deducing its lessons as pertaining to the principles of war.

The establishment of the Staff College reflected a growing sense of professionalism within the British army's officer corps as a whole, as did the emergence of professional journals such as the *United Service Journal* (later the *United Service Magazine*) (1829), the *United Service Gazette* (1833), and the *Journal of the Royal United Service Institution* (1857).[7] The *Professional Papers of the Royal Engineers* first appeared in 1837, and a volume of the *Proceedings of the Royal Artillery Institution* since 1848 was published in 1857. By the end of the nineteenth century there was a ready professional market for military history with such series as the 'Wolseley series' from Kegan Paul, Trench, Trubner & Co., or the 'Pall Mall series' from Hugh Rees. The former included George Younghusband, *Indian Frontier Warfare* (1898), and Count Yorck, *Napoelon as a General* (1902), while the latter included such titles as Lonsdale Hale, *The People's War in France* (1904), and John Gough, *Fredericksburg and Chancellorsville* (1913). Notwithstanding these productions, it is a moot point how far they were actually read. Two markedly intellectual soldiers, Sir Frederick Maurice and G. F. R. Henderson, both complained that the purchase of military books was left to mess secretaries as if they were cases of wine. Moreover, it was all too easy to get by with mutilated and abridged versions of original texts. Field Marshal Sir Evelyn Wood, who attended the Staff College in 1863–4, recalled later that one

---

7 See M. D. Welch, *Science and the British Officer: The Early Days of the Royal United Services Institute for Defence Studies, 1829–69* (London: RUSI, 1998).

fellow student required to produce an essay on Marlborough remarked that he would rely simply on Hamley's lecture notes: 'No, I shall serve up Hamley, Hamley, nothing but Hamley: that always gets me full marks.'[8]

Among the most influential of all the military histories of this period was Henderson's exhaustive two-volume study, *Stonewall Jackson and the American Civil War* (1898). Henderson taught at the Royal Military College, Sandhurst from 1890 to 1892, and then at the Staff College from 1892 to 1899. Yet, as Basil Liddell Hart later wrote, for a generation of officers 'to be able to enumerate the blades of grass in the Shenandoah valley and the yards marched by Stonewall Jackson's men is not an adequate foundation for leadership in a future war where conditions and armaments have radically changed'.[9]

The belief that military history taught practical lessons for use on the battlefield also prompted the beginnings of 'official' history. Famously, Liddell Hart was to write to the British Official Historian of the First World War, Brigadier Sir James Edmonds, that his volumes were 'official but not history'. Liddell Hart also characterised official history as parochial and patriotic.[10] The first recognisable official history was the two-volume *Journal of the Operations Conducted by the Corps of Royal Engineers*, published in 1859, and dealing with the Crimean War. The next, covering the Abyssinian expedition of 1867–8, did not appear until 1870 but, thereafter most Victorian campaigns resulted in official accounts. Though intended for a professional audience, they were not without controversy. In compiling that for the Zulu War, for example, Major John Sutton Rothwell 'uncritically incorporated the official reports on the battle of Isandlwana' and 'helped perpetuate the serious distortions they contained and the misconceptions to which they gave rise'.[11] Similarly, Frederick Maurice's official account of the Egyptian expedition of 1882, and Colonel H. E. Colvile's official account of the Gordon Relief Expedition, both took a decidedly partisan view of criticism of Garnet Wolseley's strategy.[12]

---

8 Field Marshal Sir Evelyn Wood, *From Midshipman to Field Marshal,* 2 vols. (London: Methuen & Co., 1906), I, p. 215.

9 Basil Liddell Hart, *The Remaking of Modern Armies* (London: John Murray, 1927), pp. 53–4.

10 King's College, London, Liddell Hart Centre for Military Archives (hereafter LHCMA), Liddell Hart Mss, 1/25/93 and 95, Liddell Hart to Edmonds, 6 and 13 Nov.1934.

11 John Laband, *Companion to the Narrative of the Field Operations Connected with the Zulu War of 1879* (Constantia: N & S Press, 1989), p. 13.

12 Jay Luvaas, 'The First British Official Historians', in Robin Higham (ed.), *Official Histories* (Manhattan, KS: Kansas State University Press, 1970), pp. 485–505.

Wolseley was always conscious of the value of influencing the written record, hence his sponsorship of unofficial accounts drawing on official papers such as George Huyshe, *The Red River Expedition* (1871), and Henry Brackenbury's two-volume *The Ashanti War: A Narrative* (1874). Wolseley's great rival, Frederick Roberts, was equally aware of the need to shape both contemporary and historical verdicts on his campaigns. The six-volume official history of the Second Afghan War of 1878–81 was actually suppressed, as was a subsequent two-volume version. Only a heavily bowdlerised single volume finally appeared in 1908. In part, it was due to Roberts's sensitivities, but also to subsequent political calculations in terms of the relationship between British India and Afghanistan.[13]

Controversy also dogged the official history of the South African War, the first volume written by Henderson being scrapped in its entirety in 1903 after his death. The opening chapters of the replacement volume by Frederick Maurice, dealing with the political background, suffered the same fate in 1905 amid concerns to smooth the reconciliation between Briton and Boer. The eventual four volumes, the last completed by Captain Maurice Grant after Maurice's death, were described in 1912 as 'a colourless statement of facts rather than one which might guide and form the opinions of soldiers'.[14] What might be seen as the rival six volumes of *The Times History of the War in South Africa*, edited by Leo Amery, appeared between 1900 and 1909. It began as a purely commercial venture. Amery intended to strive for accuracy and began the practice of circulating multiple drafts for comment by participants. But he was also open as to the propagandist spirit in which he compiled the text, feeling that it served the public interest, and represented the best means of forwarding the military reforms advocated by Roberts and his circle.[15]

Maurice believed that military history should educate the general public as well as the military reader. Edmonds, however, had a somewhat different purpose in mind when it came to the Official History of the Great War, publication of which stretched out from 1922 to 1948. As he wrote in March 1932, 'I want the young officers of the Army who are to occupy the high places later on to see

---

13 Brian Robson, 'The Strange Case of the Missing Official History', *SOTQ* 76 (1984), 3–6.

14 *The Times*, 13 Jan. 1912, Obituary of Maurice.

15 Ian F. W. Beckett, 'British Official History', in Craig Wilcox (ed.), *Recording the South African War: Journalism and Official History, 1899–1914* (London: Sir Robert Menzies Centre for Australian Studies, 1999), pp. 33–42; idem, 'The Historiography of Small Wars: Early Historians and the South African War', *SWI* 2 (1991), 276–98.

the mistakes of their predecessors, yet without telling the public too much.'[16] The solution was to mask criticism by hiding it in voluminous appendices. Moreover, as John Keegan has written, the prose style of Edmonds's volumes was 'so little informed by the humane spirit of general historiography that they might have been written by what the advance men for science fiction movies like to call "alien life forms" '.[17] Though some evidence was simply suppressed or massaged, Edmonds could not escape challenge altogether, duelling with the official historians of the Dominions such as C. E. W. Bean of Australia, and with some of his own assistants and collaborators. One assistant, Captain G. C. Wynne, had his name removed from the title page of the volume on Passchendaele, while Edmonds clashed repeatedly with Cecil Aspinall-Oglander, who compiled the Gallipoli volumes.[18] To be fair to Edmonds, there has been a vigorous defence of his approach and his merits as an historian in Andrew Green, *Writing the Great War: Sir James Edmonds and the Official Histories* (2003).

For many of those officers who contributed to the compilation of the Official History, but much more for the ordinary mass of wartime soldiers, regimental and divisional histories were an additional and important means by which individuals could commemorate their own role in the war.[19] Regimental history itself had originally been intended to inculcate young recruits with esprit de corps. No less than 70 volumes of *Historical Records of the British Army* by Richard Cannon had appeared between 1837 and 1853. The principal clerk in the Adjutant General's office, Cannon's work derived from a decision in January 1836 that a history of every regiment should be published 'with a

---

16 LHCMA, Liddell Hart Mss, 1/259/46, Edmonds to Liddell Hart, 8 Mar. 1932.

17 John Keegan, 'The Historian and Battle', *International Security* 3 (1978–9), 138–49, at 144.

18 There is an extensive literature on Edmonds and the Official History. See David French, 'Sir James Edmonds and the Official History: France and Belgium', in Brian Bond (ed.), *The First World War and British Military History* (Oxford: Clarendon Press, 1991), pp. 69–86; idem, ' "Official but not History": Sir James Edmonds and the Official History of the Great War', *JRUSI* 131 (1986), 58–63; Tim Travers, *The Killing Ground: The British Army, the Western Front, and the Emergence of Modern Warfare, 1900–18* (London: Allen & Unwin, 1987), pp. 203–49; idem, 'Allies in Conflict: The British and Canadian Official Historians and the Real Story of Second Ypres, 1915', *JCH* 24 (1989), 301–25.

19 Keith Grieves, 'Making Sense of the Great War: Regimental Histories, 1918–23', *JSAHR* 69 (1991), 6–15; Helen McCartney, 'Interpreting Unit Histories: Gallipoli and After', in Jenny Macleod (ed.), *Gallipoli: Making History* (London: Routledge, 2004), pp. 125–35.

view of doing the fullest justice to Regiments, as well as to Individuals who have distinguished themselves by their Bravery in Action with the Enemy'. The intention was to 'incite' the young soldier 'to emulate the meritorious conduct of those who have preceded him in their honourable career'. At the same time, the general reader would also find value in the series for, 'The fame of the deeds of the past and present generations in the various battle-fields where the robust sons of Albion have fought and conquered, surrounds the British arms with a halo of glory; these achievements will live in the page of history to the end of time.'[20]

The tradition was continued by a number of prolific authors of divisional and regimental histories after the First World War such as Christopher Thomas Atkinson, elected a Fellow of Exeter College in 1898, who served with 7th Division during the war; Reginald Everard Wyrall, a wartime subaltern, who was also known for social investigations; and Colonel Harold Carmichael Wylly, who edited the *Journal of the Royal United Service Institution* in 1913–23. As *The Times* noted after his death in 1964, Atkinson, who also produced a study of Marlborough in 1921, was 'not easily swayed by historical fashions and his interest, like his written style, had few frills'.[21]

Official and regimental history, and the work of soldiers primarily writing for other soldiers, all shared a particular characteristic with the military history increasingly also being produced by civilian authors. This was a preoccupation with the minutiae of war to the extent that it existed in a vacuum divorced from the realities of death and destruction on the battlefield. The trend was reinforced by the large numbers of memoirs and biographies emanating from both the Napoleonic Wars from the 1820s onwards, and the increasing number of colonial conflicts as the empire expanded through the course of the nineteenth century. Popular military history began to glorify the national story. A typical example was *Deeds That Won the Empire* (1897), originally written as articles for the Melbourne *Argus* by an Australian Methodist minister, W. H. Fitchett, who had a particular liking for tales of the Indian Mutiny. It was followed by Fitchett's *Fights for the Flag* (1898), drawn from another series in the *Cornhill* magazine; *How England Saved Europe: The Story of the Great War, 1793–1815* (1899–1900); and more in similar vein intended 'not to glorify war,

---

20 Richard Cannon, *Historical Record of the Twenty-Second or Cheshire Regiment of Foot* (London: Parker, Furnivall & Parker, 1849), pp. iii, xviii. All volumes had a similar preface and introduction though the wording varied slightly over the course of the series.

21 *The Times*, 19 Feb. 1964, p. 15.

but to nourish patriotism'. By 1914 *Deeds That Won the Empire* alone had gone through almost 30 impressions.[22]

In addition, however, there were also more nuanced grand narratives of the British military achievement. The first notable example was by a soldier. While influenced by Jomini, Sir William Napier was rather more interested in the drama of war than its underlying principles. Publication of his six-volume *History of the War in the Peninsula and in the South of France* began in 1828, and was completed in 1840. Some five years of research was devoted to the first volume, Napier securing copies of correspondence from British officers, and consulting French archives. The first volume, however, caused so much controversy among officers who believed that Napier had slighted them that the publishing house of John Murray refused to continue with the project: he was obliged to turn elsewhere. A lively pamphlet war ensued between Napier and his detractors, especially William, Viscount Beresford, whose conduct of the Battle of Albuera in 1811 was criticised in Napier's third volume. Napier was undeniably partisan in many of his assessments of leading figures and his political prejudices – he was a Whig – were abundantly clear. Nonetheless, he got his military facts mostly right and he was prepared to correct errors in future editions.[23] Above all, the highly melodramatic style provided memorable and enduring images of the British army at war, not least Napier's famous description of Albuera, 'But suddenly and sternly recovering, they closed on their terrible enemies, and then was seen with what a strength and majesty the British soldier fights. . . . Nothing could stop that astonishing infantry.'[24] Napier's work was widely read not only by soldiers but also by the general public to an almost unprecedented degree. It created an image of British military success that shaped the parameters of subsequent debate on military reform by constant reference to the Peninsular War, as well as inspiring future multi-volume Victorian histories of British wars.

Just as indefatigable in his search for sources as Napier was Captain William Siborn (later Siborne). Initially this was in order to construct his two remarkable scale models of the Battle of Waterloo, completed in 1838 and 1844. Unfortunately for Siborne, his detailed research, undertaken from 1830 onwards, contradicted the Duke of Wellington's version of the battle with respect to the timing and strength of the arrival of Blücher's Prussians on the field.

---

22 Craig Wilcox, *Redcoat Dreaming: How Colonial Australia Embraced the British Army* (Port Melbourne: Cambridge University Press, 2009), pp. 108–22.

23 Luvaas, *Education of an Army*, pp. 12–24.

24 William Napier, 4 vols. (US 4th edn.) *History of the War in the Peninsula and the South of France* (Philadelphia: Carey & Hart, 1842), II (book 12, chapter 6), p. 331.

Consequently, he ran into endless difficulties in completing and displaying the models: at one point he removed 40,000 Prussian figures to appease the Duke. Siborne died impoverished in 1849, and also frustrated that he had not been able to secure a permanent home for the models. They eventually found a home in the Royal United Service Institution in 1851: the larger 1838 model is now in the National Army Museum in London, and the smaller 1844 model in the Royal Armouries in Leeds. The fruits of Siborne's industry were also displayed, however, in his two-volume *History of the War in France and Belgium in 1815* (1844), and the selection from the raw material of his correspondence with participants published by his son, Herbert, as *Waterloo Letters* in 1891. So extensive was this archive, lodged in the British Library in 1894, that a further unpublished selection appeared in 2004.[25] Colonel John Gurwood published Wellington's own campaign papers and correspondence in 12 volumes as *The Dispatches of Field Marshal the Duke of Wellington* between 1837 and 1838.

Contemporary conflicts continued to inspire major descriptive works in the Napier vein such as Alexander Kinglake's eight-volume *The Invasion of the Crimea* (1863–87), Sir John Kaye's three-volume *History of the Sepoy War* (1864–67), and Colonel George Malleson's completion and expansion of Kaye, the six-volume *History of the Indian Mutiny* (1878–80). A barrister and travel writer, Kinglake witnessed the battles of the Alma and Balaclava. He had unlimited access to the papers of Lord Raglan, and also consulted French, Turkish and Russian sources. Almost inevitably perhaps, his generally favourable view of Raglan attracted the criticism of others such as Lord Cardigan: unconvinced, *The Times* characterised the first volume as 'historical romance'. But, as suggested by Hugh Small, *The Crimean War* (2007), Kinglake also misled those who relied subsequently upon his apparent wealth of detail rather than checking his original sources. Kaye was Secretary of the India Office Political and Secret Department until 1874. He had already written a three-volume history of the First Afghan War, *History of the War in Afghanistan* (1857–8). Malleson, who had held a number of posts in civilian administration in India, retired from the army in 1877. He penned biographies of both Robert Clive and Warren Hastings. The work of Kaye and Malleson has been described as 'massive, verbose, all-embracing histories: authoritative and dogmatic; entirely noble in sentiment, entirely British in attitude and sentiment'.[26]

25 Gareth Glover (ed.), *Letters from the Battle of Waterloo* (London: Greenhill Books, 2004).
26 P. J. O. Taylor (ed.), *A Companion to the 'Indian Mutiny' of 1857* (Delhi: Oxford University Press, 1996), p. 392.

The grand narrative tradition so well established in the nineteenth century characterised other magisterial histories in the early twentieth century, namely another history of the Peninsular War by Sir Charles Oman, and Sir John Fortescue's classic history of the British army from its origins until 1870. Oman's six-volume *History of the Peninsular War* appeared between 1902 and 1930, while Fortescue's *A History of the British Army* appeared in thirteen volumes (of which one had two published parts) with an additional six volumes of maps between 1899 and 1930. Oman, who was elected to the Chichele Chair of Modern History at Oxford in 1905, was certainly an 'exemplary researcher' but, unfortunately, his attitude towards documenting his sources was somewhat cavalier. Moreover, his work was suffused with the same kind of political prejudices as Napier – though Oman was a Tory where Napier had been a Whig.[27] Oman also wrote accounts of earlier warfare as *The Art of War in the Middle Ages* (1885) – later extended to the two-volume *A History of the Art of War in the Middle Ages* (1898) – and *A History of the Art of War in the Sixteenth Century* (1937)

Fortescue, a close friend of Oman, was the Royal Librarian at Windsor Castle from 1905 to 1926. Briefly, he was also the Official Historian of the Great War until removed in 1919 for his public criticism of Field Marshal Sir John French's contentious memoir, *1914*. In any case, Fortescue's belief that he had been commissioned to undertake a readable popular history was increasingly at odds with the views of Edmonds, who had been appointed as Head of the Military Branch of the Historical Section of the Committee of Imperial Defence to oversee the Official History. Fortescue had taken on the role reluctantly for patriotic reasons but he was not blind to what he saw as the value of military history. An abridged version of the early volumes of his history of the British army published in 1918, *British Campaigns in Flanders, 1690–1794*, for example, was intended as a 'portable and inexpensive' guide to enable serving officers to 'study the experiences of their forerunners in the Low Countries'.[28] Similarly, Fortescue's *The County Lieutenancies and the Army, 1803–14* (1909) had been specifically intended to demonstrate the need for R. B. Haldane's creation of the Territorial Force

---

27 Paddy Griffith, 'Oman's Peninsular War Today', in Paddy Griffith (ed.), *A History of the Peninsular War: Modern Studies of the War in Spain and Portugal, 1808–14* (London: Greenhill Books, 1999), pp. 23–46.

28 Keith Grieves, 'Early Historical Responses to the Great War: Fortescue, Conan Doyle, and Buchan', in Bond (ed.), *First World War and British Military History*, pp. 15–39, at 17.

by showing the militia and volunteers in an unfavourable light: Haldane subsidised its publication.[29]

In his wider work, Fortescue was a prisoner of prevalent Social Darwinist ideals, as is apparent in a series of lectures he delivered at Trinity College, Cambridge, and which were published in March 1914 as *Military History*.[30] He was also very much the partisan of the old pre-Cardwellian regimental system, and his dislike of political interference in the army shone through his treatment of the period prior to 1815, with which he was most comfortable.

Fortescue believed that military history gave 'insight into the character and intellectual powers of some of the most remarkable men who ever lived'.[31] Rather similarly, Oman also subscribed to the significance of 'cataclysmic figures' in history, war being 'merely the greatest of the influences that make history "cataclysmic" '.[32] Unashamedly, too, William Napier had believed that the military historian was required to 'bring the exploits of the hero into broad day-light, to show them in all their beauty of detail as well as in their grandeurs of proportion, otherwise they will be passed unheeded'.[33] All their histories fitted, therefore, into a widespread concern with the lives of the 'Great Captains', itself reflective of Thomas Carlyle's vigorous advocacy of the significance of great men in history in his *On Heroes, Hero-Worship and the Heroic in History* (1841). Cromwell figured largely in Carlyle's writings, and he also wrote a biography of Frederick the Great.

It was a trend that continued well into the twentieth century. Alongside his more theoretical works, Liddell Hart penned *A Greater than Napoleon: Scipio Africanus* (1926); *Great Captains Unveiled* (1927); *Sherman: Soldier, Realist, American* (1929); *Foch: Man of Orleans* (1932); and *T. E. Lawrence in Arabia and After* (1934), though admittedly their lives were intended to illuminate his wider theories. Similarly, Liddell Hart's contemporary theorist, J. F. C. Fuller, contributed *The Generalship of Ulysses S. Grant* (1929); *Grant and Lee: A Study*

29 The Hon. J. W. Fortescue, *The County Lieutenancies and the Army, 1803–14* (London: Macmillan, 1909), p. v.
30 Tim Travers, 'The Development of British Military Historical Writing and Thought from the Eighteenth Century to the Present', in David A. Charters, Marc Milner and J. Brent Wilson (eds), *Military History and the Military Profession* (Westport, CT: Praeger, 1992), pp. 23–44, at 32–3.
31 The Hon. J. W. Fortescue, *Military History: Lectures Delivered at Trinity College, Cambridge* (Cambridge: Cambridge University Press, 1914), p. 39.
32 Sir Charles Oman, 'A Defence of Military History', in Sir Charles Oman (ed.), *Studies in the Napoleonic Wars* (London: Methuen & Co., 1929), pp. 25–36.
33 Quoted in Luvaas, *Education of an Army*, p. 14.

in Personality and Generalship (1933); and, much later, *The Generalship of Alexander the Great* (1958); and *Julius Caesar: Man, Soldier, and Tyrant* (1965).

Interestingly, work by Liddell Hart and Fuller also fell into another 'Whiggish' category, namely a certain obsession with the concept of 'decisive' battle. Liddell Hart's *The Decisive Wars of History* appeared in 1929. Fuller's two-volume *Decisive Battles: Their Influence upon History and Civilisation* was published in 1939, followed by *The Decisive Battles of the United States* in 1942. A consolidated three-volume The *Decisive Battles of the Western World and Their Influence upon History* then appeared between 1954 and 1956. A particular way of interpreting the past in the light of contemporary events was identified by Sir Herbert Butterfield in 1931 as *The Whig Interpretation of History*. Thus, the British system of liberal parliamentary democracy was seen as the ideal system of government, and nineteenth-century historians such as Thomas Babington Macaulay interpreted British history as an inevitable progression towards this particular end. It encouraged an emphasis upon the similarities between past and present, but more particularly tended to identify some individuals and movements as history's winners and others as losers in the light of whether they were seen as pushing on towards the desirable end.

Sir Edward Creasy, *Fifteen Decisive Battles of the World*, first exemplified this approach in military history in 1851. The victors from Marathon to Waterloo had all made decisions that had changed the course of history for the better, these 'collisions' giving 'an impulse which will sway the fortunes of successive generations of mankind'.[34] Thus, for Creasy, such admirable traits as Greek wisdom, Roman virtue, European Protestantism and English liberty had all been preserved for posterity by battle. George Malleson, *Decisive Battles of India*, then appeared in 1883, and Thomas Knox, *Decisive Battles since Waterloo*, in 1887. So influential was Creasy's work that it has been argued that it accounted for the failure of British military history to embrace the philosophical and cultural approach to war, allied to scientific and critical appraisal of sources, of the Prussian military historian, Hans Delbrück. The latter's *Geschichte der Kriegskunst im Rahmen der poltitischen Geschichte* ('The History of Warfare in the Framework of Political History') appeared in four volumes between 1900 and 1920.[35]

The 'decisive battle' has never really disappeared from popular military history. A former colleague once produced a book on the 'decisive battles' of the Vietnam War, the vast majority of which were won by the United States. It calls

---

34 Quoted in Travers, 'Development of British Military Historical Writing', p. 29.
35 John Keegan, *The Face of Battle* (Harmondsworth: Penguin, 1978), pp. 55–8.

to mind the exchange between the American military theorist, Harry Summers, and a North Vietnamese Colonel named Tu in Hanoi in 1975. Summers remarked, 'You know you never defeated us on the battlefield'. Tu replied, 'That may be so but it is also irrelevant.'[36] Equally, in a speech to the American Legion on 30 August 2011, President Obama told Vietnam veterans, 'But let it be remembered that you won every major battle of that war. Every single one.'[37] Of course, soldiers have frequently sought decisive battle as usefully examined by Russell Weigley, *The Age of Battles: The Quest for Decisive Warfare from Breitenfeld to Waterloo* (1991), and Brian Bond, *The Pursuit of Victory: From Napoleon to Saddam Hussein* (1996).

Perhaps more puzzling, the Whiggish tendency is also alive in some more academic history such as interpretations of western military dominance, concepts of military revolution, and technological determinism, to which more consideration will be given in the next section. The principal problem was that, along with 'Great Captains', battle tended to be the focus of what became known as 'drum and trumpet' history. Battle, however, presented particular problems of methodology. How far could it be accurately described when the attempt to impose order on imperfect memories and experiences formed amid chaos might misrepresent them? In a pioneering book, *The Face of Battle* (1976), John Keegan ruthlessly exposed traditional battle narratives to cultural and sociological analysis. Keegan suggested that 'Napierism' survived, 'less sonorous to the ear, perhaps, certainly less xenophobic, but still trading in his limited stock of assumptions and assertions about the behaviour of human beings in extreme-stress situations'. He took a certain pleasure in selecting example of what he meant from the 'Second Empire Salon School' work of his Sandhurst colleague, David Chandler, an historian of the campaigns of both Napoleon and Marlborough.[38]

Popular history of the traditional kind certainly continued to flourish, stimulated both by the Second World War, and a revival of interest in the First World War at the time of its 50th anniversary in 1964. *Purnell's History of the Second World War*, a weekly part-work, appeared in 1966, to be followed by *Purnell's*

---

36 Harry S Summers, *On Strategy: A Critical Analysis of the Vietnam War*, 2nd edn. (New York: Random House, 1995), p.1.

37 http://www.politifact.com/truth-o-meter/statements/2011/sep/05/barack-obama/barack-obama-says-us-never-lost-major-battle-vietn/

38 Keegan, *Face of Battle*, pp. 40, 42. On tendencies towards technological determinism, see Gervase Phillips, 'The Obsolescence of the Arme Blanche and Technological Determinism in British Military History', *WH* 9 (2002), 39–59.

History of the First World War in 1969. Batsford also produced its 'British Battles series', at least 18 of which were published in the 1960s, with titles such as Austin Woolrych, *Battles of the English Civil War* (1961); Katherine Tomasson and Francis Buist, *Battles of the '45* (1962); Christopher Hibbert, *Corunna* (1961); John Terraine, *Mons: The Retreat to Victory* (1960); and Michael Carver, *El Alamein* (1962). Most then appeared in Pan paperback editions in the late 1960s and early 1970s.

Keegan acknowledged that some previous work retained its value, such as Lieutenant Colonel Alfred H. Burne's innovative approach to the study of English battles. Burne deployed what he called 'inherent military probability' based on close attention to the actual terrain as a means of reconciling conflicting and often sparse accounts from the past in *The Battlefields of England* (1951), and *More Battlefields of England* (1952). Equally, while much of the military history written in the nineteenth or early twentieth century has substantial shortcomings, it needs to be acknowledged that a work by an Oman or Fortescue often remains a useful starting point. There is still value in a work such as Arthur Broom, *History of the Rise and Progress of the Bengal Army* (1850); Sir James Sibbald Scott, *The British Army: Its Origins, Progress, and Equipment*, 3 vols. (1868–80); C. M. Clode, *The Military Forces of the Crown: Their Administration and Government* (1869); William Wilson, *History of the Madras Army* (1882); Clifford Walton, *History of the British Standing Army, 1600–1700* (1894); Sir Charles Firth, *Cromwell's Army: A History of the English Soldier during the Civil Wars, the Commonwealth and the Protectorate* (1902); Charles Dalton, *English Army Lists and Commission Registers, 1661–1714* (1904); idem, *The Scots Army, 1661–88* (1909); idem, *George the First's Army*, 2 vols. (1910–12); R. Phipps, *The Armies of the First French Republic and the Rise of the Marshals of Napoleon*, 5 vols. (1926–39); John Stuart Omond, *Parliament and the Army, 1642–1904* (1933); Winston S. Churchill, *Marlborough: His Life and Times*, 4 vols. (1933–38); Richard Pares, *War and Trade in the West Indies* (1936); J. K. Dunlop, *The Development of the British Army, 1899–1914* (1938); Sir Patrick Cadell, *A History of the Bombay Army* (1938); Sir Charles Firth and Godfrey Davies, *The Regimental History of Cromwell's Army* (1940); or G. C. Cruikshank, *Elizabeth's Army*, first published in 1946, but expanded and revised in a new edition in 1966.

Keegan wanted to refocus on the traditional battle narrative in part precisely because a new kind of military history was emerging in the 1960s and 1970s that looked well beyond the battlefield. In many respects this was the salvation of the subject as an academic discipline and endeavour, but it did undoubtedly sometimes lose sight of the essential purpose of armies, namely to fight. This was the development of the 'war and society' approach to conflict, with its emphasis upon the study of the impact of war upon states, societies, institutions and individuals. Nonetheless, it would be unjust not to acknowledge that the University of Oxford had been committed in part to a more academic Delbrück-ian approach to war since the establishment of the Chichele Chair in the History of War in 1909. Its first incumbent, Henry Spenser Wilkinson, had been a journalist on the *Manchester Guardian* but, as a leading rifle volunteer, he had established the Manchester Tactical Society for fellow volunteers in 1881. He was increasingly seen as a major proponent of military reform through publications such as *The Brain of an Army* (1890), extolling the virtues of a continental-style General Staff. At Oxford he tended to concentrate on the study of Napoleon with such publications as *The French Army before Napoleon* (1915), *The Defence of Piedmont* (1927), and *The Rise of General Bonaparte* (1930), which still repay reading. Wilkinson's successor in 1923 was a soldier, Ernest Swinton, best known for his role in the development of the tank during the Great War. Another intellectual soldier, Archibald Wavell, might well have been appointed to succeed Swinton but for the outbreak of war in 1939. The chair was then in abeyance until Cyril Falls, a Great War veteran and former journalist who had assisted Edmonds on the Official History, was appointed in 1946, although it would be many years before the post resulted in any really distinctive Oxford school of military historians emerging.

Wavell had delivered the Lees Knowles lectures on 'Generals and Generalship' at the University of Cambridge in 1939, this series of lectures on military and naval history having been inaugurated by Sir Lees Knowles in 1912. A former Conservative MP and, like Wilkinson, a volunteer soldier, Knowles was also something of an amateur military historian. His works included *Minden and the Seven Years War* (1914), and *The British on Capri, 1806–08* (1918). The Hon. J. W. Fortescue delivered four lectures at Trinity College in 1914, published as *Military History* in the Cambridge Manuals of Science and Literature series, but curiously these do not appear to have been characterised as part of the Lees Knowles lectures. The first official lecturer, therefore, was the naval historian, Sir Julian Corbett, in 1915 but the series did not become a regular event until 1922. No academic historian figured until John Ehrman in 1957, although this has been increasingly the case in a series now taking place bi-annually. Again, however, the series did not represent the emergence of a school of military history.

Keegan himself, however, had been appointed to the Royal Military Academy at Sandhurst in 1960, the Department of War Studies having been established there by Brigadier Peter Young in the previous year. Young became well known for his studies of the battles of the English Civil War, and also founded the Sealed Knot re-enactment group. At the time, Sandhurst was effectively the only major quasi-academic employer of (usually Oxford-educated) military historians such as Keegan, David Chandler and Christopher Duffy available. There was increasingly an undeniable tension between the older traditional military historians, and those schooled in 'war and society' who began to join the Sandhurst Department in the 1970s. Most of the new arrivals at Sandhurst were products of the first real British school of military historians, resulting from the establishment by Michael Howard of the Department of War Studies at King's College, London in 1962. Howard had joined King's as an assistant lecturer in 1954, and went on to become the first Professor of War Studies in 1964. In addition to the military history seminar at the Institute of Historical Research, established by Howard in 1958, and the MA in War Studies programme, begun in 1962, there was increasing doctoral research supervised by Howard and others such as Brian Bond, who joined King's in 1966 and became Professor of Military History in 1986. Few who became military historians in the 1970s and 1980s did not have a King's connection.

It is often suggested that it was Arthur Marwick, who became the first Professor of History at the Open University in 1969, who pioneered the war and society approach but there were earlier exponents. The American scholar, J. U. Nef, whose *War and Human Progress* was published in 1950, can stand representative for an earlier generation of scholars that regarded war as having a purely negative impact, in so far as it was relevant at all, to historical development. But the work of others was already suggestive of a link between war and social change. Richard Titmuss made such a connection in his volume, *Problems of Social Policy*, for the British Official History of the Second World War in that same year of 1950, while Stanislas Andrzejewski proposed a 'military participation ratio' in *Military Organisation and Society* in 1954, postulating a firm correlation between the extent of participation by society in the war effort, and the subsequent degree of levelling in social inequalities. Sir George Clark then published *War and Society in the Seventeenth Century* in 1958, arguing that war was an 'institution' in seventeenth-century Europe 'for which provision was made throughout the ordering of social life', and a 'collision of societies'.[39] The continuing debate on the existence, nature, and extent of a 'military revolution' also began with the inaugural lecture by Michael Roberts at Queen's, Belfast in 1955.

J. F. C. Fuller had also recognised the significance of industrialisation and of revolutionary ideology in the development of warfare in the nineteenth and twentieth centuries, *The Conduct of War, 1789–1961: A Study of the Impact of*

---

39 Sir George Clark, *War and Society in the Seventeenth Century* (Cambridge: Cambridge University Press, 1958), pp. 9–10, 52–75.

the French, Industrial and Russian Revolutions on War and its Conduct appearing in 1961. That same year, Cyril Falls produced the accomplished *The Art of War: From the Age of Napoleon to the Present Day*. While more focused on military than other developments that influenced the conduct of war, Falls included consideration of 'small wars', a subject widely ignored in other general accounts of the time.[40]

Then there was Michael Howard himself. In an early article in 1956, Howard called for military history to be 'directed by human curiosity about wider issues and by a sense of its relevance to the nature and development of society as a whole'.[41] In 1961 Howard published *The Franco-Prussian War*. Although appearing in some respects a traditional campaign history, in reality Howard cast the outcome of the war in the context of the military policies of France and Prussia, and the relationships of army, state and society.

Marwick, therefore, was not unique in his emphasis upon the impact of war. Nonetheless, his study of British society in the Great War, *The Deluge: British Society and the First World War* (1965), and his advancement of a framework for the analysis of 'total war' in *Britain in the Century of Total War* (1968), and *War and Social Change in the Twentieth Century: A Comparative Study of Britain, France, Germany, Russia and the United States* (1974) were immensely influential. The model became widely known through the 'War and Society' course introduced by Marwick and his colleagues at the Open University in 1973. Though criticised by some, others emulated it. There was a raft of new series from publishers in the 1980s such as 'History of European War and Society' from Fontana, and 'War, Armed Forces and Society' from Manchester University Press. There were yet further additions in the 1990s. New specialised journals also appeared such as *Journal of Strategic Studies* in Britain in 1978, *War and Society* in Australia in 1983, and *War in History* in Britain in 1994.

Military history, therefore, had been radically transformed by the 1970s, becoming the 'New Military History' in the 1980s. The phrase is still used to characterise the modern approach to the subject though it is now hardly 'new'. In more recent years, further new methodologies have begun to be applied to

---

40 Ian F. W. Beckett, 'Low-Intensity Conflict: Its Place in the Study of War', in Charters, Milner and Wilson (eds), *Military History and Military Profession*, pp. 121–30.

41 Michael Howard, 'Military History as a University Study', *History* 41 (1956), 184–91, at 186. See also Michael Howard, 'The Use and Abuse of Military History', *JRUSI* 107 (1962), 4–10; and Brian Holden Reid, 'Michael Howard and the Evolution of Modern War Studies', *JMH* 73 (2009), 869–904.

the study of war and armed forces, with examination of such issues as identity, memory and gender. Similarly, a traditional Euro-centric emphasis within military history has also now been extensively corrected. Thus, it is with the integration of the military narrative within the wider political, socio-economic and cultural context that military historians now engage though, as will be seen, in the next section, operational history has also made a distinct comeback in a much more sophisticated form. To the methodologies of modern military history, we can now turn.

Chapter 2

The Methodological Context

Those who wrote military history prior to the 1960s were not lacking in appropriate historical skills. Oman, after all, occupied one of the most prestigious chairs in British academe. Whatever the agenda behind any particular publication, most also diligently carried out essential research. There is no reason to doubt, for example, Fortescue's calculation that, for his most accomplished work, *County Lieutenancies and the Army*, he consulted 100,000 documents.[1] Similarly, those works that already appeared to have a distinctly old-fashioned air by the 1960s such as Sir Reginald Savory, *His Britannic Majesty's Army in Germany during the Seven Years War* (1966), or R. E. Scouller, *The Armies of Queen Anne* (1966), deserve respect for the sheer depth of their research: Savory's dense narrative ran to almost 600 pages.

It is more the case that the focus was nearly always a narrow one: campaigns, battles, tactics, weapons and military organisation. There were often vivid descriptions of battle drawn from personal accounts of action, though the result still tended to be one of over-written yet curiously sterile and clichéd prose that conveyed little of the actual reality. Quite often, some purely military aspects were omitted from the narratives. Fortescue, for example, had little interest in even the contributions of the Royal Artillery and Royal Engineers to the army's campaigns, let alone such wider issues as logistics, or economic factors. Rather similarly, Liddell Hart *The Real War, 1914–18* (1930), later revised as *A History of the World War, 1914–18* (1934), said nothing about the political, socio-economic or domestic contexts of the war. As Hew Strachan has remarked, 'Having read selectively and digested partially, Liddell Hart then completed the process with his penchant for simplification.'[2] C. R. M. F. Cruttwell, *A History of the Great War* (1934), and Cyril Falls, *The First World War* (1960) were equally narrowly conceived, though Falls was more aware of his limitations, and also more objective in his judgements.

---

1 Fortescue, *County Lieutenancies*, pp. vi-viii.
2 Hew Strachan, 'The Real War: Liddell Hart, Cruttwell, and Falls', in Bond (ed.), *British Military History and First World War*, pp. 41–67, at 52.

The new approach from the 1960s and 1970s onwards has borrowed heavily from other branches of history and from other disciplines. The resulting blend has not always found ready acceptance. In 1985, for example, Ian F. W. Beckett and Keith Simpson (eds), *A Nation in Arms: A Social Study of the First World War*, attempted an institutional study of the British army at war between 1914 and 1918. Attention was paid to such areas as the army's changing social composition, the demographic context of military recruitment and the impact of large numbers of troops billeted on civilian households for the first time in a century. A traditional military historian, John Terraine, wrote, 'This is a work of sociology, not military history. . .' By contrast, Gwynn Harries-Jenkins, a sociologist, proclaimed, 'Studies of the complex relationships between armed forces and society are usually works of sociology. This is not, it is military history.'[3] As the American military historian, John Lynn, observed in 1997 of the differences between even 'new' military historians and other branches of contemporary historical scholarship, ' "Deconstruction" means one thing to our "cutting edge" colleagues; to us, it just means something like carpet bombing.'[4] Lynn, it should be noted, is far from a traditional military historian. Nor was lingering wider suspicion of the academic credentials of military historians assuaged by their appropriation of new methodologies in Britain or elsewhere.[5] Nonetheless, the all-embracing 'new' military history has proven infinitely more rewarding than the old.

As indicated previously, it was the study of 'war and society' that launched the new approach, revolving around the analysis of 'total' war. The term has become generally familiar as a means of describing the nature of the two world wars of the twentieth century, and also as a means of differentiating them from other conflicts. Erich Ludendorff, Germany's First Quartermaster-General from 1916 to 1918, used the term in his memoirs in 1919. He did so again in his 1935 polemic, *Der Totale Krieg*, to characterise the total mobilisation of the

---

3 Reviews by John Terraine, *The Daily Telegraph*, 21 June 1985; G. Harries-Jenkins, *British Book News*, Sept. 1985, p. 536.

4 John A. Lynn, 'The Embattled Future of Academic Military History', *JMH* 61 (1997), 777–89, at 782.

5 See Lynn, 'Embattled Future', pp. 777–89; E. M. Coffman, 'The Course of Military History in the United States since World War II', *JMH* 61 (1997), 761–75; Wayne Lee, 'Mind and Matter: Cultural Analysis in American Military History: A Look at the State of the Field', *Journal of American History* 93 (2007), 1116–42; Matthew Hughes and William J. Philpott, 'Introduction', in Matthew Hughes and William J. Philpott (eds), *Modern Military History* (Basingstoke: Palgrave Macmillan, 2006), pp. 1–7.

state's human and material resources under the direction of the military as a necessity to ensure victory. Notably, Ludendorff argued that the First World War had not actually achieved totality, the gist of his argument being that total war would have been, as Roger Chickering has expressed it, the 'Great War done right', with an effective military dictatorship.[6]

Similarly, the term total war was used by the right-wing French writer, Léon Daudet, in 1918, echoing French prime minister Georges Clemenceau's reference to *guerre intégrale* in July 1917 as a link between home and front. The Italian theorist of strategic bombing, Guilio Douhet, referred to total warfare in 1921 in much the same way that Ludendorff had used the phrase, as mobilisation of resources. The phrase was also used in a ritualistic fashion in the Second World War by individuals as varied as Josef Goebbels, Winston Churchill and several American authors. Specifically, Goebbels made a speech on 18 February 1943 in the Berlin Sportspalast launching a call for the waging of total war primarily as a means of preparing the German population for the sacrifices required in an ideological 'fight to the death' with communism.

In its modern sense of conveying a linkage between war and social change, total war is most associated with the analytical framework postulated by Arthur Marwick. Four 'modes' outlined by Marwick in *Britain in the Century of Total War* (1968) as a framework for comparing the degree of change effected by war became a four-tier 'model' six years later in *War and Social Change in the Twentieth Century*. For Marwick, total war implied, first, enhanced destruction and disruption on an unprecedented scale; secondly, the emergence of a testing challenge to the existing social and political structures of states and societies; thirdly, greater participation in the context of the total mobilisation of a state's resources; and fourth, a cataclysmic socio-psychological impact upon existing attitudes and values. When combined, the cumulative effect would result in real and enduring social change.

What Marwick offered only as 'rough tool' was still controversial since he interpreted the Great War as an event marking a significant discontinuity with the past. He also contended that, even where change might have been attributable to longer-term evolutionary trends, war fought on a global scale was likely to accelerate the pace of changes already taking place. Some historians broadly accepted Marwick's case including Gordon Wright, *The Ordeal of Total War, 1939–45* (1968), and Peter Calvocoressi and Guy Wint, *Total War: Causes and*

---

6 Roger Chickering, 'World War I and the Theory of Total War', in Roger Chickering and Stig Förster (eds), *Great War, Total War: Combat and Mobilisation on the Western Front, 1914–18* (Cambridge: Cambridge University Press, 2000), pp. 35–53.

Courses of the Second World War (1972). Neither Calvocoressi and Wint nor Wright, however, chose to define their understanding of 'total war', the implication in Wright being that the sheer scale of the Second World War rendered it an exceptional conflict. Some social and political historians such as Angus Calder, *The People's War: Britain, 1939–45* (1969) and Henry Pelling, *Britain in the Second World War* (1971) were more cautious with respect to the experience of the Second World War. Some rejected the concept entirely, one political historian, Michael Bentley, arguing in 1985 that the concept of total war was one of the most common 'misapprehensions' in the perception of modern British social history.[7] A military historian, Trevor Wilson, also criticised the use of the term in 1986 for the Great War 'when all that is meant is something like a "bloody big war" '.[8]

Clearly, 'total war' was a relative concept akin to Carl von Clausewitz's theory of 'absolute' war. It was unrealisable in the Great War, and for much of the Second World War, through the lack of instantaneously destructive weapons. In any case, no state has yet been able to totally subordinate all civilian needs to those of the military. Wartime mobilisation, like 'universal conscription', is always necessarily partial. To quote Richard Bessel, 'No wars are total wars, no nation is totally mobilised for war, no people can have its needs totally subordinated to a war effort . . . all wartime mobilisation is necessarily partial, and the key to waging war successfully involves establishing a sustainable balance between the needs of the military and the needs of society.'[9] Similarly, Brian Bond commented in 1984, 'strictly speaking, total war is just as much a myth as total victory or total peace. What is true, however, is that the fragile barriers separating war from peace and soldiers from civilians – already eroded in World War I – virtually disappeared between 1939 and 1945.'[10]

Marwick himself further clarified his ideas in his introduction to an edited collection, *Total War and Social Change* (1988), which examined both world wars, and in the new introduction to the second edition of *The Deluge* (1991). The

---

7 Michael Bentley, 'Social Change: Appearance and Reality', in Christopher Haigh (ed.), *The Cambridge Historical Encyclopaedia of Great Britain and Ireland* (Cambridge: Cambridge University Press, 1990), p. 327.

8 Trevor Wilson, *The Myriad Faces of War: Britain and the Great War, 1914–18* (Cambridge: Polity Press, 1986), p. 669.

9 Richard Bessel, 'Mobilisation and Demobilisation in Germany, 1916–19', in John Horne (ed.), *State, Society and Mobilisation in Europe during the First World War* (Cambridge: Cambridge University Press, 1997), pp. 212–22, at 221–22.

10 Brian Bond, *War and Society in Europe, 1870–1970* (London: Fontana, 1984), p. 168.

four-tier model was recast as four 'dimensions', and social change was more explicitly characterised as including changes in social geography; economics and technology; social structure; social cohesion; social welfare and social policy; material conditions; customs and behaviour; artistic, intellectual and cultural ideas and practices; family relationships and the role and status of women; and social and political values. Marwick more closely defined participation as involving that of hitherto 'under-privileged' social groups. At the same time, Marwick made more explicit his view that servicemen under discipline were far less likely to benefit from military participation in war than those on the home front, who enjoyed greater opportunities from civil participation in the war effort.[11] Marwick was also careful to stress, however, that war was one of a number of historical processes.

Irrespective of whether Marwick's ideas were accepted or otherwise, he had recast the historical debate in terms of what social and other trends could be measured, and what changes – such as in perceptions and values – could only be gauged speculatively. The issues of change and continuity, of course, are central to much historical debate. Therefore, it was not altogether surprising that this should be reflected in much of the ensuing debate, historians of both the First and Second World Wars increasingly emphasising continuity rather than change in areas such as the development of class relationships, the position of labour, and, especially, the status of women. Given this particular focus by reference to the world wars, it was also not unexpected that it was social historians in particular who rose to Marwick's challenge. In terms of class, early publications included Jürgen Kocka, *Facing Total War: German Society, 1914–18* (1984), and Bernard Waites, *A Class Society at War: England, 1914–18* (1987). The growth of the state's role in industry and labour relations were explored by Gerald Feldman, *Army, Industry and Labor in Germany, 1914–18* (1966); Kathleen Burk (ed.), *War and the State: The Transformation of British Government* (1982); and John Godfrey, *Capitalism at War: Industrial Policy and Bureaucracy in France, 1914–18* (1987). In one sense, the on-going debate on the connection between war and the rise of the nation state in the early modern period, to be considered in a later section, is a reflection of the issues raised by Marwick as the study of 'war and society' was pursued more widely.

---

11 Arthur Marwick, 'Introduction', in Arthur Marwick (ed.), *Total War and Social Change* (London: Macmillan, 1988), pp. x–xxi; idem, 'Introduction: War and Change in Twentieth Century Britain', in Arthur Marwick, *The Deluge*, 2nd edn. (London: Macmillan, 1991), pp. 11–48.

The issue of women and war produced perhaps the greatest output of all with such works as Gail Braybon, *Women Workers in the First World War* (1981); Gail Braybon and Penny Summerfield, *Out of the Cage: Women's Experiences in Two World Wars* (1987); Summerfield, *Women Workers in the Second World War: Production and Patriarchy in Conflict* (1989); and Marwick himself in *Women at War, 1914–18* (1977). At one level, the women's history pioneered by feminist historians in the 1970s, which developed from social and labour history, simply meant a search to recover 'hidden history' given the absence of women from the perceived historical record. In much the same way, social historians in the 1960s – many of them Marxists – had also discovered 'history from below' in terms of the working class. In fact, neither women nor the poor were quite as hidden as implied, as suggested by venerable works such as J. L. Hammond and Barbara Hammond, *The Village Labourer, 1760–1832: A Study in the Government of England before the Reform Bill* (1911); the same authors' *The Town Labourer, 1760–1832: The New Civilisation* (1917); Alice Clark, *The Working Life of Women in the Seventeenth Century* (1919); and Ivy Pinchbeck, *Women Workers and the Industrial Revolution 1750–1850* (1930).

The pursuit of women's roles within society certainly required not only more careful dissection of the official record, but also the interpretation of new kinds of sources, including literary evidence, since much of the early focus was on how women had been represented. As it developed with regard to British history in the 1980s, there was an emphasis on the 'separate spheres' of men and women, with women primarily inhabiting a circumscribed 'private' sphere of home and family, and men a 'public' sphere. Interestingly, military wives like 'colonial wives' have tended to be regarded by many feminist historians as 'incorporated', being subordinated to a husband's regimental role, thereby suggesting such women lacked both influence and power. The reality was that officers' wives at least often played a significant role behind the scenes, and were not confined to any perceptions of separate public or private spheres: 'incorporation' neither automatically implied female subordination nor constrained ambition. Since the 1990s, the experience of women (and children) has been seen much more profitably within the context of the wider impact of war. In any case, it has become axiomatic that in total war out-producing an opponent was as important as outfighting an opponent, with measurable increases in women entering industrial employment, whether this resulted in changes or otherwise in their status or role.

More recently, gender history rather than women's history has been the emphasis, based on an assumption that men and women cannot be interpreted in isolation from each other, and that their respective roles are culturally determined. The roots in feminist history are obvious. A culturally constructed gender divide tended to associate masculinity with military service or other physical work, while femininity was associated with domesticity. By requiring the participation of women, war, and particularly total war, thus exposed inconsistencies in conventional constructs that men should fight and women should look to men for protection. War, therefore, was likely to result in social and cultural uncertainties. Lucy Noakes, *War and the British: Gender and National Identity, 1939–91* (1997); Susan Grayzel, *Women's Identities at War: Gender, Motherhood, and Politics in Britain and France during the First World War* (1999); Nicola Gullace, *The Blood of Our Sons: Men, Women and the Renegotiation of British Citizenship during the Great War* (2002); and Penny Summerfield and Corinna Peniston-Bird, *Contesting Home Defence: Men, Women and the Home Guard in the Second World War* (2007) are good examples of the genre. But not all men fought and the relationship between war, perceived requirements of courage, and masculinity has also seen pioneering works such as Leo Braudy, *From Chivalry to Terrorism: War and the Changing Nature of Masculinity* (2003); and three collections, Paul Higate (ed.), *Military Masculinities: Identity and the State* (2003); Stefan Dudink, Karen Hagemann and John Tosh (eds), *Masculinities in Politics and War: Gendering Modern History* (2004); and Karen Hagemann, Gisella Mettele and Jane Rendall (eds), *Gender, War and Politics: The Wars of Revolution and Liberation in Transatlantic Comparison, 1775–1820* (2009). Rather as in the case of cultural history, to be discussed later in this section, the language of gender sometimes reflects 'post-structuralist' and 'post-modernist' interpretations of history, in which historical facts or events are seen as texts being shaped by an ideological writing process. The post-modernists consciously challenged what they perceived as various 'hegemonies' such as class and race. Most military historians, however, are firmly grounded in empiricism.

In addition to the debate Marwick inspired surrounding the two world wars, other historians pointed out that elements of 'totality' existed in many previous conflicts. In *Armies and Warfare in Europe, 1648–1789* (1982), for example, John Childs suggested that the period of warfare between 1648 and 1789 could be called limited 'only when it was compared with the holocaust that had gone before and the new totality of the Napoleonic Wars'.[12] The former conflict that Childs meant, of course, was the Thirty Years War (1618–48), which may well have been the most destructive conflict in European history in proportion to total population.[13] In fact, incipient warfare throughout the 141 years that

---

12 John Childs, *Armies and Warfare in Europe, 1648–1789* (Manchester: Manchester University Press, 1982), p. 2.
13 Peter Wilson, *Europe's Tragedy: A New History of the Thirty Years War* (London: Allen Lane, 2009), pp. 786–9.

followed the Peace of Westphalia laid waste much of central Europe and the Low Countries. Compared to the 12 years of total war in the twentieth century, for example, France was involved in major wars for a total of 64 years in the seventeenth century, 52 years in the eighteenth, and 32 years in the nineteenth. In the case of the subjects of the Habsburgs, it was 77 years in the seventeenth century, 59 years in the eighteenth and 25 years in the nineteenth.[14]

Nor was it the case that 'limited' war was confined exclusively to Europe. Both the Seven Years War (1756–63) and the French Revolutionary and Napoleonic Wars (1792–1815) have been claimed as the 'real' First World War in narrative titles such as Tom Pocock, *Battle for Empire: The Very First World War, 1756–63* (1998); William Nester, *The First Global War: Britain, France and the Fate of North America, 1756–75* (2000); Paul Fregosi, *Dreams of Empire: Napoleon and the First World War, 1792–1815* (2000); and David Bell, *The First Total War: Napoleon's Europe and the Birth of Modern Warfare* (2007). In a classic 'war and society' approach to the Revolutionary and Napoleonic Wars, one of Marwick's Open University colleagues, Clive Emsley, also pointed out in *British Society and the French Wars, 1793–1815* (1979) that there was a higher proportion of the male population under arms in Britain in the Napoleonic Wars than in either world war, and that the losses were almost certainly higher in terms of men under arms. Emsley argued that, while not as 'total' as the world wars, the struggles against France were 'qualitatively and quantitatively different from their immediate predecessors'.[15]

American historians have pushed the notion of total war backwards to embrace not only the American Civil War (1861–5), but also even the American War of Independence (1775–83). The process began as early as 1948 with an article by John Walters on William T. Sherman's campaigns in Georgia and the Carolinas, followed by the ringing declaration of T. Harry Williams in 1952 that 'The Civil War was the first of the modern total wars.'[16] Williams, however, used the term

---

14 Béla Király, 'Elements of Limited and Total War', in Robert A. Kann, Béla Király and Paula Fichtner (eds), *The Habsburg Empire in World War I: Essays on the Intellectual, Military, Political and Economic Aspects of the Habsburg War Effort* (New York: Columbia University Press, 1977), pp. 135–6.

15 Clive Emsley, *British Society and the French Wars, 1793–1815* (London: Macmillan, 1979), pp. 2, 169.

16 John B. Walters, 'General William T. Sherman and Total War', *Journal of Southern History* 14 (1948), 447–80; T. Harry Williams, *Lincoln and His Generals* (New York: Alfred Knopf, 1952), p. 3.

interchangeably with that of modern war. More recently, there has been a tendency to recast this particular debate in terms of 'people's war' rather than total war, thus embracing both the War of Independence, and the French Revolutionary and Napoleonic Wars. *The Road to Total War* (1997), edited by Stig Förster and Jörg Nagler – the first of five collaborative volumes by mostly American and German historians on total war – further refined the American Civil War and the Franco-Prussian War (1870–1) as 'industrialised people's war', solving some of the undoubted difficulties in describing the Franco-Prussian War in the same terms as the Civil War.

The second volume, Manfred Boemeke, Roger Chickering and Stig Förster (eds), *Anticipating Total War* (1999), covering the period from 1871 to 1914, somewhat muddied the waters by introducing a further concept of 'unlimited wars of pacification', by which was meant colonial campaigns, particularly those in the 1890s and the first few years of the twentieth century. Such campaigns, it was argued, while representing only a variation of earlier methods, incorporated significant elements of totality in preparing nations psychologically for dehumanising the enemy. As Glenn May commented, they broke 'the fragile barriers between soldiers and civilians without pain or significant penalty'. May also argued that total war in the twentieth century was no more than 'colonial warfare writ large'.[17] The comparison was really only viable in terms of the degree of violence involved in pacification rather than the extent of industrial mobilisation.

The third volume in the series, Roger Chickering and Stig Förster (eds), *Great War, Total War: Combat and Mobilisation on the Western Front, 1914–18* (2000), displayed a range of views on whether or not the First World War was a total conflict. As the editors admitted, with regard to a definition of total war, 'a consensus has so far eluded us'.[18] The fourth volume, Roger Chickering and Stig Förster (eds), *The Shadows of Total War: Europe, East Asia and the United States, 1919–39* (2003), cast its net rather wider in considering the Sino-Japanese War (1937–45) as well as developments in Europe and the United States. But, in many respects, it abandoned the attempt to define or redefine the concept of total war. Briefly, the volume even raised the question of whether it was total

---

17 Glenn May, 'Was the Philippine-American War a Total War?', in Manfred Boemeke, Roger Chickering and Stig Förster (eds), *Anticipating Total War: The German and American Experiences, 1871–1914* (Cambridge: Cambridge University Press, 1999), pp. 437–57.

18 Stig Förster, 'Introduction', in Chickering and Förster (eds), *Great War, Total War*, pp. 1–15.

war or limited war that more properly represented the most common form of conflict in long-term historical development.

The fifth and final volume, Roger Chickering, Stig Förster and Bernd Greiner (eds), *A World at Total War: Europe, Global Conflict and the Politics of Destruction, 1937–45* (2005), acknowledged that there was still no clear consensus on the definition of total war. Even in the Second World War, there were some limitations so that the 'master narrative' of the inexorable drift towards totality in the conduct of war from the French Revolutionary Wars to the Second World War was not wholly sustainable. Total war, therefore, remained an 'ideal' concept, but there was broad agreement that totality implied a conflation of the military and civilian dimensions of war through increasing mobilisation of resources, the radicalisation of the conduct of war, and the demonisation of the 'enemy'. Hew Strachan, who contributed to a number of the volumes, made the point separately that there had been a certain conflation between modern war and total war, which were not the same for it was essentially more advanced states that had the luxury of choice: 'The economically backward belligerent has to make a greater effort to mobilise its society in order to engage a more advanced and more industrialised opponent on equal terms. In other words, total war is an option more likely to be exercised by the less modern state. By the same token, the more advanced state will engage in a war that is certainly modern but possibly not total.'[19] Arguably, the total war debate has run its course, and it remains to be seen whether much more can usefully be teased from an ever-closer attention to the over familiar parameters.

If social history and social science contributed to the war and society approach so, too, did political science. In particular, theories of civil-military relations appeared especially relevant. Generally, armies have potential political strengths in their cohesive and hierarchical natures, their discipline and their esprit de corps but potential weaknesses in terms of administrative expertise and legitimacy. They may feel a disposition to intervene in politics from fears of being politicised or in circumstances of civil war but, equally, may feel obliged to intervene from their own sense of importance or perhaps frustration. Influence, however, may be exercised either directly or indirectly. Samuel Huntington, *The Soldier and the State: The Theory and Politics of Civil-Military Relations* (1957) assumed that soldiers should accept lawful orders and that, the more professional the army, the more compliant it would become. For Morris Janowitz, *The Professional Soldier: A Social and Political Portrait* (1960), Huntington had ignored the fact that long service regulars were committed to their own careers and were almost bound to become political animals as a result of lobbying in their own

---

19 Hew Strachan, 'On Total War and Modern War', *IHR* 22 (2002), 341–69, at 351.

interests. S. E. Finer, *The Man on Horseback: The Role of the Military in Politics* (1962) suggested soldiers could influence the political system through influence, blackmail, displacement and supplantment. Accepting Janowitz's argument that all soldiers became political in some ways, he believed most armies would not actually seek to supplant a government, even if they disagreed with it strongly, provided the lawful legitimacy of that government was obvious. Amos Perlmutter, *The Military and Politics in Modern Times: On Professionals, Praetorians and Revolutionary Soldiers* (1977) also assumed that an apolitical army could not exist. In three different models of relationship, stable political systems were characterised by the classical professional soldier; unstable systems by the praetorian soldier; and a newly stable system arising from the disintegration of an older system, by the revolutionary soldier.

Janowitz was instrumental in the establishment of the Inter-University Seminar on Armed Forces and Society in 1961, and two journals appeared subsequently, *The Journal of Politics and Military Society* in 1973, and *Armed Forces and Society* in 1974. Essentially, military sociology, which had developed after the Second World War, was mostly concerned with the military as a profession and as a social institution, the primary debate since the 1970s being whether the American military was becoming less 'institutional' and more 'occupational'.[20] History, therefore, was not central to military sociology's concerns, but the methodology offered something to those military historians interested in the relationship of army and state. As will be noted below, Janowitz's initial study had been of the Wehrmacht, and all these works of military sociology were predicated on the nature of modern western national armies. Armies, however, long predated the nation state.

Certainly, a significant number of the more specialised historical studies that began to appear concentrated on civil-military relations or the development of military policy. Germany was an obvious subject in view of the troubled relationship between army and state. The classic study was that of the veteran German conservative and nationalist historian, Gerhard Ritter. Ritter became best known outside Germany for his clashes with the revisionist historian, Fritz Fischer, who argued in the 1960s for Germany's responsibility for the outbreak of the First World War. Ritter, however, also produced a massive four-volume study, *Staatskunst und Kriegshandwerk: Das Problem des 'Militarismus' in Deutschland* (1954–68), translated into English as *The Sword and the Sceptre: The Problem of Militarism in Germany* (1969–73), that traced the origins of German militarism to the radicalising nature of the First World War. Other important studies were

---

20 Guy L. Siebold, 'Core Issues and Theory in Military Sociology', *Journal of Political and Military Sociology* 29 (2001), 140–59.

also appearing such as Gordon Craig, *The Politics of the Prussian Army, 1640–1945* (1955); and Karl Demeter, *Das deutsche Offizierkorps in Gesellschaft und Staat, 1650–1945* (1962), translated into English as *The German Officer Corps in Society and State* (1965); Martin Kitchen, *The German Officer Corps, 1890–1914* (1968); F. L. Carsten, *The Reichswehr and Politics, 1918–33* (1966); and Robert O'Neill, *The German Army and the Nazi Party* (1966).

Civil-military relations elsewhere also came into focus through works such as John Erickson, *The Soviet High Command: A Military-Political History, 1918–41* (1961); J. S. Curtiss, *The Russian Army under Nicholas I, 1825–55* (1965); Dennis Ralston, *The Army of the Republic: The Place of the Military in the Political Evolution of France, 1871–1914* (1967); and John Whittam, *The Politics of the Italian Army* (1977). Many more monographs on the French, German, Austro-Hungarian, Russian and Italian armies have followed.

The amount of new research being generated enabled broad syntheses on the history of modern warfare and its impact. It was appropriate that one of the first to produce an integrated synthesis was Michael Howard, whose *War in European History* (1976) surveyed developments from the 'wars of the knights' to the 'wars of the technologists'. Howard's overview was all the more masterful for covering so much in 150 pages. Howard also made the point that 'war and society' was little different from 'war in history'. More synthesis came in the Fontana 'History of European War and Society' series, published in association with the University of Leicester. A total of five volumes were published covering the period from 1450 to 1970: John Hale, *War and Society in Renaissance Europe, 1450–1620* (1985); M. S. Anderson, *War and Society, 1618–1789* (1988); Geoffrey Best, *War and Society in Revolutionary Europe, 1770–1870* (1982); Brian Bond, *War and Society in Europe, 1870–1970* (1983); and V. G. Kiernan's *European Empires from Conquest to Collapse, 1815–1960* (1982). A Marxist, Kiernan's work was less useful than the other volumes at the time, and it has not worn well by comparison. Like his other work on early modern warfare, Hale's contribution to the series was elegantly composed, and remains a model of historical writing to which all young military historians should aspire.

Best, who edited the series, believed that 'war and society' had become 'so stretched and overworked' in only ten years that it required redefinition, suggesting that the series aimed to highlight the place of war 'in determining the standards of national societies and their political viability'. In such a task, traditional 'campaign-conscious' military historians could 'not contribute much beyond (a priceless contribution indeed, when well done) the demonstration of how the fighting part of war, once began, turned out the way it did'.[21] In his

---

21 Geoffrey Best, *War and Society in Revolutionary Europe, 1770–1870* (Leicester: Leicester University Press for Fontana, 1982), pp. 7–10.

contribution to a series of short articles that appeared in *History Today* in 1984 under the title, 'What is Military History?', Best also significantly wrote that he considered himself 'militarily engaged' rather than a military historian. He made a distinction between the history of war, and military history *per se*, which he defined as the 'history of fighting and of the proximate means of fighting: military organisation and mentality, movement and logistics, weapons and equipment, strategic planning, tactical training, and battle behaviour'.[22]

If the Fontana series was one of synthesis, the Manchester University Press 'War, Armed Forces and Society' series was intended to broaden opportunities for the dissemination of new work in terms of the organisation of armed forces, the conduct of war, the relation of armed forces to society and to politics, and the impact of war in its widest sense. A total of 16 monographs were published between 1987 and 1995 including such varied titles as Klaus-Jürgen Müller, *The Army, Politics and Society in Germany, 1933–45* (1982); Charles Esdaile, *The Spanish Army in the Peninsular War* (1988); Peter Simkins, *Kitchener's Army: The Raising of the New Armies, 1914–16* (1988); John Laband, *Kingdom in Crisis: The Zulu Response to the British Invasion, 1879* (1992); and J. Paul Harris, *Men, Ideas and Tanks: British Military Thought and Armoured Forces, 1903–39* (1995).

Studies of the causes of war form almost a sub-genre in their own right though it can be noted that the 16 monographs in the Longman 'Origins of Modern Wars' series, which ran from James Joll, *The Origins of the First World War* in 1984 to Philip Bell, *The Origins of the Second World War in Europe* in 1997, tended mostly towards diplomatic and political themes. Political science, however, could be an alternative approach as shown by John Maurer, *The Outbreak of the First World War: Strategic Planning, Crisis Decision-Making and Deterrence Failure* (1995), which utilised contemporary nuclear deterrence theory.

As Best's comments suggested, however, there was a consciousness that, as Peter Simkins wrote in 1991 with regard to the First World War, sight of war itself was being lost: 'all too few military historians . . . possess *intimate* knowledge of the tactical and sociological factors affecting the conduct of units in battle'.[23] After all, as Michael Howard also noted, 'At the centre of the history of war there must lie the study of military history – that is, the study of the central activity of the armed forces, that is, *fighting*.'[24]

---

22 Geoffrey Best, 'What is Military History', *History Today* 34:12 (1984) accessed at http://www.historytoday.com/michael-howard/what-military-history.
23 Peter Simkins, 'Everyman at War: Recent Interpretations of the Front Line Experience', in Bond (ed.), *British Military History and First World War*, pp. 289–313, at 312.
24 Michael Howard, 'Military History and the History of War', in Williamson Murray and Richard H. Sinnreich, *The Past as Prologue: The Importance of History to the Military Profession* (Cambridge: Cambridge University Press, 2006), pp. 12–20, at 20.

To some extent, an attempt had been made in the 1970s to use the techniques of oral history to remedy the deficit. This was primarily the work of non-academic authors such as Martin Middlebrook and Lyn Macdonald in Britain, Pierre Berton in Canada, and Patsy Adam-Smith and Bill Gammage in Australia, who all began to interview surviving Great War veterans. The result might add colour but, as Alistair Thomson demonstrated, in *Anzac Memories: Living with a Legend* (1994), veterans articulated a mythic past through selection, simplification and generalisation.[25] Oral history cannot be divorced from the cultural background of those contributing and, as time passes, individual memory is shaped by collective impulses within popular memory.

Rather more significant, as Keegan's *The Face of Battle* illustrated, was the application of methodologies not only from sociology but also from anthropology and psychology. Keegan also employed anthropological studies in his *A History of Warfare* (1993) to explain the origins of conflict in antiquity. The idea was not new. The French soldier, Ardant du Picq, who was killed in the Franco-Prussian War, had attempted in his posthumously published *Etudes sur les combat: Combat antique et moderne* (1880) to understand battlefield behaviour in psychological terms. Much the same approach was followed by the American combat historian, S. L. A. Marshall, in the classic *Men Against Fire: The Problem of Battle Command in Future War* (1947). Marshall's findings were based upon post-action interviews, though considerable doubt was later cast on how systematic his collection of data had been.[26] Similarly, Samuel Stouffer, *The American Soldier: Combat and Its Aftermath* (1949) embraced the Pacific theatre as well as Europe, which was more Marshall's focus. In an equally pioneering study in 1948, the sociologists, Edward Shils and Morris Janowitz, used wartime interview data from German deserters and those captured to demonstrate that the Wehrmacht fought on in 1944–5 when all appeared hopeless as a result of loyalties to the primary group.[27]

Keegan drew on Konrad Lorenz, *On Aggression* (1963), and Lionel Tiger, *Men in Groups* (1969), as well as work on combat stress such as Robert Ahrenfeldt, *Psychiatry in the British Army in the Second World War* (1958), and even studies

---

25 For a contrasting defence of oral 'military' history, see Peter Liddle and Matthew Richardson, 'Voices from the Past: An Evaluation of Oral History as a Source for Research into the Western Front Experience of the British Soldier, 1914–18', *JCH* 31 (1976), 651–74.

26 Roger Spiller, 'S. L. A. Marshall and the Ratio of Fire', *JRUSI* 133 (1988), 63–71.

27 Edward Shils and Morris Janowitz, 'Cohesion and Disintegration in the Wehrmacht', *Public Opinion Quarterly* 12 (1948), 280–315.

of mountaineering. Keegan's success led to other historically based studies such as Major General Frank Richardson, *Fighting Spirit: A Study of Psychological Factors in War* (1978); Anthony Kellett, *Combat Motivation: The Behaviour of Soldier in Battle* (1982); and Richard Holmes, *Firing Line* (1985). Holmes, a Sandhurst colleague of Keegan, collaborated with him on *Soldiers: A History of Men in Battle* (1985). As with trends in military sociology generally, it needs to be borne in mind that a great deal of attention in terms of the understanding of 'fighting spirit' has been paid to the western armies and, in particular, to the British army in the Great War, the German army in the Second World War and the United States army in Vietnam.

The 'face of battle' approach was itself widely emulated. Keegan's three case studies had been Agincourt, Waterloo and the Somme. The American historian, Victor Davis Hanson, consciously used the same methods of recreating ancient battle in *The Western Way of War: Infantry Battle in Classical Greece* (1989), and *Hoplites: The Classical Greek Battle Experience* (1991). Evaluating experience of battle has equally been the aim of Gregory Daly, *Cannae: The Experience of Battle in the Second Punic War* (2002); Anthony Goodman, *The Wars of the Roses: The Soldier's Experience* (2005); Charles Carlton, *Going to the Wars: The Experience of the British Civil Wars, 1638–51* (1992); Martyn Bennett, *The Civil Wars Experienced: Britain and Ireland, 1638–61* (2000); Christopher Duffy, *The Military Experience in the Age of Reason* (1987); Gerald Linderman, *Embattled Courage: The Experience of Combat in the American Civil War* (1987); and the contributors to Paul Addison and Angus Calder (eds), *Time to Kill: The Soldier's Experience of War in the West, 1939–45* (1997). Such an approach has become somewhat standardised and, arguably, increasingly less useful.

Another of Keegan's Sandhurst colleagues, Paddy Griffith, took a different direction, minutely analysing contemporary accounts in what he called 'tactical snippeting' for details of how battle was actually fought. His methods were first deployed in *Forward into Battle: Fighting Tactics from Waterloo to Vietnam* (1981), in which he disected phenomena such as the 'flight to the front' and the 'empty battlefield', arguing that firepower was not as significant as the willingness of men to close with the enemy. He followed it with the equally controversial *Rally Once Again: Battle Tactics of the American Civil War* (1986), which suggested that the American Civil War was the last 'Napoleonic' war rather than the first modern war. It was followed by later Griffith studies of Viking warfare, the French Revolutionary and Napoleonic Wars, and the First World War.

The two world wars have been particularly fertile ground for further studies of the impact of war on soldiers and civilians from psychological perspectives, including issues of morale and discipline. 'Shell shock', for example, now has an extensive literature including Peter Leese, *Shell Shock: Traumatic Neuroses and the British Soldier of the First World War* (2002); Peter Barham, *Forgotten Lunatics of the Great War* (2004); and Paul Lerner, *Hysterical Men: War, Psychiatry, and the Politics of Trauma in Germany, 1890–1930* (2003). Wider war disability is covered in works such as David Gerber (ed.), *Disabled Veterans in History* (2000); Deborah Cohen, *The War Come Home: Disabled Veterans in Britain and Germany, 1914–39* (2001); Antoine Prost, *In the Wake of War: Les Anciens Combattants and French Society, 1914–39* (1992); and Joanna Bourke, *Dismembering the Male: Men's Bodies, Britain and the Great War* (1996). Mark Harrison has produced excellent medical studies of both world wars, *Medicine and Victory: British Military Medicine in the Second World War* (2004), and *The Medical War: British Military Medicine in the First World War* (2010). There are also important essays in Roger Cooter, Mark Harrison and Steve Sturdy (eds), *War, Medicine and Modernity* (1998). For the Second World War there is Bill McAndrew and Terry Copp, *Battle Exhaustion: Soldiers and Psychiatrists in the Canadian Army, 1939–45* (1990), while Ben Sheppard provides an overview in *A War of Nerves: Soldiers and Psychologists, 1914–94* (2002).

The interest in military medicine may also be seen as part of what has been a growing understanding of the impact of science and technology on warfare. An early pioneer was William McNeill, *The Pursuit of Power: Technology, Armed Forces and Society since AD 1000* (1983), while Martin van Creveld, *Technology and War: From 2000 BC to the Present* (1991) was equally broad ranging. Van Creveld also published a pioneering study of logistics, *Supplying War: Logistics from Wallenstein to Patton* (1977). The contribution of science and technology to the two world wars was explored in two studies by Guy Hartcup, *The War of Invention: Scientific Developments, 1914–18* (1988), and *The Challenge of War: Scientific and Engineering Contributions to World War Two* (1970). It might be added in passing, however, that even as seemingly old-fashioned an instrument as cavalry can be reassessed in cultural terms by a through understanding of the horse itself, as shown in Louis Dimarco, *War Horse: A History of the Military Horse and Rider* (2008).

Intelligence is another important area where technology has contributed, not least in terms of the breaking of German and Japanese codes during the Second World War. The 'Ultra' secret of the breaking of the German Enigma codes was only disclosed in 1974, F. W. Winterbotham, *The Ultra Secret: The Inside Story of Operation Ultra, Bletchley Park and Enigma* (1974) being the first to reveal this hidden aspect of the Second World War. Ronald Lewin, *Ultra Goes to War* (1978); Ralph Bennett, *Ultra in the West: The Normandy Campaign, 1944–45* (1979); and Patrick Beesley, *Room 40: Naval Intelligence, 1914–18* (1984) quickly followed, the five-volume official history edited by F. H. Hinsley also being published between 1979 and 1988. In some ways publications on

Bletchley Park have become a continuing cottage industry. The field as a whole is surveyed in Michael Handel (ed.), *Intelligence and Military Operations* (1990), and by Christopher Andrew and Jeremy Noakes, *Intelligence and International Relations, 1900–45* (1987). Among many other studies of code breaking is Donald Lowman, *Magic: The Untold Story* (2000). Jim Beach, *Haig's Intelligence: GHQ and the German Army, 1916–18* (2013) is one of the most recent publications in the field, particularly demonstrating a mastery of piecing together surviving but fragmentary archives in different countries. Similar intelligence studies will be considered in later sections as appropriate.

The environmental consequences of war is a new area for research, as explored in Jay E. Austin and Carl E. Bruch (eds), *The Environmental Consequences of War: Legal, Economic and Scientific Perspectives* (2000), Richard Tucker and Edmund Russell (eds), *Natural Enemy, Natural Ally: Toward an Environmental History of Warfare* (2004), and Charles E Closmann (ed.), *War and the Environment: Military Destruction in the Modern Age* (2009). Understandably, much of the emphasis thus far has been on the destruction of landscape, flora and fauna, and other natural resources in the period since 1945. Essays in Tucker and Russell, however, also cover Mughal India and the American West. Those in Closman cover the military use of the forests of the Philippines since the sixteenth century, Sherman's march from Atlanta to the sea, and trench warfare. Nicola Lambourne, *War Damage in Western Europe: The Destruction of Historic Monuments during the Second World War* (2001); Patricia Grimsted, *Trophies of War and Empire: The Archival Heritage of Ukraine, World War II and the International Politics of Restitution* (2001); and R. Bevan, *The Destruction of Memory: Architecture and Cultural Warfare* (2004) consider the damage to the built environment and to cultural artefacts: there is a range of popular works on the looting of art by the Nazis and others. A recent publication, Chris Pearson, *Mobilising Nature: The Environmental History of War and Militarisation in Modern France* (2012) goes beyond his earlier *Scarred Landscapes: War and Nature in Vichy France* (2008) in looking at the impact of the first modern military training established in France in 1857, and the incorporation of forests in French frontier defence after 1871, before exploring the more familiar trenches of the Great War, and the post-war recovery of the landscape after both world wars. It is an approach that could readily yield dividends in terms of Britain. There is Marianna Dudley, *An Environmental History of the UK Defence Estate, 1945 to the Present* (2012), but earlier military training camps, be it those established at places such as Warley or Coxheath in the eighteenth century, or on Salisbury Plain in the nineteenth century, would make an interesting study. The Chilterns Commons Project has looked at military use of commons in a limited way, but this could be substantially extended. Current plans for centenary commemoration of the

Great War are also drawing attention to the many practice trenches dug in Britain to help prepare new recruits for front line service.

Commemoration, of course, equally has an impact on landscape as suggested by the monuments and cemeteries of the Great War. In regard to the latter, Hugh Clout, *After the Ruins: Restoring the Countryside of Northern France after the Great War* (1996) was an earlier pioneering study of the impact of modern warfare. The annual 'iron harvest' of unexploded munitions so familiar to visitors to the Western Front is dwarfed in many respects by the legacy of munitions and mines from more recent conflicts elsewhere in the modern world.

Environment itself may also have an impact, and there have been a number of studies of the effect of terrain and climate on warfare as in Harold Winters et al, *Battling the Elements: Weather and Terrain in the Conduct of War* (1998) and Anthony Clayton, *Warfare in Woods and Forests* (2011). Lisa Brady, *War Upon the Land: Military Strategy and the Transformation of Southern Landscapes during the American Civil War* (2012) is particularly successful in uniting operational factors with wider environmental issues. Kathryn Meier, *Nature's Civil War: Common Soldiers and the Environment in 1862 Virginia* (2013) draws down to the impact of environment on early campaigning in the eastern theatre. Ecological issues are also raised in J. R. McNeill (ed.), *Mosquito Empires: Ecology and War in the Greater Caribbean, 1620–1914* (2010) and, more controversially, in Jared Diamond, *Guns, Germs, and Steel: The Fates of Human Societies* (1998), which proposed what was seen as a measure of environmental determinism as a significant factor in European colonisation and dominance. The latter can be contrasted with George Raudzens (ed.), *Technology, Disease, and Colonial Conquests, Sixteenth to Eighteenth Centuries: Essays Reappraising the Guns and Germs Theories* (2001). Matthew Restall, *Seven Myths of the Spanish Conquest* (2003), emphasises the role of European diseases as well as native allies in the Spanish colonisation of Central and Latin America. In another exercise marrying 'ethnohistory' with military history, Ian Steele, *Warpaths: Invasions of North America* (1994) argued, by contrast, that the military balance between Europeans and American Indians was much more finely balanced than usually suggested with constant adaptation on both sides. It might be added that a variation on the theme of the impact of disease on indigenous peoples was the corrective offered by Glenn May, *Battle for Batangas: A Philippine Province at War* (1991). Rather than the depopulation of this area of the Philippines being the result of American 'resettlement' policies targeted at guerrilla opposition after 1900, the 'demographic disaster' was the product of a malarial epidemic that predated even the beginning of the Filipino struggle against the Spanish in 1896.

Civilians, however, were most likely to suffer from the scientific and technological extension of war through the ability to target the 'home front', and the plight of civilians generally has increasingly attracted attention. This has also been approached from a psychological perspective in terms of the propensity for soldiers to commit war crimes. Joanna Bourke, *An Intimate History of Face-to-Face Killing in Twentieth Century Warfare* (1999), with a focus on British, American and Australian evidence, included discussion of the more gruesome acts of soldiers' 'trophy hunting'. It was not without controversy, however, since the sheer mass of material presented did not always necessarily support the conclusions drawn: it was clear, for example, that the men (and women) whose testimony was included did not always find pleasure in the act of killing. By contrast, David Grossman in *On Killing: The Psychological Cost of Learning to Kill in War and Society* (1995), and *On Combat: The Psychology and Physiology of Deadly Conflict in War and in Peace* (2004) suggested that humans had a natural aversion to killing fellow humans, and soldiers had to be conditioned to do so. The conduct of the Wehrmacht has been scrutinised by Omar Bartov *in The Eastern Front, 1941–45: German Troops and the Barbarisation of Warfare* (1985) and his *Hitler's Army: Soldiers, Nazis and War in the Third Reich* (1992), as well as that of other Germans on the Eastern Front in Christopher Browning, *Ordinary Men: Reserve Police Battalion 101 and the Final Solution in Poland* (1993). John Horne and Alan Kramer have examined German conduct in the Great War in *German Atrocities, 1914: A History of Denial* (2001), and Isabel Hull has delved further back into Imperial Germany's colonial record in *Absolute Destruction: Military Culture and the Practices of War in Imperial Germany* (2004). However, racially motivated aspects of the Second World War in the Pacific have also been covered in John Dower, *War Without Mercy: Race and Power in the Pacific War* (1986), and Iris Chang, *The Rape of Nanking: The Forgotten Holocaust of World War II* (1997). The civilian experience generally is covered in three valuable collections, Mark Grimsby and Clifford Rogers (eds), *Civilians in the Path of War* (2002); Linda Frey and Marsha Frey (eds), *Daily Lives of Civilians in Wartime Europe, 1618–1900* (2007); and Nicholas Atkin (ed.), *Daily Lives of Civilians in Wartime Twentieth Century Europe* (2007). Looting has always been a feature of war and, while this has become somewhat associated with Nazi occupation of Europe during the Second World War, it was by no means confined to German soldiers as indicated by Kenneth Alford, *Allied Looting in World War II: Thefts of Art, Manuscripts, Stamps and Jewellery in Europe* (2011). Mary Louise Roberts, *What Soldiers Do: Sex and the American GI in World War II France* (2013) also explores the darker aspects of prostitution and rape. Soviet depredations in Europe, including systematic rape, however, were on an even larger scale, as examined by Norman Naimark, *The Russians in Germany: A History of the Soviet Zone of Occupation, 1945–49* (1995) and Catherine Merridale, *Ivan's War: Life and Death in the Red Army, 1939–45* (2006).

Such studies impinge upon cultural issues and, arguably, cultural history and cultural studies have made the greatest impact on the study of war since the appearance of 'war and society' as cultural historians began to apply their own methodologies to military affairs. One example is the study of 'Revolutionary and Napoleonic Wars in European Experience' bringing together a number of European institutions as part of a still wider 'Nations, Borders and Identities' project. There is Palgrave's associated 'War, Culture and Society, 1750–1850', and the trend is also evident in the 'Cultural History of Modern War' series from Manchester University Press; 'Warfare, Society and Culture' from Pickering & Chatto; 'War, Culture and Society' from Continuum; and 'War and Culture' from New York University Press. The emphasis of the 'cultural turn' has been upon language, semiotics, representations and meanings, studying how ideas and practices are communicated and how popular and collective memory and identity are shaped by history. Military historians have been wary of 'tropes', 'discourses' and 'remediations' but, as John Lynn has argued in *Battle: A History of Combat and Culture from Ancient Greece to Modern America* (2003), the practice of war itself can be regarded as an expression of culture, being rooted in cultural assumptions and values of the participants. These, however, will vary significantly among participants since differing military cultures may well be alien to each other. Jeremy Black, *War and the Cultural Turn* (2011) is a typically stimulating introduction.

Initially, works such as Eric Leed, *No Man's Land: Combat and Identity in World War I* (1979), and Robert Wohl, *The Generation of 1914* (1980), were seriously misleading in attempting to weave a common universality of experience for the 'war generation' of 1914–18. Equally contentious were suggestions in works such as Modris Eksteins, *Rites of Spring: The Great War and the Birth of the Modern Age* (1990), and Samuel Hynes, *A War Imagined: The First World War and English Culture* (1990) that the Great War was a product of modernism. In reality, the war fitted both within the context of existing cultural movements as well as pushing them into new directions. As Jay Winter has argued in *Sites of Memory, Sites of Mourning: The Great War in European Cultural Memory* (1995), the war did not mark a triumph of modernism. Even more disingenuous was Paul Fussell's literary conclusions concerning the experience of war in *The Great War and Modern Memory* (1975), most of his assumptions about the way the war was fought being entirely wrong. His *Wartime: Understanding and Behaviour in the Second World War* (1989) was equally misconceived.[28] Doubts were

---

28 See the justifiably scathing attack in Robin Prior and Trevor Wilson, 'Paul Fussell at War', *WH* 1 (1994), 63–80.

raised by another typical cultural product. While Guy Pedronici, *Les mutineries de 1917* (1967), for example, had characterised the French army mutinies in 1917 as resulting from what might be termed 'bread and butter' issues, Leonard Smith, *Between Mutiny and Obedience: The Case of the French Fifth Infantry Division during World War I* (1994), stressed politicised 'dialogue' in the power relationship between officers and soldiers. By contrast to Smith, however, André Loez, *14–18: Les Refus de la Guerre – Une histoire des mutins* (2010) turns to a detailed social profile of the mutineers, and their many varied motivations.

At its best, cultural interpretation can be illuminating, as in highlighting issues of memory, commemoration and identity. Jay Winter has been in the forefront of this work. Initially, it was his demographic approach that was innovative, as in *The Great War and the British People* (1985), which examined both the demographic basis of British wartime recruitment in the context of general public health, and also the 'demographic deficit' as a result of the war. Winter contended that the war was dysgenic in its impact in Britain, and that the demographic gain outweighed the demographic loss, with a marked improvement in public health.

It was in his subsequent work on memory and commemoration, however, that Winter had his greatest impact in *Sites of Memory, Sites of Mourning* and also in *Remembering War: The Great War between Memory and History in the Twentieth Century* (2006). In addition, there was his joint work with Antoine Prost, *The Great War in History: Debates and Controversies, 1914 to the Present* (1999), which, although a bibliographical introduction, had a cultural emphasis, and his collaboration with Emmanuel Sivans, *War and Remembrance in the Twentieth Century* (1999). Prost and other French scholars such as Jean-Jacques Becker, Annette Becker and Stéphane Audoin-Rouzeau have worked along similar lines to Winter. Their associates and postgraduates have also published extensively so that there has been a growing literature on war memorials, acts of commemoration and popular memory. In addition, a large number of collaborative works have appeared including Richard Wall and Jay Winter (eds), *The Upheaval of War: Family, Work, and Welfare in Europe, 1914–18* (1988); Aviel Roshwald and Richard Stites (eds), *European Culture in the Great War: The Arts, Entertainment and Propaganda, 1914–18* (1999); and the two-volume Jean-Louis Robert and Jay Winter (eds), *Capital Cities at War: London, Paris, Berlin, 1914–19* (1997 and 2007).

There has been a general trend, for academic (as opposed to popular) study of the Second World War to lag behind that of the First World War in most areas. Memory and culture, however, are not among them. Alongside work looking at the popular memory of the Great War by the military historians such as Brian Bond, *The Unquiet Western Front: Britain's Role in Literature and History*

(2002), and Dan Todman, *The First World War: Myth and Memory* (2005), there are examples by cultural historians such as Pat Kirkham and David Thoms (eds), *War Culture: Social Change and Changing Experience in World War Two* (1995); and Helen Jones, *British Civilians in the Front Line: Air Raids, Productivity and Wartime Culture* (2006). Other work has also extended beyond the First World War including James Mayo, *War Memorials as Political Landscape: The American Experience and Beyond* (1984); Edward Linenthal, *Sacred Ground: Americans and their Battlefields* (1991); Timothy Ashplant, Graham Dawson and Michael Roper (eds), *The Politics of War Memory and Commemoration* (2000); Luc Capedevila and Daniele Voldman (eds), *War Dead: Western Societies and the Casualties of War* (2006); Michael Keren and Holger Herwig (eds), *War, Memory and Popular Culture: Essays on Modes of Remembrance and Commemoration* (2009); P. J. Rhodes, Polly Low and Graham Oliver (eds), *Cultures of Commemoration: War Memorials, Ancient and Modern* (2010); and Martin Gegner and Bart Ziino (eds), *The Heritage of War* (2012).

It might be noted that battlefield tourism is far from a twentieth-century phenomenon, for it played a role in earlier commemorative activities as explored by Thomas Chambers, *Memories of War: Visiting Battlegrounds and Bonefields in the Early American Republic* (2012). In the case of Britain, as will be explored in another section, the field of Waterloo was equally a popular tourist attraction in the nineteenth century. Chris Ryan (ed.), *Battlefield Tourism: History, Place and Interpretation* (2007) provide a wide-ranging series of essays on the preservation and presentation of battlefields as heritage from Britain to China, New Zealand and the United States. An interesting earlier polemical stimulus to what was then the beginning of the battlefield preservation lobby in the United State is Georgie Boge and Margie Boge, *Paving Over the Past: A History and Guide to Civil War Battlefield Preservation* (1993). In passing, a wholly original approach is to be found in Peter Svenson, *Farming a Civil War Battleground* (1994), recounting his experiences of owning an historical farm, alongside the story of the action at Cross Keys fought over his land in 1862.

A slightly different aspect of cultural memory is explored in two highly entertaining popular works, Tony Horwitz, *Confederates in the Attic: Dispatches from the Unfinished Civil War* (1998), examining the obsessions of battlefield re-enactors in the United States; and Harry Pearson, *Achtung Schweinehund! A Boy's Own Story of Imaginary Combat* (2007), dealing with the developing memory of the Second World War in 1950s and 1960s Britain as seen through the lens of film, childrens' comics and Airfix plastic kits. A more serious analysis of re-enactment is to be found in Iain McCalman and Paul Pickering (eds), *Historical Re-enactment: From Realism to the Affective Turn* (2010).

Certain military episodes that have had a lasting cultural impact have also caught the attention of historians, particularly in the United States. Examples include Brian W. Dippie, *Custer's Last Stand: The Anatomy of an American Myth* (1976); Carol Reardon, *Pickett's Charge in History and Memory* (1997); Neil Longley York, *Fiction and Fact: The Horse Soldiers and Popular Memory* (2001); and Frank Thompson, *Alamo: A Cultural History* (2001). The 'Lost Cause' of the Southern Confederacy has been a particular focus, as explored in Thomas Connelly and Barbara Bellows, *God and General Longstreet: The Lost Cause and the Southern Mind* (1982); Gaines Foster, *Ghosts of the Confederacy: Defeat, the Lost Cause and the Emergence of the New South, 1865–1913* (1989); Gary Gallagher, *Lee and His Generals in War and Memory* (1998); Gary Gallagher and Alan T. Nolan (eds), *The Myth of the Lost Cause and Civil War History* (2000); and William C. Davis, *The Cause Lost: Myths and Realities of the Confederacy* (2003). All such works are invariably stimulating.

Another exception to the concentration on the First World War by European historians is the depiction of war on film, primarily because the cinema was so much more developed by the Second World War. There has been study of the cinema of the Great War and the cinematic depiction of that conflict thereafter as in Karel Dibbets and Bert Hogenkamp (eds), *Film and the First World War* (1995); Andrew Kelly, *Cinema and the Great War* (1997); and Michael Paris, *The First World War and Popular Cinema, 1914 to the Present* (1999). For the Second World War, however, the many published works include general titles such as J. W. Chambers and D. Culbert (eds), *World War Two, Film and History* (1996), and S. P. Mackenzie, *British War Films, 1939–45* (2001). The treatment of war in the media generally is the subject of Ian Stewart and Susan Carruthers (eds), *War, Culture and the Media* (1995); Peter Young and Peter Jesser, *The Media and the Military: From the Crimea to Desert Strike* (1999); and Mark Connelly and David Welch (eds), *War and the Media: Reportage and Propaganda, 1900–2003* (2005).

Film might be regarded as a kind of material culture, and the study of material culture in general has also turned to war. At one level, it might be the larger remains of military activity, be it fortifications or barracks, studied in the case of Britain in such works as James Douet, *British Barracks, 1600–1914: Their Architecture and Role in Society* (1998); Austin Ruddy, *British Anti-Invasion Defences, 1940–45* (2003); and Mike Osborne, *Always Ready: The Drill Halls of Britain's Volunteer Forces* (2006). They may appear to some a little like train spotting or compiling laundry lists – 'pillbox measurers' is one term, used for enthusiasts – but they do have value. At another level, it might be battlefields, conflict archaeology being a growing area of study, as suggested by the launching of the *Journal of Conflict Archaeology* in 2005. General issues have been explored by John Schofield, William Gray Johnson and Colleen Beck (eds), *Matériel Culture: The Archaeology of Twentieth Century Conflict* (2002), and John Schofield, *Combat Archaeology: Material Culture and Modern Conflict* (2005), though it is questionable whether inclusion of some of the post-1945 sites discussed such as Robben Island or Greenham Common can really be justified. More historically based, with a particular emphasis on the nineteenth century, is Clarence Geier, Lawrence Babits, Douglas Scott and David Orr (eds), *The Historical Archaeology of Military Sites: Method and Topic* (2010). Specific to England is Glenn Foard and Richard Morris, *The Archaeology of English Battlefields: Conflict in the Pre-industrial Landscape* (2012).

In the case of Custer's Last Stand, as shown in Richard A. Fox, *Archaeology History and Custer's Last Battle: The Little Big Horn Re-examined* (1993), and Douglas Scott, Richard Fox, Melissa Connor and Dick Harmon, *Archaeological Perspectives in the Battle of Little Big Horn* (2000), archaeological investigation has entirely revised the record by demonstrating that the Sioux and Cheyenne significantly outgunned Custer's troops, being armed with repeating rifles compared to the single-shot breechloaders of the cavalry. Similarly, as indicated in Glenn Foard and Anne Curry, *Bosworth, 1485: A Battlefield Rediscovered* (2013), excavation has fixed the 1485 battlefield, the precise location of which had been contested, as well as revealing the largest number of early artillery rounds yet found on any English battlefield.[29] The 1461 battlefield of Towton has also been subjected to archaeological investigation, resulting in the discovery of a mass grave from which much has been gleaned, as suggested by Veronica Fiorato, Anthea Boylston and Christopher Knüsel (eds), *Blood Red Roses: The Archaeology of a Mass Grave from the Battle of Towton, 1461* (2000).[30] A similar mass grave relating to military victims of Napoleon's retreat from Moscow was discovered in Vilnius in Lithuania in 2002.[31]

Archaeology on the Western Front can add little to the historical record by comparison. The trenches of the Great War, however, have produced artefacts that contribute to the study of material cultures, as shown by Nicholas Saunders, *Trench Art: Materialities and Memories of War* (2003); and in the two collections edited by him, *Matters of Conflict: Material Culture, Memory and the First World*

---

29 Glenn Foard, 'Discovering Bosworth', *British Archaeology* 112 (2010), 26–31; idem, 'Bosworth Uncovered', *BBC History Magazine* 11:3 (2010), 23–30.

30 See also T. L. Sutherland, 'The Towton Battlefield Archaeological Survey Project: An Integrated Approach to Battlefield Archaeology', *Landscapes* 4:2 (2003), 15–25.

31 Michel Signoli et al., 'Discovery of a Mass Grave of Napoleonic Period – Lithuania (1812 Vilnius)', *Human Paleontology and Prehistory* 3 (2004), 219–27.

War (2004), and *Materialities of Conflict: Anthropology and the First World War* (2003). In addition, there are Bernard Finn, Bart Hacker, Robert Bud and Helmuth Trischler (eds), *Materialising the Military* (2005); and Nicholas Saunders and Paul Cornish (eds), *Contested Objects: Material Memories of the Great War* (2009). *Materialising the Military* includes essays on such diverse topics as fourteenth-century Burgundian gunpowder weapons, prosthetics for the war disabled in the United States since 1860, Second World War occupation relics from the Channel Islands, and women's uniforms.

Uniform is seen as part and parcel of a culture of soldiering in Scott Hughes Myerly, *British Military Spectacle: From the Napoleonic Wars through the Crimea* (1996), and T. S. Abler, *Hinterland Warriors and Military Dress: European Empires and Exotic Uniforms* (1999). Soldering as a cultural activity is also explored by Yuval Noah Harari in *Renaissance Military Memoirs: War, History and Identity, 1450–1600* (2004), and his *The Ultimate Experience: Battlefield Revelations and the Making of Modern War Culture, 1450–2000* (2008), both of which focus on memoirs as a means of suggesting the potential for war to provide revelatory and privileged experiences. Drill, too, has been seen in cultural terms as in William McNeil, *Keeping Together in Time: Dance and Drill in Human History* (1977).[32]

Artistic representation of war has also been a fruitful area for research as shown by such works as John Hale, *Artists and Warfare in the Renaissance* (1990); Peter Harrington, *British Artists and War: The Face of Battle in Paintings and Prints, 1700–1914* (1993); Peter Paret, *Imaging Battles: Reflections of War in European Art* (1997); Alan McNairn, *Behold the Hero: General Wolfe and the Arts in the Eighteenth Century* (1997); Phil Shaw (ed.), *Romantic War: Studies in Culture and Conflict, 1789–1815* (2000); John Bonehill and Geoff Quilley (eds), *Conflicting Visions: War and Visual Culture in Britain and France, c.1700–1830* (2005); Holger Hoock, *Empires of the Imagination: Politics, War and the Arts in the British World, 1750–1850* (2010); Theodore Rabb, *The Artist and the Warrior: Military History Through the Eyes of the Masters* (2011); and Eleanor Jones Harvey, *The Civil War and American Art* (2012). Other visual representation is covered in Terence Freeman, *Dramatic Representations of British Soldiers and Sailors on the London Stage, 1660–1800: Britons Strike Home* (1995), and Gillian Russell, *The Theatres of War: Performance, Politics and Society, 1793–1815* (1995).

---

32 See also Matthew McCormack, 'Dance and Drill: Polite Accomplishments and Military Masculinities in Eighteenth Century Britain', *Cultural and Social History* 8 (2011), 315–30.

Cultural assumptions raise a contentious issue in that there have been attempts to offer cultural explanations for supposed military success in war. The historian most associated with this argument is Victor Davis Hanson. Apart from following the Keegan model in recreating battle, Hanson's *The Western Way of War* also interpreted Hoplite warfare as the origin of 'modern battle'. His *Why the West Has Won: Carnage and Culture from Salamis to Vietnam* (2001), which was entitled *Carnage and Culture: Landmark Battles in the Rise of Western Power* in the United States, then suggested that democracy and technology explained the 'triumph' of western arms. Hanson ignored periods of non-European dominance in presenting a series of case studies from antiquity to the contemporary world to illustrate his thesis. In *Carnage and Culture*, for example, the choice includes the Greek naval victory over the Persians at Salamis in 480 BC, Alexander the Great's victory over the Persians at Gaugamela in 331 BC, Cortes's victory over the Aztecs at Tenochtitlan in 1521, the Western naval victory over the Ottoman Turks at Lepanto in 1571, the British repulse of the Zulu at Rorke's Drift in January 1879, the American naval victory over the Japanese at Midway in 1942 and the US military victory over the Viet Cong during the Tet offensive in 1968. The Vietnam War alone might suggest that western military methods are not predestined to succeed but, in leaping from 331 BC to 1521, Hanson failed to recognise the weakness of Europe in the face of Mongol incursions between 400 and 1400. It might also be noted that the Moors invaded Spain in 711, only being stopped in their further advance into France at Poitiers in 732. Nor was it until 1492 that the *reconquista* swept away the final vestiges of Moorish power in Spain.

In a large measure, Hanson's work was predicated on technological determinism. Hanson's thesis was passionately rejected by John Lynn's *Battle*, and by Jeremy Black, *Rethinking Military History* (2004). Both Lynn and Black were unconvinced by either technological determinism, or by cultural explanations for the apparent rise of the West. Black has revisited technological determinism in a wide-ranging, if sometimes slightly confusing way, in *War and Technology* (2013). Such scepticism similarly marks John France's sweeping history of warfare, *Perilous Glory: The Rise of Western Military Power* (2011), which argues that the rise of the 'Western' style of warfare to international significance was largely fortuitous, coinciding with the decline and stagnation of the Ottomans and the Mughals, the inheritors of the previously dominant form of steppe warfare that had emerged from Eurasia in antiquity. The historical essays in Hew Strachan and Sibylle Scheipers (eds), *The Changing Character of War* (2011) display similar reservations about Hanson.

More significantly, Lynn and Black argued for a corrective to the Euro-centric view of military history. It is a theme that the industrious Black has continued to pursue in such books as *War in the Modern World* (2003), and *An Introduction to Global Military History* (2005). As will become apparent in later sections, military developments were not confined to the West. To give another example, a great deal of attention has been given to the West's struggle with the Ottomans after the fall of Constantinople in 1453. The Ottomans took Belgrade in 1526 and besieged Vienna both in 1529 and 1683. But the Ottomans themselves devoted most attention between 1514 and 1743 to their rivalry with Safavid Persia. Equally, the Chinese invented gunpowder weapons, and it was their artillery that played a decisive part in their expulsion of the Japanese from the Korean peninsula between 1592 and 1598 following an attempt by the Japanese to overrun it. The war in Korea involved perhaps half a million men in all, a far greater number than involved in any contemporary European conflict. Indeed, it has been suggested by Black that China was the greatest military power in the world in the mid-eighteenth century following the campaigns of the Qianlong Emperor between 1747 and 1799 to consolidate his power over China, Taiwan, Tibet, Mongolia, Manchuria and that part of Central Asia later known as Xinjiang. He also carried war into Burma and Vietnam.

The work of Lynn and Black, indeed, as indicated by the latter's *An Introduction to Global Military History*, clearly contributes to the evolving trend for global history generally. Comparisons between different cultures with differing concepts of social and cultural organisation and values over long time frames pose particular difficulties. As suggested by the approach of the Oxford Centre for Global History in 2011, transnational interpretation requires co-operation between historians of different periods as well as interdisciplinary skills. Significantly, while the first conference of the Oxford Centre was on consumerism, the second is scheduled to be on 'War in Global History'. While globalisation appears more relevant to the contemporary world – the 'Global War on Terror' proclaimed by President George W. Bush on 20 September 2011 comes readily to mind – the age of European imperialism equally involved transnational encounters. An example of the value of a global approach for an earlier period is Felipe Fernandez-Armesto, *1492: The Year Our World Began* (2010), which deals with much more than Columbus's voyage to the New World. More specific to the theme of war, however, is Geoffrey Parker, *Global Crisis: War, Climate Change and Catastrophe in the Seventeenth Century* (2013), which sees the 'Little Ice Age' as a catalyst for such events as the British Civil Wars, the Thirty Years War, the Pequot War in North America, the civil war in Mughal India, conflict in Qing China and large-scale rural revolt in Japan.

The issue of strategic culture returns us to the business of waging war, for operational history itself has also been transformed by the steady absorption of all the methodological developments in the historiography since the 1970s. It would now be unthinkable for a serious academic study of a campaign not to take account of the whole historical context. One result has been sophisticated studies of the 'learning curve' on the Western Front during the First World War by historians such as Tim Travers, Robin Prior and Trevor Wilson, as will be considered in a later section.

Modern warfare has also lent itself to the application of models drawn from organisational theory as espoused by Barry Posen, *The Sources of Military Doctrine: France, Britain and Germany between the World Wars* (1984); Stephen Rosen, *Winning the Next War: Innovation and the Modern Military* (1991); Kimberley Zisk, *Engaging the Enemy: Organisational Theory and Soviet Military Innovation, 1955–91* (1993); Deborah Avant, *Political Institutions and Military Change: Lessons from Peripheral Wars* (1994); Elizabeth Kier, *Imagining War: French and British Military Doctrine between the Wars* (1997); Richard Downie, *Learning from Conflict: The US Military in Vietnam, El Salvador and the Drug War* (1998); and Victoria Nolan, *Military Leadership and Counter-insurgency: The British Army and Small War Strategy since World War II* (2012).

A multiplicity of interdisciplinary approaches is apparent in such works as Karl Erik Haug and Ole Jørgen Maaø (eds), *Conceptualising Modern War* (2011), and the previously mentioned Strachan and Scheipers (eds), *The Changing Character of War*, the publication resulting from a five-year Leverhulme-funded project of the same name. The latter calls upon historians, political and social scientists, and specialists in law and philosophy to distinguish between change and continuity in warfare. Unfortunately, some of its essays are all but incomprehensible.

In reality, military history today is a vibrant field of study. Indeed, as well as those series already mentioned that are still being published, there are at least 15 other series from various publishers, as well as others who publish military history without having a dedicated series. All this is without taking into account the large number of general publishers with military history lists, some of which, such as Pen & Sword, and Osprey Publishing, specialise in military history. Though much of the latter's output is concerned with uniforms and weaponry, mention should be made of Osprey's 'Essential Histories' series, in which mostly academic historians provide concise summaries of major wars. Those few soldier-historians who laboured to understand the history of their profession in the past would have been astonished at the variety of military history now available.

Chapter 3

The British Context

Perhaps inevitably, there are more popular than academic histories of the British army. Many of the former are now badly outdated such as Corelli Barnett, *Britain and Her Army, 1509–1970: A Military, Political and Social Survey* (1970), and Peter Young and J. P. Lawford (eds), *History of the British Army* (1970). The best recent popular history is Allan Mallinson, *The Making of the British Army: From the English Civil War to the War on Terror* (2009). The late Richard Holmes wrote a number of fine studies of the British soldier aimed at the general reader including *Redcoat: The British Soldier in the Age of Horse and Musket* (2001), *Tommy: The British Soldier on the Western Front, 1914–18* (2004), and *Sahib: The British Soldier in India, 1750–1914* (2006). His last book, a consolidated compendium, *Soldiers: Army Lives and Loyalties from Redcoats to Dusty Warriors*, was published posthumously in 2011. The only academic history that covers the whole period of the army's history is David Chandler and Ian F. W. Beckett (eds), *The Oxford Illustrated History of the British Army* (1994).[1]

It is noticeable that, when sociologists were constructing their theories of civil-military relations, some additional explanation had to be made for why Britain did not fit the proffered model. Huntington's *The Soldier and the State*, for example, argued that political compliance in Britain rested on the aristocracy's dominance in the army. Finer's *The Man on Horseback* suggested the British political culture was such that there were fewer opportunities for the army to exercise power other than by influence. Perlmutter's *The Military and Politics in Modern Times* characterised Britain as a stable political system but where the army was coming into increasing contact with the politicians through both its corporate existence in striving for protection from the politicians, and as a bureaucratic existence as a key partner in formulating and implementing policy. The army and politics had become more intertwined as Ireland became more troublesome, but the army had always been kept under firm political leadership.

---

1 A paperback version was published as *The Oxford History of the British Army* in 1996, with a revised 2nd edn. in 2003.

Certainly, the consensus among soldiers and military historians in the past was that the British army was apolitical within the steady evolution over a long period of time of a constitutional monarchy and representative democracy, characterised in many respects by the political settlement of the 'Glorious Revolution' of 1689. No officer had been dismissed for his political views since 1764. Nonetheless, there had been the tension in the seventeenth century over control of a standing army, which Parliament wrested from the Crown in 1689, although the Crown continued to actively assert its influence over aspects of administration until at least the end of the nineteenth century. The development of the army frequently illustrated the conflict, from the profusion of administrative agencies in the seventeenth and eighteenth centuries to the emergence of a duality between Commander-in-Chief and Secretary of State for War in 1855, and to the centralisation of military advice through twentieth-century creations such as the Chiefs of Staff Committee and the Ministry of Defence. Financial control and the constant pressure for economies has been a constant feature of the army's existence, as has parliamentary control of the army's discipline from the Mutiny Act of 1689 through the Army (Annual) Act of 1881, to the Army Acts of the twentieth century. It is often suggested that the existence of the purchase system, by which most but not all commissions in the infantry and cavalry were obtained between 1660 and 1871, was of particular political significance in giving officers a stake in the status quo.

Clearly, there have been politically charged episodes such as the Curragh Incident in March 1914 and the Chanak Crisis in 1922. Hew Strachan's important study, *The Politics of the British Army* (1997) rejected the notion of an apolitical army altogether, arguing that armies were inherently political through being embedded within the state, and intimately involved in the formation and implementation of policy, eroding any real demarcation between military and political spheres. Strachan saw increasing convergence between the military and political leaders in a process that commenced during the seventeenth century, highlighting such aspects as the politics of the regiment as well as inter-service rivalry. Its direct role in politics remains open to debate. There are some useful essays on civil-military relations in Paul Smith (ed.), *Government and the Armed Forces in Britain, 1856–1990* (1996).

As the issue of civil-military relations suggests, there has always been a sense in which the British experience of armed forces has been regarded as an exception. That exceptionalism has derived from Britain's island status and its absence of vulnerable land frontiers once the union of the two parliaments of England and Scotland was effected in 1707, for all that the Jacobites contrived to invade England from Scotland in 1715 and 1745, and that continental powers sometimes saw Ireland as a backdoor to Britain, as in 1798. The Royal Navy's 'wooden walls' protected the British Isles from invasion in the modern era – the last hostile landing on British soil was at Fishguard in Pembrokeshire in 1797 – even after steam power had been thought to have 'bridged the Channel' in the 1840s. Security at home was the concomitant to expansion overseas, access to the sea in itself conferring enormous advantages for the possession of colonies, both formal and informal empire in the Americas, Africa, Asia and Australasia being denied purely continental powers. Command of the sea likewise enabled the British army not only to garrison a far-flung empire but also to be what one admiral characterised as a 'projectile' fired by the Navy.

That in itself led to an assumption of a British 'way in warfare', a concept revived by Basil Liddell Hart, in a lecture at the Royal United Services Institution in 1931,[2] and his subsequent book, *The British Way in Warfare* (1932). The idea had been advanced first by the naval historian, Sir Julian Corbett, in *Some Principles of Maritime Strategy* (1911), developing from his two-volume earlier study, *England in the Seven Years War* (1907). Thus, British maritime power had enabled Britain to avoid manpower-costly continental entanglements, bankrolling continental allies to undertake the main fighting on land, while seizing enemy colonies to augment her own resources. This idea of a 'British Way in Warfare' became embedded in the historiography but, in reality, it had only ever applied to a brief period in the early eighteenth century. Britain could not afford to neglect land participation in any of the major continental wars, and always required continental allies in order to prevail, but there was at all times a tendency to view the army as essentially a small imperial constabulary out of sight and out of mind. Certainly, there was no belief in the need for continental-style conscription and, other than relatively briefly in the early eighteenth century, during the two world wars of the twentieth century, and for a short period after 1945, the army was enlisted on a purely voluntary basis.

Michael Howard, *The Continental Commitment: The Dilemma of British Defence Policy in the Era of Two World Wars* (1972) was more a statement of the continuing struggle between imperial and European commitments that bedevilled the formulation of a coherent defence policy between 1900 and the fall of Singapore in 1942 than a direct critique of the concept. A naval historian, Paul Kennedy then offered a different 'mixed paradigm' of a combination of army, a strong navy and continental allies over the longer period in *The Rise and Fall of British Naval Mastery* (1976), as a critique of the Mahanian interpretation of seapower. It was an oblique contribution to the emerging debate on the British way in

---

2 Basil Liddell Hart, 'Economic Pressure or Continental Victories', *JRUSI* 76 (1931), 486–503.

warfare. In another illuminating study, Hew Strachan rejected Liddell Hart's interpretation though acknowledging its potency as a theory in 1983.[3] David French's full-length study, *The British Way in Warfare, 1688–2000* (1990) carefully analysed the patterns and distribution of defense spending, suggesting that British policymakers never consistently preferred isolation to continental engagement, nor consistently adopted either a 'British way in warfare' or the mixed paradigm. French's ideas were further explored in Keith Neilson and Greg Kennedy (eds), *The British Way in Warfare: Power and the International System, 1856–1956: Essays in Honour of David French* (2010). Generally, the concept of what might be termed strategic culture and whether the national strategy was shaped by the nature of the political, social and economic order has been elevated to a predictive tool in modern strategic analysis by political and social scientists rather than by historians. As William Fuller observed in a sweeping survey of the relationship between military strategy and political power in Russia between 1600 and 1914, however, historians 'have a duty to be wary of any technique that substitutes theoretical elegance for complex truth'.[4]

Generally, British military thought as it developed through the nineteenth century was a poor imitation of continental theory so the idea of a British way in warfare at least suggested exceptionalism. Indeed, only in two respects could it be argued that the British army made a lasting impact on military thought, namely the theory of armoured warfare, and that of counter-insurgency. Liddell Hart and J. F. C. Fuller are the two individuals most prominently associated with the development of armoured warfare. Liddell Hart was more an advocate of mechanisation than of armour, and, in his own writings, also greatly exaggerated his influence over subsequent German and Israeli use of armour. Not surprisingly, both Liddell Hart and Fuller were closely studied in such works as A. J. Trythall, *'Boney' Fuller: The Intellectual General, 1878–1966* (1977); Brian Holden Reid, *J. F. C. Fuller: Military Thinker* (1987); Brian Bond, *Liddell Hart: A Study of His Military Thought* (1977); John Mearsheimer, *Liddell Hart and the Weight of History* (1988); and Alex Danchev, *Alchemist of War: The Life of Basil Liddell Hart* (1998). Brian Holden Reid brought a number of his essays together in *Studies in British Military Thought: Debates with Fuller and Liddell Hart* (1998). Mearsheimer is particularly hostile to Liddell Hart but Danchev more sympathetic for all that he acknowledges Liddell Hart's limitations as an historian.

---

3 Hew Strachan, 'The British Way in Warfare Revisited', *HJ* 26 (1983), 447–61.
4 William Fuller, *Strategy and Power in Russia, 1600–1914* (New York: Free Press, 1992), p. xiii.

The lessons of the long British experience of 'small wars' throughout the empire was most famously summarised by Charles Callwell in two articles on the strategy and tactics of small wars contributed to the *Proceedings of the Royal Artillery Institution* in 1884 and 1885; his prize winning entry for the gold medal essay competition of the RUSI in 1887; and the classic *Small Wars: Their Principles and Practice*, first published in 1896 and then in revised editions in 1899 and 1906.[5] As Tim Moreman showed in *The Army in India and the Development of Frontier Warfare, 1849–1947* (1998), Callwell was not seen as especially relevant to the Indian army. Nonetheless, Callwell's influence was apparent in the British army at least until the late 1920s, and he can be characterised as the true father of British counter-insurgency practice.[6]

The British imperial experience certainly established the contemporary idea that an 'imperial school' of thought was a valid alternative to slavish imitation of continental practices.[7] So far as the British army was concerned, Callwell was eventually replaced by Sir Charles Gwynn, *Imperial Policing* (1934), and Hugh Simson, *British Rule, and Rebellion* (1937). Gwynn in particular suggested that the four principles of British practice were the primacy of the civil power, the use of 'minimum force', the need for firm and timely action, and the need for civil-military co-operation. The body of influential British work on counter-insurgency was then continued after the Second World War by Sir Robert Thompson, *Defeating Communist Insurgency: Experiences from Malaya and Vietnam* (1966), and Sir Frank Kitson, *Low-Intensity Operations* (1971): Kitson was a critic of aspects of the more traditional approach taken by Thompson

---

5 Charles E. Callwell, 'Notes on the Tactics of our Small Wars', *Minutes of the Proceedings of the Royal Artillery Institution* 12 (1884), 531–52; idem, 'Notes on the Strategy of Our Small Wars', *Minutes of the Proceedings of the Royal Artillery Institution* 13 (1885), 403–20; idem, 'Lessons to be Learnt from the Campaigns in which British Forces have been employed since the year 1865', *JRUSI* 31 (1887–88), 357–411.

6 Ian F. W. Beckett, 'Another British Way in Warfare: Charles Callwell and Small Wars', in Ian F. W. Beckett (ed.), *Victorians at War: New Perspectives* (Society for Army Historical Research Special Publication, 16, 2007), pp. 89–102. See Daniel Whittingham, 'Savage Warfare: C. E. Callwell, the Roots of Counter-insurgency and the Nineteenth Century Context', *Small Wars and Insurgencies* 23 (2012), 591–607; idem, 'The Military Thought of Charles E. Callwell', PhD dissertation, University of London, 2013.

7 See Howard Bailes, 'Patterns of Thought in the Late Victorian Army', *JSS* 4 (1981), 29–45; idem, 'Technology and Tactics in the British Army, 1866–1900', in Ronald Haycock and Keith Neilson (eds), *Men, Machines and War* (Waterloo, ON: Wilfrid Laurier Press, 1988), pp. 23–47.

towards the primacy of the civil power. The idea that minimum force has been
sacrosanct underpinned some early analyses of British post-1945 operations such
as the two studies by Tom Mockaitis, *British Counter-Insurgency, 1919–60* (1990),
and *British Counter-Insurgency in the Post-Imperial Era* (1995). As will be discussed in a later section, however, this interpretation of British exceptionalism
has now come under sustained academic criticism.

If, as sometimes suggested in the past, armies are mirrors of their parent
society then it is the case that the British army has certainly reflected the often-
paradoxical attitudes of the British towards it. The subtitle of George Stanley,
Canada's Soldiers: The Military History of an Unmilitary People (1954) could
well stand for Britain as well. There are certainly ambiguities. John Brewer's
influential *The Sinews of Power: War, Money and the English State, 1688–1783*
(1988), to be considered again in a later section, has provoked debate on the
nature of state development in England and its relationship to warfare. David
Edgerton, *Warfare State: Britain, 1920–70* (2005) has provoked another debate
by characterising twentieth-century Britain as a warfare state rather than a
welfare state in terms of the impact of the interaction of science, technology
and industry. Essentially, however, these debates concern the nature of the state
apparatus rather than society's perception of the nature and conduct of war.

There have been attempts in the past to sum up the English or British attitudes to war, often through means of anthologies for a popular readership such
as Cyril Field, *Old Times Under Arms* (1939); Thomas Gilby, *Britain at Arms*
(1953); Eric Bush, *Salute the Soldier* (1966); and Roy Palmer, *The Rambling
Soldier* (1977). That particular literary tradition lingers in popular accounts such
as E. Sanger, *Englishmen at War: A Social History in Letters, 1450–1900* (1993);
Lawrence James, *Warrior Race: The British at War* (2001); and John Lewis-
Stempel, *The Autobiography of the British Soldier: From Agincourt to Basra in
His Own Words* (2007). Rather more important is Michael Paris, *Warrior Nation:
Images of War in British Popular Culture, 1850–2000* (2000), which presents a
serious analysis of how military values have been projected, Paris arguing that
'the overriding national image is of an aggressively militant warrior nation'.[8] An
interesting contribution was that of Lewis Winstock, *Songs and Music of the
Redcoats: A History of the War Music of the British Army, 1642–1902* (1970),
now supplemented by an important study, Trevor Herbert and Helen Barlow,
Music and the British Military in the Long Nineteenth Century (2013), that

---

8 Michael Paris's *Warrior Nation: Images of War in British Popular Culture, 1850–2000*
  (London: Reaktion, 2000), p. 11.

demonstrates not only the impact of the military on the development of music making in Britain but also the impact of military music on civilian and social life.

An anti-militarist tradition certainly predated the establishment of the standing army, and there was always a fear of the threat that such an army might pose to civil liberties. The long-standing military role in aid of the civil power prior to the creation of constabularies in the mid-nineteenth century contributed to the distrust. Useful studies of this particular aspect of the army's role have included Kenneth O. Fox, *Making Life Possible: A Study of Military Aid to the Civil Power in Regency England* (1971); Tony Hayter, *The Army and the Crowd in Mid-Georgian England* (1978); S. H. Palmer, *Police and Protest in England and Ireland, 1780–1850* (1988); Keith Jeffery and Peter Hennessy, *States of Emergency: British Governments and Strike Breaking since 1919* (1983); and Anthony Babington, *Military Intervention in Britain* (1991), although the latter was aimed more at the general reader. The last civilian killed by a civilian on the British mainland on such service was as recent as 1919, apart from those terrorists killed by the Special Air Service (SAS) in the siege of the Iranian embassy in 1980.

There was also friction between soldiers and society over issues such as billeting, which continued long after the Billeting Act of 1679 supposedly outlawed the practice and the construction of large barracks towards the end of the eighteenth century. The interaction of British garrisons and local society in Britain has been generally neglected beyond the discursive essays in Peter Dietz (ed.), *Garrison: Ten British Military Towns* (1986), which largely concentrated on the post-1945 period, and a doctoral dissertation on early nineteenth-century Windsor, from which two journal articles have been extracted, and on Colchester.[9]

By contrast, there are a number of useful studies of British garrisons overseas. The British soldier in North America has been especially well covered as in Sylvia Frey, *The British Soldier in America: A Social History of Military Life in the Revolutionary Period* (1981); John Shy, *Toward Lexington: The Role of the British Army in the Coming of the American Revolution* (1965); Stephen Brumwell, *Redcoats: The British Soldier and War in the Americas, 1755–63* (2002); Michael

---

9 Brigitte Mitchell, 'Problems of a Garrison Town: Windsor, 1815–55', PhD dissertation, University of Reading, 2001; eadem, 'The Control of Smallpox in the British Army during the Nineteenth Century based on records from the Windsor Garrison', *JSAHR* 83 (2005), 152–57; eadem, 'The Health of Recruits for the British Army during the Early Nineteenth Century', *JSAHR* 83 (2005), 215–27; A. F. F. H. Robertson, 'The Army in Colchester and Its Influence on the Social, Economic and Political Development of the Town, 1854–1914', PhD dissertation, University of Essex, 1992.

McConnell, *Army and Empire: British Soldiers on the American Frontier, 1758–75* (2004); and Richard Archer, *As if in an Enemy's Country: The British Occupation of Boston and the Origins of Revolution* (2010). The Victorian period is also reasonably covered as in M. Austin, *The Army in Australia, 1840–50* (1979); Elinor Kyte Senior, *British Regulars in Montreal: An Imperial Garrison, 1832–54* (1981); Elizabeth Muenger, *The British Military Dilemma in Ireland: Occupation Politics, 1886–1914* (1991); and Con Costello, *A Most Delightful Station: The British Army on the Curragh of Kildare, Ireland, 1855–1922* (1996). There are doctoral theses available for the garrisons on the Cape Frontier, at Pietermaritzburg in Natal, Auckland in New Zealand, and one regiment's experience in Canada.[10] There have also been some richly illustrated studies including Peter Stanley, *The Remote Garrison: The British Army in Australia, 1788–1870* (1986); Clem Sargent, *The Colonial Garrison, 1817–24: The 48th Foot in the Colony of New South Wales* (1996); and Geoff Blackburn, *Conquest and Settlement: The 21st Regiment in Western Australia, 1833–40* (1999). Particularly noteworthy is the excellent catalogue with supporting specialist essays that accompanied a major exhibition at the National Army Museum, namely Peter Boyden, Alan Guy and Marion Harding (eds), *Ashes and Blood: The British Army in South Africa, 1795–1914* (1999). Craig Wilcox, *Redcoat Dreaming: How Colonial Australia Embraced the British Army* (2009) is a particularly interesting study of the lingering cultural impact of British regulars after their withdrawal from Australia in 1870.

Other than Richard Holmes's *Sahib*, the British – as opposed to the Indian army – in India has been generally neglected, though it is touched upon in Tony Heathcote's introduction, *The Military in British India: The Development of British Land Forces in South Asia, 1600–1947* (1995). Heathcote also contributed to the valuable essays collected in Alan J Guy and Peter Boyden (eds), *Soldiers of the Raj: The Indian Army, 1600–1947* (1997), based on another major exhibition at the National Army Museum, while there is a popular history of the Indian army, Philip Mason, *A Matter of Honour: An Account of the Indian Army,*

---

10 J. B. Scott, 'The British Soldier on the Eastern Cape Frontier, 1800–50', PhD dissertation, University of Port Elizabeth, 1974; Graham Dominy, 'The Imperial Garrison in Natal with Special Reference to Fort Napier, 1843–1914: Its Social, Cultural and Economic Impact', PhD dissertation, University of London, 1995); R. A. V. Fox, 'The Rifle Brigade, Imperial Gracious and Canadian Society, 1861–70', DPhil dissertation, University of Oxford, 1993; Adam Davis, 'The Imperial Garrison in New Zealand, 1840–70 with particular reference to Auckland', PhD dissertation, University of Luton, 2004). See also Hannah Muller, 'The Garrison Revisited: Gibraltar in the Eighteenth Century', *JICH* 41 (2013), 353–76.

its Officers and Men (1974). More recent interpretations can be found in Partha Sarath Gupta and Anirudh Deshpande (eds), *The British Raj and its Indian Armed Forces, 1857–1939* (2002); DeWitt Ellinwood and Kaushik Roy (eds), *War and Society in Colonial India, 1807–1945* (2006); and Daniel Marston and Chandra Sundaram (eds), *A Military History of India and South East Asia: From the East India Company to the Nuclear Era* (2007). Kaushik Roy (ed.), *War and Society in Colonial India, 1807–1945* (2006) has an excellent introduction on the impact of 'agrarian', 'subaltern' and 'cultural' studies on the specific historiography of the Indian army. Roy is also responsible for *The Army in British India: From Colonial Warfare to Total War, 1857–1947* (2013). Stephen Peter Rosen, *Societies and Military Power: India and its Armies* (1996) puts the British experience in the much longer context of Indian history from antiquity to the post-independence era. The longer time frame is also presented in Pradeep Barua, *The State at War in South Asia* (2005). Rosen tends to follow the theme of inherent western dominance then current in the historiography, suggesting that Indian social structures determined military capability, thus rendering indigenous military systems vulnerable to the East India Company. By contrast, Barua looks beyond societal and cultural interpretations to analyse the military effectiveness of successive Indian states, arguing that they tried unsuccessfully to copy European methods. In some respects, however, this still leads back to greater European military prowess in later periods. The latest 'longue durée' approach is Kaushik Roy, *Military Manpower, Armies and Warfare in South Asia* (2013), which argues that class and culture have shaped the composition of South Asian armies from antiquity to the present.

Rather less known are the details of the British presence in the East Indies and on the China coast, for which there are three studies by Alan Harfield, *British and Indian Armies in the East Indies, 1685–1935* (1984), *British and Indian Armies on the China Coast, 1785–1985* (1990), and *Bencoolen: A History of the Honourable East India Company's Garrison on the West Coast of Sumatra, 1685–1825* (1995).

The unrepresentative nature of the army given the system of voluntary enlistment and the unattractiveness of military service also distanced the army from society. Yet, there was a certain interdependence between army and society that co-existed with the often popular indifference to the army. The presence of soldiers invariably meant trade for local businesses but the army also provided spectacle and considerable inspiration for the purveyors of popular culture. At times of major military disasters or, of course, during periodic invasion scares, soldiers would also find themselves suddenly popular. As will become apparent in later sections, there are fine studies of the army and society for most periods. Attention should be drawn here, however, to another unique aspect of the

British army, namely its regimental tradition. Military tradition, however, can be manufactured just like any other tradition.[11] One need only look at the way in which West Germany's *Bundeswehr* and East Germany's *Nationale Volksarmee* manufactured entirely different military traditions from a common military past, the former searching for appropriate democratic traditions and the latter discovering equally revolutionary traditions whilst also embracing the Convention of Tauroggen in December 1812 as a model of Russo-German co-operation.

In fact, the British regimental tradition – seen as such an essential ingredient of English county and national identity – is entirely bogus in terms of continuity and spurious in terms of county lineage. Often only nicknames and customs were transmitted from one creation to another as regiments were raised and disbanded as needs dictated, and regimental numbers simply reallocated. County affiliation was only briefly established for the first time in 1782, and not systematically applied until the localisation scheme introduced by Edward Cardwell in 1872 reached its logical conclusion in the territorialisation scheme of Hugh Childers in 1881. Little logic was applied, however, in allocating the regiments to counties.

As illustrated by David French's forensic if sometimes complex examination of the regimental tradition in *Military Identities: The Regimental System, the British Army, and the British People, c. 1870–2000* (2005), the county regiment effectively disappeared in the changes wrought between 1948 and 1958. Though French rejected criticism of the supposedly resulting parochial military culture deriving from the regiment as unsuited to major war fighting, it was all but impossible to maintain realistic county links in wartime drafting policy once casualties began to mount. Arguably, the division rather than the regiment became the real focus of loyalty in two world wars. Indeed, the disappearance of once cherished titles has had increasingly less capacity to mobilise public support outside Scotland.

Mention of Scotland raises the issue of what might be termed the Celtic factor in the British experience. While Wales was incorporated into the English military model in 1536, Scotland remained independent until the union of the English and Scottish Crowns in 1603. Even then, Scotland retained a separate military establishment until the Act of Union in 1707. Ireland also maintained a separate military establishment from 1661 until 1801. Similarly, the county lieutenancy – effectively established in England and Wales in the 1540s and 1550s – was not extended to Scotland until 1794, or to Ireland until 1831. Wales

---

11 See John Keegan, 'Regimental Ideology', in Geoffrey Best and Andrew Wheatcroft (eds), *War, Economy and the Military Mind* (London: Croom Helm, 1976), pp. 3–18.

remains distinctly neglected other than in Matthew Cragoe and Chris Williams (eds), *Wales and War: Society, Politics and Religion in the Nineteenth and Twentieth Centuries* (2007), but there are excellent overviews of Scottish and Irish military history, including their separate military traditions and mediaeval antecedents in two volumes, Thomas Bartlett and Keith Jeffery (eds) *A Military History of Ireland* (1996); and Edward Spiers, Jeremy Crang and Matthew Strickland (eds), *A Military History of Scotland* (2012). Inevitably perhaps, the treatment is occasionally uneven. Bartlett and Jeffery, for example, needed a more substantial chapter on the early twentieth century and the impact of the Great War. Spiers, Crang and Strickland have rather too much on antiquity, and no separate chapter on Scottish auxiliary forces.

There is a useful if diverse selection of subjects covered in Norman Mac-Dougall (ed.), *Scotland and War, AD79-1918* (1991). In addition, there is a brief but important overview of the Scottish military identity by Hew Strachan.[12] A thematic study of how military service has shaped the image of the Scottish soldier was presented by Stuart Allan and Allan Carswell, *The Thin Red Line: War, Empire and Visions of Scotland* (2004), based on an exhibition at Edinburgh's National War Museum of Scotland. Edward Spiers contributed further to the contemporary image in *The Scottish Soldier and Empire, 1854–1902* (2006).

Of course, the Scots and the Irish have frequently plied the military trade outside Britain. The subject lends itself to popular treatments but among academic studies are Brendan Jennings (ed.), *Wild Geese in Spanish Flanders, 1582–1700* (1964); G. Henry, *The Irish Military Community in Flanders, 1586–1621* (1992); G. G. Simpson (ed.), *The Scottish Soldier Abroad, 1247–1967* (1992); R. A. Stradling, *The Spanish Monarchy and Irish Mercenaries: The Wild Geese in Spain, 1618–68* (1994); M. E. Ailes, *Military Migration and State Formation: The British Military Community in Seventeenth Century Sweden* (2002); Matthew Glozier, *Scottish Soldiers in France in the Reign of the Sun King: Nursery for Men of Honour* (2004); and D. Worthington, *Scots in Habsburg Service, 1618–48* (2004).

Other specialised works on the Scottish and Irish experience will be included in later sections but one other aspect should be raised here. In some respects, Scots and Irish soldiers came to be regarded as 'martial races', and this has been a general theme examined by a number of historians. Heather Streets, *Martial Races: The Military, Race and Masculinity in British Imperial Culture, 1857–1914* (2004) was a case in point in linking the image of the Highlander with those of

---

12 Hew Strachan, 'Scotland's Military Identity, *Scottish Historical Review* 85 (2006), 311–32.

Sikhs and Gurkhas. She also contributed to Steve Murdoch and Andrew Mack-illop (eds), *Fighting for Identity: Scottish Military Experience, c. 1550–1900* (2002). Her efforts can be supplemented by works looking at the more obvious manifestations in Britain's colonial forces, as examined by David Omissi, *The Sepoy and the Raj: The Indian Army, 1860–1940* (1994); Lionel Caplan, *Warrior Gentlemen: Gurkhas in Western Imagination* (1995); and those essays concerning the British empire to be found in the wide-ranging collections, De Witt Ellinwood and Cynthia Enloe (eds), *Ethnicity and the Military in Asia* (1981); David Killingray and David Omissi (eds), *Guardians of Empire: The Armed Forces of the Colonial Powers, c. 1700–1964* (1999); and Tobias Rettig and Karl Hack (eds), *Colonial Armies in Southeast Asia* (2009).

Just as Scotland and Ireland have a military history predating the establishment of a standing army, this is obviously the case for England and Wales as well. In England the free man's obligation of military service was well established in medieval legislation that owed its origin to the pre-feudal period. The principle was enshrined in the first militia statutes in 1558, the 'amateur military tradition' thus long predating the appearance of a standing army in the seventeenth century. Again, the various manifestations of the amateur military tradition will be covered in subsequent sections. An overview is available in Ian F. W. Beckett, *The Amateur Military Tradition, 1558–1945* (1991). Not surprisingly, the model of such citizen soldiers serving in militias and a variety of volunteer units spread to the British Empire. It became the model for the early colonial forces in North America and the Caribbean. As might be expected, the historiography on such colonial units in North America is substantial, a useful introduction being provided by the classic work of Marcus Cunliffe, *Soldiers and Civilians: The Martial Spirit in America, 1775–1865* (1969). Typical specialised studies among many include Fred Anderson, *A People's Army: Massachusetts Soldiers and Society in the Seven Years' War* (1984); and Harold Selesky, *War and Society in Colonial Connecticut* (1990). The local forces raised elsewhere in the 'First Empire', however, have been neglected.

For the 'Second Empire', there are the essays in Ian F. W. Beckett (ed.), *Citizen Soldiers and the British Empire, 1837–1902* (2012). Among the settled colonies, South Africa has no overall modern study beyond Geoffrey Tylden's now out-dated *The Armed Forces of South Africa, 1659–1954* (1954). The development of citizen military forces in Australia, Canada and New Zealand, however, is well covered in Craig Wilcox, *For Hearths and Homes: Citizen Soldiering in Australia, 1854–1945* (1998); D. McCarthy, *The Once and Future Army: A History of the Citizen Military Forces, 1947–74* (2003), which also looks at Australia; James Wood, *Militia Myths: Ideas of the Canadian Citizen Soldier, 1896–1921*

(2010); and Peter Cooke and John Crawford, *The Territorials: The History of the Territorial and Volunteer Forces of New Zealand* (2011).[13] For the Far East, apart from Harfield's work, there is also Barry Renfrew, *Forgotten Regiments: Regular and Volunteer Units of the British Far East* (2009). Among more general studies of the military history of the dominions, the Australian army is especially well served by two general accounts by Jeffrey Grey, *The Australian Army: A History* (2006), and *A Military History of Australia* (2008). For Canada there is J. M. Hitsman, *Safeguarding Canada, 1763–1871* (1968); Desmond Morton, *A Military History of Canada* (2001); and Bernd Horn (ed.), *Forging a Nation: Perspectives on the Canadian Military Experience* (2002). More specialised studies of India and the white dominions will be included in subsequent sections.

---

13 See also H. J. Zwillenberg, 'Citizens and Soldiers: The Defence of South Australia, 1836–1901', MA dissertation, University of Adelaide, 1970; C. Neumann, 'Australia's Citizen Soldiers, 1919–39', MA dissertation, University of New South Wales, 1978; William Beahen, 'A Citizen Army: The Growth and Development of the Canadian Militia, 1904–14', PhD dissertation, University of Ottawa, 1979; J. A. B. Crawford, 'The Role and Structure of the New Zealand Volunteer Force, 1885–1910', MA dissertation, University of Canterbury, 1986; Gary Clayton, 'Defence Not Defiance: The Shaping of New Zealand's Volunteer Force', PhD dissertation, University of Waikato, 1990; Paul James Maroney, 'The Peaceable Kingdom Reconsidered: War and Culture in English Canada 1884–1914', PhD dissertation, Queen's University, 1996; R. J. Marmion, 'The Victorian Volunteer Force on the Central Victorian Goldfields, 1858–83', MA dissertation, Latrobe University, 2003; idem, 'Gibraltar of the South: Defending Victoria – An Analysis of Colonial Defence in Victoria, Australia, 1851–1901', PhD dissertation, University of Melbourne, 2009.

PART II
Research Areas and Issues

Chapter 4

1500–1702

The early modern period has been one of the most dynamic in recent decades, primarily through the debate on the 'military revolution'. In terms of older general texts already mentioned, Hale's *War and Society in Renaissance Europe, 1450–1620* (1985) from the Fontana series remains an elegantly written introduction to the period, as is Hale's *Renaissance War Studies* (1983). It can be supplemented by the relevant sections of John Childs, *Armies and Warfare in Europe, 1648–1789* (1982), and the other Fontana volume, M. S. Anderson, *War and Society, 1618–1789* (1988). André Corvisier, *Armies and Societies in Europe, 1494–1789* (1979) was another early synthesis. More recent are Frank Tallett, *War and Society in Early Modern Europe, 1495–1715* (1992), and several works by Jeremy Black: *European Warfare, 1660–1815* (1994), *European Warfare, 1494–1660* (2002), and *European Warfare in a Global Context, 1660–1815* (2006). Black has also edited *War in the Early Modern World, 1450–1815* (1999), and *European Warfare, 1453–1815* (1999), and produced a bibliographical guide, *War in European History, 1494–1660* (2006). In keeping with his mission to draw attention to the wider global context and developments beyond Europe, Black has published two further short surveys, *War in the World: A Comparative History, 1450–1600* (2011), and *Beyond the Military Revolution: War in the Seventeenth Century World* (2011). Black also contributes to Geoffrey Mortimer (ed.), *Early Modern Military History, 1450–1815* (2004), while another useful collection is Paul Hammer (ed.), *Warfare in Early Modern Europe, 1450–1660* (2007), which reprints key journal articles. The well illustrated Cassell 'History of Warfare' series has Thomas Arnold, *The Renaissance at War* (2003) and John Childs, *Warfare in the Sixteenth Century* (2001). The most recent overview are the essays in Frank Tallett and David Trim (eds), *European Warfare, 1350–1750* (2010), which take a broad ranging view encompassing the fringes of Europe.

The conflicts of the era have been well served in Michael Mallett, *Mercenaries and Their Masters: Warfare in Renaissance Italy* (1974); Michael Mallett and Christine Shaw, *The Italian Wars, 1494–1559: War, State and Society in Early Modern Europe* (2012); Christine Shaw (ed.), *Italy and the European Powers: The Impact of War, 1500–30* (2006); Stewart Oakley, *War and Peace in the Baltic, 1560–1790* (1992); Mack Holt, *The French Wars of Religion, 1562–1629* (1995);

Robert Knecht, *The French Civil Wars, 1562–98* (2000); Geoffrey Parker, *The Dutch Revolt* (1977); Marco van der Hoeven (ed.), *Exercise of Arms: Warfare in the Netherlands, 1568–1648* (1998); Ronald Asch, *The Thirty Years War: The Holy Roman Empire and Europe, 1618–48* (1997); Geoffrey Parker (ed.), *The Thirty Years War* (1984); Peter Wilson, *Europe's Tragedy: A New History of The Thirty Years War* (2009); and Robert Frost, *The Northern Wars: War, State and Society in Northeastern Europe, 1558–1721* (2000). There are also the relevant sections of Peter Wilson, *German Armies: War and German Politics, 1648–1806* (1998); John Lynn, *The Wars of Louis XIV, 1667–1714* (1999), and Michael Hochedlinger, *Austria's Wars of Emergence: War, State and Society in the Habsburg Monarchy, 1683–1797* (2003). The Habsburg struggle with the Ottomans, including the siege and relief of Vienna in 1683, is covered in Andrew Wheatcroft, *The Enemy at the Gate: Habsburgs, Ottomans and the Battle for Europe* (2009).

The wider world is covered in more specialised works such as Carol Stevens, *Russia's Wars of Emergence, 1460–1730* (2007); Jos Gommans, *Mughal Warfare: Imperial Frontiers and Highroads to Empire, 1500–1700* (2002); Rhoads Murphey, *Ottoman Warfare, 1500–1700* (1999); Brian L. Davies (ed.), *Warfare in Eastern Europe, 1500–1800* (2012); S. R. Turnbull, *Samurai Invasion: Japan's Korean War, 1592–98* (2002); Caroline Finkel, *The Administration of Warfare: Ottoman Campaigns in Hungary, 1593–1606* (1988); Gábor Ágoston, *Guns for the Sultan: Military Power and the Weapons Industry in the Ottoman Empire* (2005); Virginia Aksan, *Ottoman Wars, 1700–1870: An Empire Besieged* (2007); Brian L. Davies, *Warfare, State and Society on the Black Sea Steppe, 1500–1700* (2007); Weston Cook, *The Hundred Years War for Morocco: Gunpowder and the Military Revolution in the Early Modern Muslim World* (1994); and John Laband, *Bringers of War: The Portuguese in Africa during the Age of Gunpowder and Sail from the Fifteenth to the Eighteenth Century* (2013).

One specialised area is covered by a number of essays in David Trim and Mark C. Fissel (eds), *Amphibious Warfare, 1000–1700: Commerce, State Formation and European Expansion* (2005), while David Trim (ed.), *The Chivalric Ethos and the Development of Military Professionalism* (2003) explores the emergence of the profession of arms in the early modern period. Other impacts of warfare are explored in J. R. Mulryne and Margaret Shewring, *War, Literature and the Arts in Sixteenth Century Europe* (1989); John Hale, *Artists and Warfare in the Renaissance* (1990); and Sydney Anglo, *The Martial Arts of Renaissance Europe* (2000). The causes of conflict are examined in Jeremy Black (ed.), *The Origins of War in Early Modern Europe* (1987). For siege warfare, there is Christopher Duffy, *Siege Warfare: The Fortress in Early Modern History, 1494–1660* (1979), and

Simon Pepper and Nicholas Adams, *Firearms and Fortifications: Military Archi-tecture and Siege Warfare in Sixteenth Century Siena* (1986). On logistics, see the relevant sections of Martin van Creveld, *Supplying War: Logistics from Wallenstein to Patton* (1977) and John Lynn (ed.), *Feeding Mars: Logistics in Western Warfare from the Middle Ages to the Present* (1993). John Lynn, *Women, Armies and Warfare in Early Modern Europe* (2008), suggests women were central to the functioning of armies. The demographic impact of warfare is also covered in Myron Gutt-man, *War and Rural Life in the Early Modern Low Countries* (1980).

As reflected in the general texts, the principal theme has been the 'military revolution'. The identification of a military revolution in the early modern period is not new, having been advanced first by Michael Roberts as long ago as 1955 in his inaugural lecture at Queen's, Belfast, *The Military Revolution, 1560–1660* (1956).[1] Roberts contended that the introduction of effective musketry around 1560 paved the way for a century of change. According to Roberts, the Dutch first recognised the importance of bringing the largest possible number of fire-arms to bear upon an opposing formation, but it was the Swedish King, Gustavus Adolphus, who refined the emerging linear tactics by extending the frontages of his forces and using them far more aggressively. The decrease in the depth of formations and the increase in the length of the line necessitated both more officers to supervise firing along an extended line but also better training and discipline. This stimulated growth in the size of armies and in the administrative machinery required to maintain an army. As a consequence of the changes, Sweden played a decisive role in the Thirty Years War of 1618–48, safeguarding the permanence of the Protestant reformation and leading to major alterations in state structures in order to pay for the new weapons and to train men in their use.

Geoffrey Parker returned to the theme in a journal article in 1976,[2] subse-quently producing *The Military Revolution: Military Innovation and the Rise of the West, 1500–1800* (1988). Parker, who had established his reputation with *The Army of Flanders and the Spanish Road, 1567–1659* (1972), pushed the time frame back to the period between 1450 and 1530, relating the changes in warfare to the development of artillery, notably the use of a highly mobile artillery train by Charles VIII of France when he invaded Italy in 1494. Parker argued that the challenge posed to masonry fortifications forced military engineers into

---

1 It was reproduced in Michael Roberts (ed.), *Essays in Swedish History* (London: Weidenfeld & Nicolson, 1967), pp. 195–225.
2 Geoffrey Parker, 'The Military Revolution, 1560–1660: a Myth?' *Journal of Modern History* 47 (1976), 195–214.

radical solutions based on complex and extensive earthworks and angled bastions. The attempt to keep the enemy from the walls led to ever larger systems of fortifications that had stimulated the growth of armies and administration for defending and besieging these works demanded troops of better quality with better equipment. It thus forced major changes on European states, the resulting military power then being translated into world power.[3] Artillery itself is covered in Bert Hall, *Weapons and Warfare in Renaissance Europe: Gunpowder, Technology and Tactics* (1997).

This argument, in turn, was countered by Jeremy Black, *A Military Revolution? Military Change and European Society, 1550–1800* (1991). For Black, both Roberts and Parker had placed the significant changes far too early and he argued that it was only after 1660 and more particularly after 1720 that European armies began to take a decisive lead. He suggested that the real growth in the size of armies was not driven by technological changes but by social and political developments in Europe linked to the emergence of royal absolutism and a more stable relationship between monarchies and aristocratic elites, who became servants of the state. Black suggested that it was only after European kings and aristocracies found themselves safely back in power after the disfiguring wars of religion that dominated most of the seventeenth century that there was time, capital and a sense of security sufficient to consolidate into exploitation and refinement of technology. Moreover, Black maintained that, although there were qualitative advances in weaponry, it was not so much technology as technique that was decisive on the battlefield with better battlefield discipline and manoeuvrability through complex evolutions giving Europe the advantage.

The debate has widened well beyond tactical, technological and organisational issues into one of growing sophistication concerning the complexity of the relationship between warfare, the rise and formation of the state, and the instruments of state power. Indeed, most early modern historians are agreed that some form of transformation or, rather, evolution in military affairs was crucial to the outcome of European history in terms of the emergence of modern state systems, even if they might hold varying opinions on precisely where and when it occurred. A useful summary with key journal articles, including important early work by John Lynn and David Parrott, is Clifford J. Rogers (ed.), *The Military Revolution Debate: Readings on the Military Transformation of Early Modern Europe* (1995).

---

3 See also Geoffrey Parker, 'The "Military Revolution", 1955–2005: From Belfast to Barcelona and The Hague', *JMH* 69 (2005), 205–10.

Subsequent monographs relating to the impact of the military revolution and the relationship between war and the rise of the modern state have been many. More general treatments include Michael Duffy (ed.), *The Military Revolution and the State, 1500–1800* (1980); Brian Downing, *The Military Revolution and Political Change: Origins of Democracy and Autocracy in Early Modern Europe* (1990); and David Eltis, *The Military Revolution in Sixteenth Century Europe* (1995) that, as the title implies, suggests the military revolution was confined to the sixteenth century. There are relevant essays in John Lynn (ed.), *Tools of War: Instruments, Ideas and Institutions of Warfare, 1445–1871* (1990). David Parrott, *The Business of War: Military Enterprise and Military Revolution in Early Modern Europe* (2012) points to the survival of what might be termed private sector networks in the management of warfare alongside emerging state bureaucracies. There have also been a large number of studies of specific states too numerous to mention here.

The concept of the military revolution also attracted the attention of medieval historians. Clifford Rogers, for example, writing in 1993, argued that the transformations of the early modern period were in fact built upon medieval developments.[4] Thus, for Rogers, after about 1300 foot soldiers became more important than mounted ones especially through the firepower revolution of the longbow. Though some argued for an 'infantry revolution' in the medieval period,[5] Rogers thought that these developments did not constitute a revolution: rather there were a series of points of accelerated change, which eventually came together. The medieval 'military revolution' was then examined in Andrew Ayton and John Price (eds), *The Medieval Military Revolution: State, Society and Military Change in Medieval and Early Modern Europe* (1998). It emphasises the evolutionary development of warfare, suggesting, for example, that the Dutch Republic fought 'modern' wars with 'medieval' political institutions.

In some respects, the debate was further distorted by a concern with a 'revolution in military affairs' (RMA) postulated by contemporary, especially American, military theorists in the 1990s and their ahistorical attempt to push it backwards to the debate on the early modern period, as in Williamson Murray and MacGregor Knox (eds), *The Dynamics of Military Revolution, 1300–2050* (2001), and Colin Gray, *Strategy for Chaos: Revolutions in Military Affairs and the Evidence of History* (2004). Technology became something of a byword for

---

4 Clifford J. Rogers, 'The Military Revolution of the Hundred Years War', *JMH* 57 (1993), 241–78.

5 John Stone, 'Technology, Society and the Infantry Revolution of the Fourteenth Century', *JMH* 68 (2004), 361–80.

military revolution in the context of the RMA debate, the assumption that technology was decisive being a throwback to Whiggish history. In any case, some new technologies might prove a blind alley while their adoption might also be shaped by cultural peculiarities.

Certainly, the assumption – particularly explicit in Parker – is that the military revolution was essentially a phenomenon in the West and explained western dominance as Europe began to expand. It has become increasingly clear, however, that in expanding their empires, Europeans adapted to local conditions, including existing patterns of warfare. There are two useful introductions. Douglas Peers (ed.), *Warfare and Empires: Contact and Conflict between European and Non-European Military and Maritime Forces and Cultures* (1997), covers aspects of European military interaction with Africa, Asia and the Americas from 1415 onwards. The equally wide-ranging Wayne Lee (ed.), *Empires and Indigenes: Intercultural Alliance, Imperial Expansion, and Warfare in the Early Modern World* (2011) concentrates on evidence of European adaptation of indigenous military and diplomatic norms. In India in particular, the East India Company conformed to traditional means of raising armed forces within the existing military labour market, as suggested by Dirk Kolff, *Naukar, Rajput, and Sepoy: The Ethnohistory of the Military Labour Market of Hindustan, 1450–1850* (1990). In Central America, indigenous manpower was just as significant for the Spanish conquest as new technology, as illustrated by Laura Matthews, *Indian Conquistadors: Indigenous Allies in the Conquest of Mesoamerica* (2007)

European involvement in North America has attracted particular interest as in Patrick Malone, *The Skulking Way of War: Technology and Tactics among the New England Indians* (1991); Ian Steele, *Warpaths: Invasions of North America* (1994); Armstrong Starkey, *European and Native American Warfare, 1675–1815* (1998); William Nester, *The Great Frontier War: Britain, France and the Imperial Struggle for North America, 1607–1755* (2000); Guy Chet, *Conquering the American Wilderness: The Triumph of European Warfare in the Colonial Northeast* (2003); and John Grenier, *The First Way of War: American War Making on the Frontier, 1607–1814* (2005). The early clashes between settlers and Indians in New England have been covered in Alfred Cave, *The Pequot War* (1996), and James Drake, *King Philip's War: Civil War in New England, 1675–76* (1975). Somewhat ambitiously, Wayne Lee, *Barbarians and Brothers: Anglo-American Warfare, 1500–1865* (2011), suggests parallels between Elizabethan Ireland, Civil War England and North America.

Inevitably, the issues of the military revolution and the relationship of war have been raised in connection with the emergence of the British state. An ambitious overview is Roger Manning, *An Apprenticeship in Arms: The Origins of the British Army, 1585–1702* (2006), which sought to establish the significance of the influence on an evolving professional officer corps of those who had experienced overseas service.

While the establishment of the standing army is variously ascribed to different dates in the latter half of the seventeenth century, it is clear that the first real standing forces emerged during the reign of Henry VII, as suggested by Anita Hewerdine, *The Yeomen of the Guard and the Early Tudors: The Formation of a Royal Bodyguard* (2012). G. C. Cruiskshank covered two of Henry's overseas expeditions in *Army Royal: Henry VIII's Invasion of France, 1513* (1969) and *The English Occupation of Tournai, 1513–19* (1971), both well written campaign narratives, and it will be recalled that his *Elizabeth's Army* (1946) was updated 20 years after its original publication. The emergence of standing forces slowly eclipsed the earlier reliance upon mercenaries, as shown in Gilbert Millar, *Tudor Mercenaries and Auxiliaries, 1485–1547* (1980). As suggested earlier, too, local auxiliary forces predated standing forces, and these were covered by another older work, Lindsay Boynton, *The Elizabethan Militia, 1558–1638* (1967), which cast some glances back to the pre-Elizabethan period. It can now be supplemented by Neil Younger, *War and Politics in the Elizabethan Counties* (2012), which concentrates on counties in Southeast England.[6] Henrician military organisation is also covered in a number of articles.[7]

The only permanent garrison, however, was that at Calais, the subject of David Grummitt, *The Calais Garrison: War and Military Service in England, 1436–1558*

---

6 See also A. Hassell Smith, 'Militia Rates and Militia Statutes, 1558–1663', in Peter Clarke, A.G. R. Smith and N. Tyacke (eds), *The English Commonwealth, 1547–1640: Essays in Politics and Society presented to Joel Hurstfield* (Leicester: Leicester University Press, 1979), pp. 93–110; Joyce Youings, 'Bowman, Billmen and Hackbutters: The Elizabethan Militia in the South West', in R. Higham (ed.), *Security and Defence in South-west England before 1800* (1987), pp. 51–68; E. J. Bourgeois, 'Meeting the Demands of War: Late Elizabethan Militia Management in Cambridgeshire', *The Local Historian* 26 (1996), 130–41; Michael Braddick, ' "Uppon this instant extraordinaire occasion": Military Mobilisation in Yorkshire before and after the Armada', *Huntington Library Quarterly* 61 (2000), 429–55.

7 See Steve Gunn, 'The Duke of Suffolk's March on Paris in 1523', *EHR* 101 (1986), 596–634; idem, 'The French Wars of Henry VIII', in Jeremy Black (ed.), *The Origins of War in Early Modern Europe* (Edinburgh: John Donald, 1987), pp. 28–47; idem, 'The Army of Henry VIII: A Reassessment', *JSAHR* 75 (1997), 9–23; Gervase Phillips, 'To cry "Home! Home!": Mutiny, Morale, and Indiscipline in Tudor Armies', *JMH* 65 (2001), 313–32.

(2008), its defence also immediately raising issues of technological development.[8] In terms of the wider debate, there is also Steven Gunn, David Grummitt and Hans Cool, *War, State, and Society in England and the Netherlands, 1477–1559* (Oxford, 2007), which saw war as a significant factor in shaping social and political change.[9] They broadly concur with the analysis for the later period of Michael Braddick, *State Formation in Early Modern England, c. 1550–1700* (2000), Braddick having also specifically addressed the issue of a military revolution in England.[10]

Mark C. Fissel provides a useful overview of the Henrician, Elizabethan and Stuart periods in *English Warfare, 1511–1642* (2001), and there are also some valuable essays on such matters as logistics and the projection of Elizabethan power overseas in Mark C. Fissel (ed.), *War and Government in Britain, 1598–1650* (1991). Slightly less extensive in its periodisation is the excellent Paul Hammer, *Elizabeth's Wars: War, Government and Society in Tudor England, 1544–1604* (2003), which covers naval as well as military affairs. Fissel suggests sustained progress in an 'English art of war' that established the foundations of British military power. By contrast, Hammer sees less evidence of a military revolution than of a minimal adaptation of continental practice sufficient to achieve the government's aims before a rapid decline in the capacity of English military and financial structures that endured until the political crisis of the 1640s.

A useful summary of overseas campaigns over a lengthy period with emphasis upon the role of contingency in Ireland, North America, the Caribbean and India, is Bruce Lenman, *England's Colonial Wars, 1550–1688: Conflicts, Empire and National Identity* (2001). Contrasting Elizabethan campaigns were covered in R. B. Wernham (ed.), *The Expedition of Sir John Norris and Sir Francis Drake to Spain and Portugal, 1589* (1988), and Howell Lloyd, *The Rouen Campaign, 1590–92: Politics, Warfare and the Early Modern State* (1973). John Nolan, *Sir John Norreys and the Elizabethan Military World* (1997) reviews the career of a prominent soldier, but it is not free of errors. R. B. Wernham's two volumes, *After the Armada: Elizabethan England and the Struggle for Western Europe, 1588–95* (1984) and *The Return of the Armadas: The Last Years of the Elizabethan*

---

8 See also David Grummitt, 'The Defence of Calais and the Development of Gunpowder Weaponry in England in the Late Fifteenth Century', *WH* 7 (2000), pp. 253–72.

9 See also Steven Gunn, David Grummitt and Hans Cool, 'War and the State in Early Modern Europe: Widening the Debate', *WH* 15 (2008), 371–88.

10 Michael Braddick, 'An English Military Revolution?' *HJ* 36 (1993), 965–75.

War against Spain, 1595–1603 (1994) provide a majestic narrative. The Earl of Leicester's expedition to the Netherlands has also been examined by Simon Adams, who is critical of Cruickshank's influence on the historiography of the Elizabethan army.[11] For many years, the standard work on the Elizabethan campaigns in Ireland was Cyril Falls, *Elizabeth's Irish Wars* (1950) but this can now be supplemented by Nicholas Canny, *The Elizabethan Conquest of Ireland: A Pattern Established, 1565–76* (1976); and two works by John McGurk, *The Elizabethan Conquest of Ireland: The 1590s Crisis* (1997), and *The Recruitment and Transport of English Troops and their Service in Ireland, 1594–1603* (1982). Like Hammer, McGurk raises the extent of any military revolution in English practice, suggesting that the Elizabethan state did consciously emulate other monarchical states' military trends, albeit only slowly. The extent of military knowledge was covered in Henry Webb, *Elizabethan Military Science: The Books and the Practice* (1965), while the political attitudes of an emerging group of professional soldiers is examined in Rory Rapple, *Martial Power and Elizabethan Political Culture: Military Men in England and Ireland, 1558–94* (2009). Rapple suggests that experience of warfare in Ireland was less significant in radicalising soldiers than their frustrations with Elizabethan foreign policy. Militarisation generally is discussed by John Nolan, as previously indicated.[12] Though naturally principally concerned with naval matters, there was some coverage of the armies that might have come to blows in the catalogue of the tercentenary exhibition at Greenwich, *Armada, 1588–1988* (1988).

There are implications, too, for the supposed peripheral nature of warfare in Ireland in James Raymond, *Henry VIII's Military Revolution: The Armies of Sixteenth Century Britain and Europe* (2007), and Gervase Phillips, *The Anglo-Scots Wars, 1513–50: A Military History* (1999), both of which argue that the

---

11 Simon Adams, 'A Puritan Crusade? The Composition of the Earl of Leicester's Expedition to the *Netherlands*, 1585–1586', in Paul Hoftijzer (ed.), *The Dutch in Crisis, 1585–1588: People and Politics in Leicester's Time* (Leiden: Sir Thomas Browne Institute, 1988), pp. 7–34. See also W. T. McCaffrey, 'The Newhaven Expedition, 1562–63', *HJ* 40 (1997), 1–23; David Trim, 'The "Foundations of the British Army"? The Normandy Campaign of 1562', *JSAHR* 77 (1999), 74–81; and Tracy Borman, 'Sir Francis Vere in the Netherlands, 1589–1603: A Re-evaluation of his Career as Sergeant-Major of Elizabeth I's Troops', PhD dissertation, University of Hull, 1997.

12 John Nolan, 'The Militarisation of the Elizabethan State', *JMH* 58 (1994), 391–420. See also David Trim, 'Fighting "Jacob's Warres": The Employment of English and Welsh Mercenaries in the European Wars of Religion: France and the Netherlands, 1562–1610', PhD dissertation, University of London, 2002.

accreditation of military adaptation in England and Scotland was in the main-stream of European development, although Phillips emphasises the persistent appearance of the longbow in English practice.[13] Some claim has been made for the modernisation of Irish forces in Darren McGettigan, *Red Hugh O'Donnell and the Nine Years War* (2005) and Hiram Morgan, *Tyrone's Rebellion: The Outbreak of the Nine Years' War in Tudor Ireland* (1993). The general assumption has been that the Gaelic world remained apart from progressive military developments in Europe, the prolongation of offensive tactics that emphasised the efficacy of blade weapons into an increasingly technological age condemning Irish and Highland armies to catastrophic defeat in the face of overwhelming defensive firepower. Many Irishmen were to serve abroad, however, and absorb continental military practices.[14] It was also argued in James Michael Hill, *Celtic Warfare, 1595–1763* (1986) that firearms were integrated fully into 'Celtic' offensive tactics, whereas British and continental armies saw firepower as primarily defensive, thus prolonging the 'Celtic charge' until improved muskets, socket bayonets and light field artillery in the eighteenth century sufficiently increased defensive power to blunt the shock impact. Hill's thesis has been attacked both in terms of the supposed uniqueness of the Celtic charge, and also as to the extent to which the Scots in particular relied on cold steel. As suggested by Frost's *The Northern Wars*, and by essays in Steve Murdoch (ed.), *Scotland and the Thirty Years War, 1618–48* (2001), the Swedes also employed similar shock infantry tactics. Recent archaeological investigations at Culloden, as reported in Tony Pollard (ed.), *Culloden: The History and Archaeology of the Last Clan Battle* (2009) have also demonstrated that there were far more muskets available to the Jacobite army and the fighting was at far closer quarters than previously thought.[15] Moreover, Padraig Lenihan, *Confederate Catholics at War, 1641–1649* (2001), and essays in Padraig Lenihan (ed.), *Conquest and Resistance: War in Seventeenth Century Ireland* (2001), stress far more evidence of evolving

---

13 See also Gervase Phillips, 'In the Shadow of Flodden: Tactics, Technology and Scottish Military Effectiveness, 1514–1550', *Scottish Historical Review* 77 (1998), 162–82.

14 Rolf Loeber and Geoffrey Parker, 'The Military Revolution in Seventeenth Century Ireland', in Jane Ohlmeyer (ed.), *Ireland from Independence to Occupation* (Cambridge: Cambridge University Press, 1995), pp. 66–88.

15 See also James Michael Hill, 'The Distinctiveness of Gaelic Warfare, 1400–1750', *EHQ* 221 (992), 323–45; idem, 'The Origins and Development of the Highland Charge, *c.* 1650–1646', *Militärgeschichtliche Mitteilungen* 53 (1994), 295–307; idem, 'Killiecrankie and the Evolution of Highland Warfare', *WH* 1 (1994), 125–39.

military modernity than elements of antiquity and Irish military adaptation to the changing nature of warfare.

Lenihan views the introduction of Cromwellian military and financial organisation, coupled with the sheer ruthlessness of the suppression of resistance, as the real moment of military revolution in Ireland. Cromwellian financial innovation is also stressed by James Scott Wheeler, *The Making of a World Power: War and the Military Revolution in Seventeenth Century England* (1999). The intrusion on the Irish scene by the English parliamentary war machine is in itself also a useful reminder of the wider context. Where military historians tended once to write of the English Civil Wars between 1642 and 1660, the wider approach is now reflected in the preferred terminology of some in referring to the Wars of the Three Kingdoms. The military aspects of the conflict have been well covered by a number of overviews, each in turn drawing upon recent research including John Kenyon, *The Civil Wars of England* (1988); Martyn Bennett, *The Civil War in Britain and Ireland, 1638–1651* (1997); the wide-ranging John Kenyon and Jane Ohlmeyer (eds), *The Civil Wars: A Military History of England, Scotland, and Ireland, 1638–1660* (1998); James Scott Wheeler, *The Irish and British Wars, 1637–1654: Triumph, Tragedy and Failure* (2002); David Scott, *Politics and War in Three Stuart Kingdoms, 1637–1649* (2004); Malcolm Wanklyn and Frank Jones, *A Military History of the English Civil War, 1642–46: Strategy and Tactics* (2005); Ian Gentles, *The English Revolution and the Wars in the Three Kingdoms, 1638–1652* (2007); and Michael Braddick, *God's Fury, England's Fire: A New History of the English Civil Wars* (2008).

The issue of the control of both the standing army and the militia was crucial to the growing rift between Crown and Parliament, as explored by L. G. Schwoerer.[16] The county lieutenancies have figured in many of local studies, including editions of lieutenancy or other military papers published by county record societies. Examples include W. P. D. Murphy (ed.), *The Earl of Hertford's Lieutenancy Papers, 1603–12* (1969) for Wiltshire; Jeremy Goring and Joan Wake (eds), *Northamptonshire Lieutenancy Papers, 1580–1614* (1974); and B. W. Quinnell (ed.), *The Maynard Lieutenancy Book, 1608–39* (1993) for Essex. The lieutenancy takes centre stage in Victor Stater, *Noble Government:*

---

16 L. G. Schwoerer, 'The Fittest Subject for a King's Quarrel: An Essay on the Militia Controversy, 1642', *JBS* 2 (1971), 187–212. See also Lawson C. Nagel, 'The Militia of London, 1641–49', PhD dissertation, University of London, 1982; idem, ' "A Great Bouncing at Everyman's Door": The Struggle for London's Militia in 1642', in Stephen Porter (ed.), *London and the Civil War* (Basingstoke: Macmillan, 1996), pp. 68–83.

The Stuart Lieutenancy and the Transformation of English Politics (1994).[17] Matters first came to a head in the Bishops' Wars against the Scots in 1638–9 as covered in Mark C. Fissel, *The Bishops' Wars* (1994). One specialist study of value is Richard W. Stewart, *The English Ordnance Office, 1585–1625: A Case Study in Bureaucracy* (1996), while David Lawrence, *The Complete Soldier: Military Books and Military Culture in Early Stuart England, 1603–45* (2009) usefully extends the discussion of Elizabethan military cultures by Webb and Rapple mentioned previously.

In terms of the Wars of the Three Kingdoms, there have been an increasing number of studies of individual battles, campaigns, military leaders and county studies of the course and impact of the conflict: too many, indeed, to attempt to summarise. Mention should be made, however, of the pioneering efforts of Brigadier Peter Young to reconstruct orders of battle and battle itself in *Edgehill, 1642: The Campaign and the Battle* (1967); *Marston Moor, 1644: The Campaign and the Battle* (1970); (with Margaret Toynbee) *Cropredy Bridge, 1644: The Campaign and the Battle* (1970); and *Naseby, 1645: The Campaign and the Battle* (1985). Peter Newman, *Marston Moor* (1981); Glenn Foard, *Naseby: The Decisive Campaign* (1995) and Martin Matrix Evans, Peter Burton and Michael Westaway, *Naseby: English Civil War – June 1645* (2002) all make full use of evolving archaeological investigations.

Equally, a pioneering framework for local studies was established by John Morrill, *The Revolt of the Provinces: Conservatives and Radicals in the English Civil War, 1630–50* (1976), not least in its examination of the terms of rival local taxation and committee systems.[18] The process was perhaps started by Alan Everitt, who wrote on the local county communities in both Suffolk and Kent in the 1960s, as well as *The Local Community and the English Civil War* (1969).[19] Again, publications by record societies should not be neglected. Examples include H. G. Tibbutt (ed.), *The Letter Books of Sir Samuel Luke, 1644–45: Parliamentary Governor of Newport Pagnell* (1963), a joint venture between the Historical Manuscripts Commission and Bedfordshire; and Alan Thomson (ed.), *The Impact of the First Civil War on Hertfordshire, 1642–47* (2007).

---

17 See also Henrik Langelüddecke, '"The Chieftest Strength and Glory of this Kingdom": Arming and Training the "Perfect Militia" in the 1630s', *EHR* 118 (2003), 124–53.

18 See also Martyn Bennett, 'Contribution and Assessment: Financial Extractions in the English Civil War, 1642–46', *W&S* 4 (1986), 1–11.

19 Originally an Historical Association pamphlet, it is reprinted in R. C. Richardson (ed.), *The English Civil Wars: Local Aspects* (Basingstoke: Palgrave/Macmillan, 1997).

Royalist military organisation is the focus of Ronald Hutton, *The Royalist War Effort, 1642–46* (1982); Joyce Malcolm, *Caesar's Due: Loyalty and King Charles, 1642–45* (1983); and Peter Newman, *The Old Service: Royalist Regimental Colonels and the Civil War, 1642–46* (1993).[20] A number of doctoral theses also address the Royalist armies.[21] For Parliamentary organisation, there is Clive Holmes, *The Eastern Association in the English Civil War* (1974), and other unpublished theses extending to the overwhelming military presence during the Interregnum.[22] Beyond the many popular biographies of leading military figures, generalship as a whole has also received attention, as have tactics.[23]

Of course, that military presence reflected the emergence of the New Model Army. Mark Kishlansky, *The Rise of the New Model Army* (1979), and Ian Gentles, *The New Model Army in England, Ireland and Scotland, 1645–53* (1991) take opposing views on the character of the new army since Kishlansky sees it as differing little from its predecessors. The impact of militarisation is also covered in Roger Manning, *Swordsmen: The Martial Ethos in the Three Kingdoms* (2003); Austin Woolrych, *Soldiers and Statesmen: The General Council of the Army and its Debates, 1647–48* (1987), and R. Hainsworth, *The Swordsmen in*

---

20 See also Joyce Malcolm, 'A King in Search of Soldiers: Charles I in 1642', *HJ* 21 (1978), 251–74; Malcolm Wanklyn and Peter Young, 'A King in Search of Soldiers: Charles I in 1642: A Rejoinder', *HJ* 24 (1981), 147–54; Malcolm Wanklyn, 'Royalist Strategy in the South of England, 1642–44', *Southern History* 3 (1981), 54–79.

21 Ian Roy, 'The Royalist Army in the First Civil War', DPhil dissertation, University of Oxford, 1963; Peter Newman, 'The Royalist Army in Northern England, 1642–45', DPhil dissertation, University of York, 1978; Martyn Bennett, 'The Royalist War Effort in the North Midlands, 1642–46', PhD dissertation, University of Loughborough, 1986. See also Malcolm Wanklyn, 'The King's Armies in the West of England, 1642–46', MA dissertation, University of Manchester, 1966.

22 Jennifer Jones, 'The War in the North: The Northern Parliamentary Army in the English Civil War, 1642–45', PhD dissertation, York University (Canada), 1991; and J. G. A. Ive, 'The Local Dimensions of Defence: The Standing Army and the Militia in Norfolk, Suffolk and Essex, 1949–60', PhD dissertation, University of Cambridge, 1986.

23 Roger Manning, 'Styles of Command in Seventeenth Century English Armies', *JMH* 71 (2007), 701–42; Malcolm Wanklyn, 'A General Much Maligned: The Earl of Manchester as Army Commander in the Second Newbury Campaign', *WH* 14 (2007), 133–56; Aaron Graham, 'The Earl of Essex and Parliament's Army at the Battle of Edgehill: A Reassessment', *WH* 17 (2010), 276–93; Gavin Robinson, 'Equine Battering Rams? A Reassessment of Cavalry Charges in the English Civil War', *JMH* 75 (2011), 718–32.

Power: War and Politics in the English Republic, 1649–60 (1997). Later memories of the brief rule of the Major Generals can be contrasted with the reality as examined by Christopher Durston *Cromwell's Major Generals: Godly Government during the English Revolution* (2001), and Henry Reece, *The Army in Cromwellian England, 1649–60* (2013).[24] Important essays on the army's politics by John Morrill are reproduced in John Morrill (ed.), *The Nature of the English Revolution* (1993), while he also contributes to Michael Mendle (ed.), *The Putney Debates of 1647: The Army, the Levellers and the English State* (2001). A lingering autocratic tendency on the part of the military overseas is detected in Stephen Saunders Webb, *The Governors General: The English Army and the Definition of Empire, 1569–1682* (1979). Webb went on to illustrate the same theme in succeeding studies, *The Governors-General, 1676: The End of American Independence* (1984); *The Governors-General, Lord Churchill's Coup: The Anglo-American Empire and the Glorious Revolution Reconsidered* (1995); and *Marlborough's America* (2013), which suggests officers nominated by Marlborough to American provincial appointments continued to shape American development well into the eighteenth century.

Specialised aspects are covered in Anne Laurence, *Parliamentary Army Chaplains, 1642–51* (1990); Stephen Porter, *Destruction in the English Civil Wars* (1994); Eric Gruber von Arni, *Justice to the Maimed Soldier: Nursing, Medical Care and Welfare for the Sock and Wounded Soldiers and Their Families during the English Civil Wars and Interregnum, 1642–60* (2001); Peter Edwards, *Dealing in Death: The Arms Trade and the British Civil Wars, 1638–52* (2000); Ben Coates, *The Impact of the English Civil War on the Economy of London* (2004); Mark Stoyle, *Soldiers and Strangers: An Ethnic History of the English Civil War* (2005); John Ellis, *To Walk in the Dark: Military Intelligence in the English Civil War, 1642–46* (2011); Gavin Robinson, *Horses, People and Parliament in the English Civil War: Extracting Resources and Constructing Allegiances* (2012); Barbara Donagan, *War in England, 1642–49* (2008), which builds on earlier articles to examine such issues as accepted codes of military conduct and atrocities; and Andrew Hopper, *Turncoats and Renegadoes: Changing Sides during the English Civil War* (2012).[25]

---

24 See also Austin Woolrych, 'The Cromwellian Protectorate: A Military Dictatorship?' *History* 72 (1990), 207–33; G. Catemario, 'The Political Making of the New Model Army, 1644–47', PhD dissertation, University of London, 2002; Henry Midgley, 'The Political Thinking of the New Model Army, 1647–54', PhD dissertation, University of Cambridge, 2008.

25 See also Ian Roy, 'England Turned Germany? The Aftermath of the Civil War in its European Context', *Transactions of the Royal Historical Society* 5th ser. 28 (1978), 127–44; Stephen Porter, 'The Fire Raid in the English Civil War', *W&S* 2 (1984), 27–40; Michael O'Siochrui, 'Atrocity, Codes of Conduct and the Irish in the British Civil Wars, 1641–53', *P&P* 195 (2007), 55–86.

There are useful articles and dissertations on logistics such as horse supply.[26] Two publications by the Oxfordshire Record Society are also very relevant, Ian Roy (ed.), *The Royalist Ordnance Papers, 1642–46*, 2 vols. (1964 and 1975); and Margaret Toynbee (ed.), *The Papers of Captain Henry Stevens, Waggonmaster to King Charles I* (1960–1). Ordnance is also covered by Stephen Bull, *The Furie of the Ordnance: Artillery in the English Civil Wars* (2008), based in part on his 1989 Swansea doctoral dissertation on the development of ordnance in Britain between 1580 and 1655.

Surviving field remains of the war are covered in Peter Harrington, *English Civil War Archaeology* (2004), which provides a useful introduction. It can now be supplemented by a substantial overview, Glenn Foard, *Battlefield Archaeology of the English Civil War* (2012). One account informed by archaeological investigation is Foard's own *Naseby: The Decisive Campaign* (1995). Similarly, archaeological investigation in a Northamptonshire deer park used by cavalry for target practice has resulted in D. F. Harding, *Lead Shot of the English Civil War: A Radical Study* (2012).

The Restoration in 1660 was predicated on a constitutional settlement – so far as the standing army was concerned – that remained to be clarified, ultimately being resolved between 1689 and 1702. L. G. Schwoerer, *No Standing Armies: The Anti-Army Ideology in Seventeenth Century England* (1974) covers the continuing debate.[27] There is a useful overview in Alan Guy and Jenny Spencer-Smith (eds), *Glorious Revolution? The Fall and Rise of the British Army, 1660–1704* (1988), a catalogue of a major exhibition at the National Army Museum for the tercentenary of 1688, including a bibliographical essay. The evolution of the army, however, is best traced in the successive studies of John Childs: *The Army of Charles II* (1976); *The Army, James II and the Glorious Revolution* (1980); and

---

26 James Scott Wheeler, 'The Logistics of the Cromwellian Conquest of Scotland, 1650–51', *W&S* 10 (1992), 1–18; Peter Edwards, 'The Supply of Horses to the Parliamentarian and Royalist Armies in the English Civil War', *Historical Research* 68 (1995), 49–66; Aryeh Nusbacher, 'Civil Supply in the Civil War: Supply of Victuals to the New Model Army in the Naseby Campaign, 1645', *EHR* 115 (2000), 145–60; idem, 'Triple Thread: The Supply of Victuals to the Army under Sir Thomas Fairfax, 1645–46', DPhil dissertation, University of Oxford, 2001; Gavin Robinson, 'Horse Supply and the Development of the New Model Army, 1642–46', *WH* 15 (2008), 121–40; idem, 'Horse Supply in the English Civil War, 1642–46', PhD dissertation, University of Reading, 2001.

27 See, however, a corrective in Ian Roy, 'The Army and its Critics in Seventeenth Century England', in Brian Bond and Ian Roy (eds), *War and Society Yearbook* (London: Croom Helm, 1976), pp. 141–50. See also Hannah Smith, 'Politics, Patriotism and Gender: The Standing Army Debate on the English Stage, c. 1689–1720', *Journal of British Studies* 50 (2011), 48–75.

The British Army of William III, 1689–1702 (1987). Childs has provided a valuable guide to the officer corps in *Nobles, Gentlemen and the Profession of Arms in Restoration Britain, 1660–88: A Biographical Dictionary of British Army Officers on Foreign Service* (Society for Army Historical Research Special Publication 13, 1987), and also contributed an essay on the Huguenots within the English army to Matthew Glozier and David Onnekink (eds), *War, Religion and Service: Huguenot Soldiering, 1685–1713* (2007). Most recently, he has also revisited the period through the career of Percy Kirke in *General Percy Kirke and the Later Stuart Army* (2014).[28] Matthew Glozier has also written a biography of William III's leading Huguenot general, *Marshal Schomberg, 1615–90: International Soldiering and the Formation of State Armies in the Seventeenth Century* (2005). Childs can be supplemented with a number of articles examining differing aspects of the constitutional struggles involving the army.[29]

Studies of other individual campaigns, though they tend towards being popular accounts, include A. J. Smither, *The Tangier Campaign: The Birth of the British Army* (2003), and David Chandler, *Sedgemoor 1685: An Account and an Anthology* (1985). Tangier would certainly merit an academic study. Better grounded in primary sources is Jonathon Riley, *The Last Ironsides: The English Expedition to Portugal, 1662–68* (2014). Mention should also be made of a useful booklet for the earlier period, Paul Sutton, *Cromwell's Jamaica Campaign: The Attack on the West Indies, 1654–55* (1990). The Anglo-Dutch Wars of 1652–54, 1665–67 and 1672–74 spanned the Protectorate and the Restoration. Though they were entirely maritime wars, there is a good summary in J. R. Jones, *The Anglo-Dutch Wars of the Seventeenth Century* (1996). The only land element was the Dutch

---

28 See also John Childs, 'War, Crime Waves and the English Army in the late Seventeenth Century', *W&S* 15 (1997), 1–17.

29 David Allen, 'The Role of the London Trained Bands in the Exclusion Crisis, 1678–81', *EHR* 87 (172), 287–303; John Miller, 'Catholic Officers in the Late Stuart Army', *EHR* 88 (1973), 35–53; idem, 'The Militia and the Army in the Reign of James II', *HJ* 16 (1973), 659–79; D. P. Carter, 'The Lancashire Militia, 1660–88', in J. L. Kermode and C. B. Phillips (eds), *Seventeenth Century Lancashire: Essays Presented to J. J. Bagley* (Liverpool: Historical Society of Lancashire and Cheshire, 1982), pp. 155–81; Christopher Scott, 'The Military Effectiveness of the West Country Militia at the Time of the Monmouth Rebellion', PhD dissertation, Cranfield University, 2011; George H. Jones, 'The Recall of the British from the Dutch Service', *HJ* 25 (1982), 423–35; A. M. Coleby, 'Military-Civilian Relations on the Solent, 1651–88', *HJ* 29 (1986), 949–61; and Neil Garnham, 'The Establishment of a Statutory Militia in Ireland, 1692–1716: Legislative Processes and Protestant Mentalities', *HR* 84 (2011), 266–87.

attacks upon the Medway and upon Landguard Fort in Suffolk in June and July 1667, the latter the subject of a local publication, F. Hussey, *Suffolk Invasion: The Dutch Attempt on Landguard Fort, 1667* (1983).

As might be expected, the Williamite campaign in Ireland – the 'War of the Two Kings' – has attracted some wider interest, not least the Battle of the Boyne. Again, there is a tendency towards popular narrative but there is more academic treatment in Padraig Lenihan, *1690: Battle of the Boyne* (2003). Commendable, too, is W. A. Maguire (ed.), *Kings in Conflict: The Revolutionary War in Ireland and its Aftermath, 1689–1750* (1990), the catalogue of a major commemorative exhibition in Belfast. Kjeld Hald Galster, *Danish Troops in the Williamite Army in Ireland, 1689–91* (2012) offers a distinctly new perspective. John Childs has covered both the continental and Irish campaigns following William's accession in great detail in *The Nine Years' War and the British Army, 1688–97: The Operations in the Low Countries* (1991); and *The Williamite Wars in Ireland, 1688–1691* (2007).[30] K. A. J. McLay covers amphibious operations.[31]

---

30 See also J. M. Stapleton, 'Forging a Coalition Army: William III, the Grand Alliance and the Confederate Army in the Spanish Netherlands, 1688–97', PhD dissertation, Ohio State University, 2003.

31 See K. A. J., McLay, 'Combined Operations and the European Theatre during the Nine Years War, 1688–97', *HR* 78 (2005), 506–39, idem, 'Wellsprings of a World War? An Early English Attempt to Conquer Canada during King William's War, 1688–97', *JICH* 34 (2006), 144–75; idem, 'Sir Francis Wheeler's Caribbean and North American Expedition, 1693: A Case Study of Combined Operational Command during the reign of William III', *WH* 14 (2007), 383–407; idem, 'Combined Operations: British Naval and Military Co-operation in the Wars of 1688–1720', PhD dissertation, University of Glasgow, 2003.

Chapter 5

1702–1815

In the light of the argument that the changes in the sixteenth and seventeenth centuries paved the way for an unintended consequence of British involvement in continental warfare after 1689, it makes sense to view a 'long' eighteenth century, beginning with the accession of Queen Anne in 1702 and extending to the end of the French Revolutionary and Napoleonic Wars in 1815, as a continuous period of military conflict. War-driven policies and resulting global expansion in the case of Britain had a profound and lasting impact upon the activities of the state. In the process, it has been contended, a specifically 'British' national identity also emerged though one tempered by differing national and local agendas.

Some of those general texts previously mentioned remain relevant to the period between 1702 and 1815, including John Childs, *Armies and Warfare in Europe, 1648–1789* (1982); M. S. Anderson, *War and Society, 1618–1789* (1988); André Corvisier, *Armies and Societies in Europe, 1494–1789* (1979); Jeremy Black, *European Warfare, 1660–1815* (1994); and the two compilations edited by Black, *War in the Early Modern World, 1450–1815* (1999) and *European Warfare, 1453–1815* (1999). In addition, however, there are general texts that take the story on into the nineteenth century, including Black's *Western Warfare, 1775–1882* (2001). In the Fontana series, there is Geoffrey Best, *War and Society in Revolutionary Europe, 1770–1870* (1982), which sees post-1815 developments in the light of the experience of Napoleonic warfare. Geoffrey Wawro, *Warfare and Society in Europe, 1792–1914* (2000) also sees the Napoleonic Wars as a starting point as does, naturally, David Gates, *Warfare in the Nineteenth Century* (2001). Rather similarly, John Gooch, *Armies in Europe* (1980) and Hew Strachan, *European Armies and the Conduct of War* (1983) take 1789 and 1700 respectively as a starting point for surveys extending to 1945. There are relevant sections on the actual conduct of war in Russell Weighley, *The Age of Battles: The Quest for Decisive Warfare from Breitenfeld to Waterloo* (1991), and Brent Nosworthy, *The Anatomy of Victory: Battle Tactics, 1689–1763* (1990).

The only texts specifically related to the eighteenth century, however, are Armstrong Starkey, *War in the Age of Enlightenment, 1700–89* (2003), and two works by Jeremy Black, *Warfare in the Eighteenth Century* (1999), an entry in the Cassell series, and *War in the Eighteenth Century World* (2012). As with Black's other work, these have the merit of considering both warfare between Europeans and non-Europeans and 'war without Europeans'.[1] A kind of epilogue to the five German-American collaborative volumes on total war with which they were previously associated, Roger Chickering and Stig Förster (eds), *War in an Age of Revolution, 1775–1815* (2010) looks back to the 'military revolution', as well as forward to the debate on the evolution of 'total war'.[2] The adoption of the *levée en masse* by the French Republic in 1792, of course, has been seen traditionally as a distinct moment of transition between 'limited' or 'cabinet' wars in the eighteenth century and 'people's wars'. As previously suggested, warfare between 1648 and 1789 was only limited if compared with the Thirty Years War and the French Revolutionary Wars.

Curiously, of the wars fought in the eighteenth century, the first major European conflict, the War of Spanish Succession (1702–15), has no modern overall synthesis. By contrast, for the War of Austrian Succession (1740–8), there is Reed Browning, *The War of Austrian Succession* (1994), and M. S. Anderson, *The War of Austrian Succession, 1740–48* (1995), Anderson being less confident on combat detail than Browning. Dennis Showalter, *The Wars of Frederick the Great* (1996) embraces both the War of Austrian Succession and the Seven Years War (1756–63). The latter has also been covered in the relevant sections of Peter Wilson, *German Armies: War and German Politics, 1648–1806* (1995), and Michael Hochedlinger, *Austria's Wars of Emergence: War, State and Society in the Habsburg Monarchy, 1683–1797* (2003). Specifically there is also Franz Szabo, *The Seven Years War in Europe, 1756–63* (2008); Matt Schumann and Karl Schweizer, *The Seven Years War: A Transatlantic History* (2010); Daniel A. Baugh, *The Global Seven Years War, 1754–63: Britain and France in a Great Power Contest* (2011); and Mark Danley and Patrick Speelman (eds), *The Seven Years War: Global Views* (2013). The story of Russia's continuing struggles with the Ottoman Empire is taken up in Brian Davies, *Empire and Military Revolution in Eastern Europe: Russia's Turkish Wars in the Eighteenth Century* (2011).

As might be expected, much of the focus of the studies of Schumann and Schweizer, and of Baugh is on North America, for which there is also the very detailed Fred Anderson, *Crucible of War: The Seven Years War and the Fate of*

---

1 Black also addresses the 'limited' nature of warfare in 'Eighteenth Century Warfare Reconsidered', *WH* 1 (1994), 215–33.
2 See also Michael Broers, 'The Concept of "Total War" in the Revolutionary-Napoleonic Period', *WH* 15 (2008), 247–68.

the Empire in British North America, 1754–66 (2001). Anderson has summarised his account in *The War That Made America: A Short History of the French and Indian War* (2005). Maarten Ultee (ed.), *Adapting to Conditions: War and Society in the Eighteenth Century* (1986) is primarily concerned with warfare in North America and the Caribbean. Complementing his study of the period prior to 1688, there is Bruce Lenman, *Britain's Colonial Wars, 1688–1783* (2001), which covers North America, the Caribbean and India.

In carrying his account into the immediate post-war period, Anderson is suggestive of those tensions arising from Britain's attempt to claw back the costs of the war from the colonists that led to the subsequent revolution. There are many surveys of the American War of Independence (1775–83), but among the best academic studies are Piers Mackesy, *The War for America, 1775–83* (1964), which views the war from the perspective of policymakers in London; Don Higginbotham, *The War of American Independence: Military Attitudes, Policies and Practice* (1971); Robert Middlekauf, *The Glorious Cause: The American Revolution, 1763–89* (1985); Stephen Conway, *The War of American Independence, 1775–83* (1995); and Richard Middleton, *The War of American Independence, 1775–83* (2011). There is an excellent catalogue of the bicentenary exhibition at Greenwich, *1776: The British Story of the American Revolution* (1976).

As might be expected, the French Revolutionary and Napoleonic Wars have also generated a large literature. The best guide to the French Revolutionary Wars is T. C. W. Blanning, *The French Revolutionary Wars, 1787–1802* (1996), who has also contributed *The Origins of the French Revolutionary Wars* (1986), though Owen Connelly also covers the earlier period in *The Wars of the French Revolution and Napoleon, 1792–1815* (2006). On the Napoleonic Wars, the academic general texts are Charles Esdaile, *The Wars of Napoleon* (1995); Esdaile's updated *Napoleon's Wars: An International History, 1803–15* (2007); and David Gates, *The Napoleonic Wars, 1803–15* (1997). Esdaile is more revisionist than Gates, particularly questioning the idea of 'people's wars'. On the overall impact of war, see also Alan Forrest, Karen Hagemann and Jane Rendall (eds), *Soldiers, Citizens and Civilians: Experiences and Perceptions of the Revolutionary and Napoleonic Wars, 1790–1820* (2008); and Alan Forrest, Étienne François and Karen Hagemann (eds), *War Memories: The Revolutionary and Napoleonic Wars in Modern European Culture* (2012). All these texts have full bibliographies and cover the wide impact of war between 1792 and 1815 upon states, societies, institutions and individuals.

There is no overall account of the British army in the period under consideration but there is a useful overall survey of the socio-economic impact of war in H. V. Bowen, *War and British Society, 1688–1815* (1998), and in Jeremy Black, *Britain as a Military Power, 1688–1815* (1998). Suggestive of new trends in identity and gender is Kevin Linch and Matthew McCormack (eds), *Britain's Soldiers: Rethinking War and Society, 1715–1815* (2014). The modern historiography has been increasingly shaped by the argument that England and (from 1707) Britain was transformed by the experience of war. The significance of war for the expansion of British global political and economic power had long been acknowledged as well as the impact upon the domestic economy and society amid the world's first industrial revolution.

As already suggested, ultimate British success was attributed to a mythic version of a 'British Way in Warfare' established in the eighteenth century. In reality, Britain was forced to commit troops to the continent in major conflicts in order to secure victory. The only war that was 'lost' – that for America between 1775 and 1783 – was the only one fought in this period without a continental ally. The continental basis of British power in terms of the central significance of Hanover for the alliance with Prussia, indeed, is the theme of Brendan Simms, *Three Victories and a Defeat: The Rise and Fall of the First British Empire, 1714–83* (2007).[3] That Britain could sustain large financial subsidies to continental allies and wage war effectively on a global scale was testament to the ability to raise substantial revenue through taxation, loans and, above all, a funded national debt: the Bank of England, of course, was established in 1694 during the Nine Years War. John Brewer, *The Sinews of Power: War, Money and the English State, 1688–1783* (1990) contended that England and Britain did not experience a military revolution in the sixteenth and seventeenth centuries, but that involvement in continental wars established a 'fiscal-military state' by which the exigencies of wartime requirements intruded into every aspect of state and society. Brewer's argument has not escaped criticism, as reflected in the essays in Laurence Stone (ed.), *An Imperial State at War: Britain from 1689 to 1815* (1994).[4] Other reflections on the issue are to be found in P. G. M. Dickson and C. Storrs (eds), *The Fiscal-Military State in Eighteenth Century Europe: Essays in Honour of P. G. M. Dickson* (2009). D. W. Jones, *War and Economy in the Age of William III and Marlborough* (1988) testifies to the frequent financial improvisations of government in the war years. Gordon Bannerman, *Merchants and the Military in Eighteenth Century Britain: British Army Contracts and Domestic Supply, 1739–63* (2008), however, sees private contractors, without whom the army could not have functioned, as the nexus of the fiscal-military state.

---

3 See also Daniel Baugh, 'Great Britain's "Blue Water" Policy, 1689–1815', *IHR* 10 (1988), 33–58.
4 See also Patrick O'Brien and P. A. Hunt, 'The Rise of a Fiscal State in England, 1485–1815', *HR* 66 (1993), 129–76.

Clearly, the army was as much a partner as the navy in the expansion of British global influence even if it was slow to adapt to overseas campaigning while politicians and public displayed scant interest in the conditions of service life. Indeed, the pattern of wartime expansion and immediate post-war reduction reflected continuing antipathy towards the standing army. This was something particularly experienced by soldiers in their frequent domestic role in aid of the civil power. Tony Hayter, *The Army and the Crowd in Mid-Georgian England* (1978), and John Houlding, *Fit for Service: The Training of the British Army, 1715–1795* (1981) both stress that it was to the army's detriment that it was seen more as a guardian of civil order than as an instrument of foreign policy.[5] Though the army performed its domestic tasks remarkably well in the circumstances, the dispersal of units deprived the army of time and opportunity to undertake serious military training that was to prove costly in wartime. Accordingly, the army's reputation fluctuated, the decline in popularity following the successes in the War of Spanish Succession being rescued by the army's role in securing new victories in the Seven Years War to the extent that it was able to survive the subsequent shock of defeat in North America.

The British role in the War of Spanish Succession is well covered from the perspective of the campaigns of the Duke of Marlborough. David Chandler, *The Art of War in the Age of Marlborough* (1975) is a starting point. It can be supplemented by the collection of Chandler's essays, *Blenheim Preparation: The English Army on the March to the Danube* (2004), which range more widely over the army's administration than the title suggests. More general accounts of the impact on Britain can be found in John Hattendorf, *England in the War of Spanish Succession: A Study of the English View and Conduct of Grand Strategy, 1702–12* (1987), which deals primarily with strategy, and D. W. Jones, *War and Economy in the Age of William III and Marlborough* (1989). The classic account of the army's administration remains R. E. Scouller, *The Armies of Queen Anne* (1960), and one of the better among many biographies of Marlborough himself is still Ivor Burton, *The Captain-General: The Career of John Churchill, Duke of Marlborough from 1702 to 1711* (1968). However, there is now a major re-assessment in John Hattendorf, Augustus Veenendaal and Rolof van Hovell tot Westerflier (eds), *Marlborough: Soldier and Diplomat* (2012). Similarly, Marlborough's battles have been covered in several popular accounts. There has been rather less interest in the British campaigns in Portugal and Spain though A. D. Francis, *The First Peninsular War, 1702–13* (1975) takes a British perspective, and Henry Kamen, *The War of*

---

5 See also S. H. Palmer, 'Calling Out the Troops: The Military, the Law and Public Order in England, 1650–1850', *JSAHR* 56 (1978), 198–224.

Succession in Spain, 1700–15 (1969) and J. A. C. Hugill, *No Peace Without Spain* (1991) provide general overviews of the theatre.

The army between 1715 and 1756 has attracted relatively little interest but there is the indispensable Alan Guy, *Oeconomy and Discipline: Officership and Administration in the British Army, 1714–1783* (1984).[6] Guy has also edited *Colonel Samuel Bagshawe and the Army of George II, 1731–62* (1990), enabling him to highlight more aspects of military administration, while Tony Hayter (ed.), *An Eighteenth Century Secretary at War: The Papers of William, Viscount Barrington* (1988) does similar service for the period between 1755 and 1778. Andrew Cormack and Alan Jones (eds), *The Journal of Corporal William Todd, 1745–62* (2001) equally illuminates the experience of other ranks. Jennine Hurl-Eamon, *Marriage and the British Army in the Long Eighteenth Century* (2014) is a particularly welcome new study.

Richard Harding, primarily a naval historian, covers amphibious aspects of British involvement in the War of Jenkins' Ear and its continuation as the War of Austrian Succession in *Amphibious Warfare in the Eighteenth Century: The British Expedition to the West Indies, 1740–42* (1991), and *The Emergence of Britain's Global Naval Supremacy: The War of 1739–48* (2010). Although now dated, Rex Whitworth, *Field Marshal Lord Ligonier: A Story of the British Army, 1702–70* (1958) still has its uses, as does the same author's *William Augustus Duke of Cumberland: A Life* (1992), but the Duke of Cumberland badly needs an updated academic study. The one aspect of his career that has generated most attention is his part in the defeat of the third of the Jacobite interventions in Britain in 1745. An overview of all the Jacobite risings is to be found in Bruce Lenman, *The Jacobite Risings in Britain, 1689–1745* (1980). Daniel Szechi, *1715: The Great Jacobite Rebellion* (2006) supersedes the earlier narrative by John Baynes, *The Jacobite Rising of 1715* (1970). The definitive account of the '45 is Christopher Duffy, *The '45: Bonnie Prince Charlie and the Untold Story of the Jacobite Rising* (2003), based on exhaustive archival research. There are relevant essays in Robert C. Woosnam-Savage (ed.), *1745: Prince Charles Edward Stuart and the Jacobites* (1995), a publication accompanying a 250th anniversary exhibition in Glasgow. A similar endeavour was the broad narrative offered by Michael Hook and Walter Ross, *The Forty-Five: The Last Jacobite Rebellion* (1995) for the National Library of Scotland. There is much detail on local defence

---

6 See also Alan Guy, 'Minions of Fortune: The Regimental Agents of Early Georgian England, 1714–63', *Army Museum '85* (1986), pp. 31–42; D. W. Bailey, 'The Board of Ordnance and Small Arms Supply: The Ordnance System, 1714–83', PhD dissertation, University of London, 1989.

arrangements in England in Rupert C. Jarvis (ed.), *Collected Papers on the Jacobite Risings*, 2 vols. (1971–2). Culloden is also well covered in Stuart Reid, *Like Hungry Wolves: Culloden Moor, 16 April 1746* (1994) though, as suggested in an earlier section, the picture has been modified by recent archaeological investigation, as outlined in Tony Pollard (ed.), *Culloden: The History and Archaeology of the Last Clan Battle* (2009).

The '45 raises the issue of the increasing Scottish contribution to the army notwithstanding the Jacobite risings. A key text is Andrew Mackillop, *'More Fruitful than the Soil': Army, Empire and the Scottish Highlands, 1715–1815* (2000), as is Victoria Henshaw, *Scotland and the British Army, 1700–50: Defending the Union* (2014).[7] By contrast, Peter Simpson, *The Independent Highland Companies, 1603–1760* (1996) lacks rigour, while John Prebble, *Mutiny: Highland Regiments in Revolt, 1743–1804* (1975) is outdated. There are relevant essays in both N. Macdougall (ed.), *Scotland and War, AD79-1918* (1991), and Steve Murdoch and Andrew Mackillop (eds), *Fighting for Identity: Scottish Military Experience, c. 1550–1900* (2002). The Scottish military settlers who defended the new colony of Georgia are covered in Anthony Parker, *Scottish Highlanders in Colonial Georgia; The Recruitment, Emigration and Settlement at Darien, 1735–48* (1997); and Larry Ivers, *British Drums on the Southern Frontier: The Military Colonisation of Georgia, 1733–49* (1974). Wayne Lee has also contrasted the British military use of the Irish and American Indians.[8]

There are a number of useful contributions on Ireland.[9] The recruitment of Irish Catholics posed particular issues.[10] A wider survey of religious issues is

---

7 See also Andrew Mackillop, 'Continuity, Coercion and Myth: The Recruitment of Highland Regiments in the Later Eighteenth Century', *Scottish Traditions* 26 (2001), 30–55; and Stana Nenadic, 'The Impact of the Military Profession on Highland Gentry Families, 1730–1830', *Scottish Historical Review* 85 (2006), 75–99.

8 Wayne Lee, 'Subjects, Clients, Allies or Mercenaries? The British Use of Irish and Amerindian Military Power, 1500–1800', in H. V. Bowen, Elizabeth Mancke and John Reid (eds), *Britain's Oceanic Empire: Atlantic and Indian Ocean Worlds, c. 1550–1850* (Cambridge: Cambridge University Press, 2012), pp. 179–217.

9 See Kenneth P. Ferguson, 'The Army in Ireland from the Restoration to the Act of Union', PhD dissertation, Trinity College, Dublin, 1980; and Terry Denman, '*Hibernia officina militum*: Irish Recruitment to the British Regular Army, 1660–1815', *Irish Sword* 78 (1996), 148–67.

10 Arthur N. Gilbert, 'Ethnicity and the British Army in Ireland during the American Revolution', *Ethnic and Racial Studies* 1 (1978), 475–83; Thomas Bartlett, 'A Weapon of War Yet Untried: Irish Catholics and the Armed Forces of the Crown, 1760–1830', in T. G. Fraser and Keith Jeffery (eds), *Men, Women and War* (Dublin: Lilliput, 1993), pp. 66–85; and Paul Kopperman, 'Religion and Religious Policy in the British Army, c.1700–96', *Journal of Religious History* 14 (1987), 390–405.

found in Michael Snape, *The Redcoat and Religion: The Forgotten History of the British Soldier from the Age of Marlborough to the First World War* (2005).

Recruitment generally has been well covered in journal articles and it is something of a tragedy that Glenn Steppler's thesis on the British soldier between 1760 and 1792 remains unpublished.[11] Military discipline is also covered in articles.[12] Soldiering as a cultural activity is the subject of a number of essays in Catriona Kennedy and Matthew McCormack (eds), *Soldiering in Britain and Ireland, 1750–1850: Men of Arms* (2013).

The Seven Years War has been exhaustively covered from the British perspective. Strategic policy is considered by Richard Middleton, *The Bells of Victory: The Pitt-Newcastle Ministry and the Conduct of the Seven Years War, 1757–62* (1985); and Karl Schweizer, *England, Prussia and the Seven Years War: Studies in Alliance Politics and Diplomacy* (1989). Middleton is highly critical of the traditional view that British victory was due to William Pitt the Elder, arguing

---

11 Arthur N. Gilbert, 'An Analysis of Some Eighteenth Century Army Recruiting Records', *JSAHR* 54 (1976), 38–47; Alan Guy, 'Reinforcements for Portugal, 1762: Recruiting for Rank at the End of the Seven Years' War', *Annual Report of the National Army Museum* (1978), pp. 29–34; Richard Middleton, 'The Recruitment of the British Army, 1755–62', *JSAHR* 68 (1989), 226–38; Stephen Brumwell, 'Rank and File: A Profile of One of Wolfe's Regiments', *JSAHR* 79 (2001), 3–24; Thomas Bartlett, 'The Augmentation of the Army in Ireland, 1767–69', *EHR* 96 (1981), 540–59; Stephen Conway, 'The Recruitment of Criminals into the British Army, 1775–81', *BIHR* 58 (1985), 46–58; A. N. Gilbert, 'Charles Jenkinson and the Last Army Press, 1779', *MA* 42 (1978), 7–11; idem, 'Why Men Deserted from the Eighteenth Century British Army', *Armed Forces and Society* 6 (1980), 553–67; and Philip D. Morgan and Andrew Jackson O'Shaughnessy, 'Arming Slaves in the American Revolution', in Christopher Leslie Brown and Philip D. Morgan (eds), *Arming Slaves: From Classical Times to the Modern Age* (London: Yale University Press, 2006), pp. 180–208. See also Glenn A. Steppler, 'The Common Soldier in the Reign of George III, 1760–92', PhD dissertation, University of Oxford, 1984.

12 E. E. Steiner, 'Separating the Soldier from the Citizen: Ideology and Criticism of Corporal Punishment in the British Armies, 1790–1815', *Social History* 8 (1983), 19–35; Glenn Steppler, 'British Military Law, Discipline and the Conduct of Regimental Courts Martial in the Later Eighteenth Century', *EHR* 102 (1987), 859–86; Armstrong Starkey, 'War and Culture: A Case Study in the Enlightenment and the Conduct of the British Army in America 1755–81', *W&S* 8 (1990), 1–28; K. R. Stacy, 'Crime and Punishment in the 84th Regiment of Foot, 1775–84', *JSAHR* 79 (2001), 108–18; P. E. Kopperman, 'The Cheapest Pay: Alcohol Abuse in the Eighteenth Century British Army', *Military History Review* 60 (1996), 445–70; idem, 'The British High Command and Soldiers' Wives in America, 1755–83', *JSAHR* 60 (1982), 14–34.

instead for the significance of the Duke of Newcastle and King George II. Varying demands arising from the scale of the conflict are covered in Jenny West, *Gunpowder, Government and War in the Mid Eighteenth Century* (1991).[13]

The war effort in Germany is the subject of the weighty but rather old-fashioned narrative, Sir Reginald Savory, *His Britannic Majesty's Army in Germany during the Seven Years War* (1966), while the court martial of Lord George Sackville following Minden is examined by Piers Mackesy, *The Coward of Minden* (1979). The Caribbean also receives coverage in David Syrett, *The Siege and Capture of Havana, 1762* (1970). Syrett has considered amphibious operations more generally and there are other useful contributions.[14] Perhaps surprisingly, the campaign in Portugal in 1762 has also been well covered, while there is the impressive Erica Charters, *Disease, War and the Imperial State: The Welfare of the British Armed Forces during the Seven Years' War* (2014).[15]

Much of the attention, however, has been on North America. In addition to those texts already cited above, many of those studies of warfare in North America previously mentioned are also relevant including Ian Steele, *Warpaths: Invasions of North America* (1994); Armstrong Starkey, *European and Native American Warfare, 1675–1815* (1998); William Nester, *The Great Frontier War: Britain, France and the Imperial Struggle for North America, 1607–1755* (2000); and Guy Chet, *Conquering the American Wilderness: The Triumph of European Warfare in the Colonial Northeast* (2003). There are also some useful essays in Julie Flavell and Stephen Conway (eds), *Britain and America Go to War: The Impact of War and Warfare in Anglo-America, 1754–1815* (2004). More specifically related to

---

13 See also E. J. S. Fraser, 'The Pitt-Newcastle Coalition and the Conduct of the Seven Years War, 1757–60', DPhil dissertation, University of Oxford, 1976; H. M. Little, 'The Treasury, the Commissariat and the Supply of the Combined Army in Germany during the Seven Years War, 1756–63', PhD dissertation, University of London, 1981; Reed Browning, 'The Duke of Newcastle and the Financial Management of the Seven Years War in Germany', *JSAHR* 39 (1971), 20–45; idem, 'The Duke of Newcastle and the Financing of the Seven Years War', *Journal of Economic History* 31 (1971), 344–77.

14 David Syrett 'The Methodology of British Amphibious Operations during the Seven Years and American Wars', *Mariner's Mirror* 48 (1972), 269–80; Richard Harding, 'Sailors and Gentlemen of Parade: Some Professional and Technical Problems concerning the Conduct of Combined Operations in the Eighteenth Century', *HJ* 32 (1989), 35–55.

15 A. D. Francis, 'The Campaign in Portugal, 1762', *JSAHR* 59 (1981), 25–43; and Jeremy Black, 'The British Expeditionary Force to Portugal in 1762', *British Historical Society of Portugal Annual Report* 16 (1989), 66–75.

the Seven Years' War are accounts of the British army's experience in North America, notably Stephen Brumwell, *Redcoats: The British Soldier and War in the Americas, 1755–63* (2002), a major revisionist account of the transformation of the army in America into a highly flexible and innovative fighting force. Brumwell suggests that an unintended ironic consequence of successful adaptation was to provide a blueprint for the Continental Army that ultimately triumphed over the British. Indeed, the adaptation of British tactics has attracted some attention.[16] Brumwell has also examined the career of Robert Rogers in *White Devil* (2004), and the equally enigmatic figure of James Wolfe in *Paths of Glory: The Life and Death of General James Wolfe* (2006). Not surprisingly, the struggle for Quebec has generated a considerable literature over the years, not least for the 250th anniversary in 2009, which saw several new popular accounts. The best study, however, remains Matthew Ward, *The Battle for Quebec 1759: Britain's Conquest of Canada* (2005).[17] As suggested previously, Alan McNairn, *Behold the Hero: General Wolfe and the Arts in the Eighteenth Century* (1997) is an engaging study illustrating what Simon Schama once called the many deaths of James Wolfe in all their varied forms from art to monuments, ceramics and exceedingly bad poetry.

A number of other episodes in the campaigns in North America have attracted attention. The early setback to the force commanded by Edward Braddock in 1755 is the subject of Paul Kopperman, *Braddock at the Monongahela* (1977), and Thomas Crocker, *Braddock's March* (2010). The fall of Fort William Henry in 1757 and the subsequent killing of members of its garrison by the Indian allies of the French is covered in Ian Steele, *Betrayals: Fort William Henry and the 'Massacre'* (1990). The actions around Fort Ticonderoga are the subject of William Nester, *The Epic Battle for Ticonderoga 1758* (2008), a more academic study than the title suggests. Louisburg is also the subject of a fine modern account, Hugh Boscawen, *The Capture of Louisburg 1758* (2011). Amherst's

---

16 P. E. Russell, 'Redcoats in the Wilderness: British Officers and Irregular Warfare in Europe and North America, 1740–60', *WMQ* 35 (1978), 629–52; Daniel Beattie, 'The Adaptation of the British Army to Wilderness Warfare, 1755–63', in Maarten Ultee (ed.), *Adapting to Conditions: War and Society in the Eighteenth Century* (Tuscaloosa, AL: University of Alabama Press, 1986), pp. 56–83; M. C. Ward, 'The European Method of Warring is Not Practiced Here: The Failure of British Military Policy in the Ohio Valley, 1755–59', *WH* 4 (1997), 249–63; and Brumwell's own 'A Service Truly Critical: The British Army and Warfare with the North American Indians, 1754–64', *WH* 5 (1998), 146–75.

17 See also Erica Charters, 'Disease, Wilderness Warfare and Imperial Relations: The Battle for Quebec, 1759–60', *WH* 16 (2009), 1–24.

concluding campaign in 1760 is the subject of Douglas Cubbison, *All Canada in the Hands of the British: General Jeffrey Amherst and the 1760 Campaign to Conquer New France* (2014). The Pontiac rising that followed the conclusion of the war in North America has also attracted attention as in Gregory Dowd, *War Under Heaven: Pontiac, the Indian Nations, and the British Empire* (2002), and Richard Middleton, *Pontiac's War: Its Causes, Course and Consequences* (2007). Middleton has also edited a selection of the papers of Jeffrey Amherst, *Amherst and the Conquest of Canada* (2003), a soldier whose career is well worth a modern biography.

The British victory in North America had particular repercussions when its economic costs were passed on to the American colonists. As already mentioned previously, John Shy, *Toward Lexington: The Role of the British Army in the Coming of the American Revolution* (1965); Michael McConnell, *Army and Empire: British Soldiers on the American Frontier, 1758–75* (2004); and Richard Archer, *As if in an Enemy's Country: The British Occupation of Boston and the Origins of Revolution* (2010) all deal with aspects of the British military presence between the Seven Years War and the outbreak of hostilities in 1775. There is also Douglas E. Leach, *Roots of Conflict: British Armed Forces and Colonial Americans, 1677–1763* (1986). Also previously mentioned is a study that still has value, Sylvia Frey, *The British Soldier in America: A Social History of Military Life in the Revolutionary Period* (1981). Of course, the War of American Independence has an enormous literature of its own, to which those general texts listed earlier are the best guide.

On specific British military aspects, there has been less modern work than might be anticipated. Some more recent works, however, have illuminated the conduct of operations. British officership has been investigated by Stephen Conway,[18] while Ira Gruber, *Books and the British Army in the Age of the American Revolution* (2010) looks at one aspect of professionalism. Gruber has also edited an outstanding officer's memoir, *John Peebles' American War, 1776–82* (1997).[19] A major reassessment of British military performance on the battlefield is Matthew Spring, *With Zeal and Bayonets Only: The British Army on Campaign in North America, 1775–83* (2010), which demonstrates

---

18 Stephen Conway, 'British Army Officers and the American War of Independence', *WMQ* 41 (1984), 265–76; idem, 'To Subdue America: British Army Officers and the Conduct of the Revolutionary War', *WMQ* 43 (1986), 381–407

19 See also P. D. Nelson, 'The British Officer Corps, 1754–83', PhD dissertation, University of Michigan, 1988; A. G. Jamieson, 'War in the Leeward Islands, 1775–83', DPhil dissertation, University of Oxford, 1981.

the increasingly effective reliance upon looser formations suited to the terrain, and to shock action.[20]

In addition, however, warfare in North America both in the Seven Years War and the American Revolutionary War has specific importance for the other significant debate concerning the impact of war on the evolving British state in the eighteenth century, namely the emergence of a British national identity. While much of this debate has centred on the Revolutionary and Napoleonic Wars, Linda Colley, *Britons: Forging the Nation, 1707–1837* (1992) viewed it as originating with a sense of a Protestant state under threat from Catholic France before becoming fully developed between 1793 and 1815. On the other hand, Stephen Conway, *War, State and Society in Mid-Eighteenth Century Britain and Ireland* (2006) suggests a partnership of government and private interests was fundamental to British success in the Seven Years War, a conflict in which he sees evidence of an emerging 'Britishness' subtlety different from that detected by historians for the period of the late eighteenth century. John Cardwell, *Arts and Arms: Literature, Politics and Patriotism during the Seven Years War* (2004) is also relevant to the theme. In *The British Isles and the War of American Independence* (2000), Conway also argues that wartime mobilisation was greater than usually supposed and, though it proved a divisive conflict in terms of domestic politics, invasion fears strengthened the sense of 'Britishness' though mobilisation also strengthened localism in Britain so that it actually negated national power to some extent.[21]

Concentration on North America tends to mean that less attention is often paid to the consolidation of British power in India that followed from victory in the Seven Years War. Nonetheless, there has been an increasing body of scholarly work on warfare in India that leads back to the debate on the military revolution and the adaptation of European methods to the sub-continent. Some aspects of this have been mentioned in the previous section. Thus, Douglas Peers (ed.), *Warfare and Empires: Contact and Conflict between European and Non-European Military and Maritime Forces and Cultures* (1997), and Dirk Kolff, *Naukar, Rajput, and Sepoy: The Ethnohistory of the Military Labour Market of Hindustan, 1450–1850* (1990) remain relevant to the later period. So, too, are those general histories of the Indian army previously mentioned, The most

---

20 See also Armstrong Starkey, 'War and Culture, a Case Study: The Enlightenment and the Conduct of the British Army in America, 1775–81', *W&S* 8 (1990), 1–28.

21 See also Stephen Conway, 'War and Nationality in the Mid-Eighteenth Century British Isles', *EHR* 116 (2001), 863–93; idem, 'The Mobilisation of Manpower for Britain's Mid-Eighteenth Century Wars', *HR* 77 (2004), 377–404.

detailed coverage of the early period of the East India Company (EIC) army is in G. J. Bryant's unpublished thesis, although much has appeared in articles as will become apparent from succeeding footnotes. Equally unpublished is John Bourne's thesis on the Company's civil and military patronage.[22]

There have been a number of suggestive general surveys of the merging of western and Indian systems, although a number suggest that the decisive factor was the cultural differences between the Company's approach to war and that of its opponents with the emphasis upon superior organisation and infantry firepower.[23] Bryant in particular sees a kind of Indian 'military revolution' in India in the 1760s as a result of the Company's military success, a theme echoed in Peter Lorge, *The Asian Military Revolution: From Gunpowder to the Bomb* (2008). By contrast, Kaushik Roy, *War, Culture and Society in Early Modern South Asia, 1740–1849* (2011) sees more evidence of evolutionary transformation, and a paradox in Company military practices being shaped by Indian methods at the very same time as Indian states were endeavouring to emulate western military organisation. He also emphasises that victory for the Company was not inevitable, as the events of the Maratha, Mysore and even Sikh Wars demonstrated. Just as the military revolution debate has been applied to Indian military history so, too, has the concept of the fiscal-military state to India as considered in C. A. Bayly (ed.), *Origins of Nationality in South Asia: Patriotism and Ethical Government in the Making of Modern India* (1998).

---

22 G. J. Bryant, 'The East India Company and its Army, 1600–1778', PhD dissertation, University of London, 1975; John Bourne, 'The Civil and Military Patronage of the East India Company, 1784–1858', PhD dissertation, University of Leicester, 1978.

23 Gary Ness and William Stahl, 'Western Imperialist Armies in Asia', *Comparative Studies in Society and History* 19 (1977), 1–20; Peter J. Marshall, 'Western Arms in Maritime Asia in the Early Phases of Expansion', *MAS* 14 (1980), 13–28; Dirk Kolff, 'The End of an Ancien Regime: Colonial War in India, 1798–1818', in J. A. de Moor and H. L. Wesseling (eds), *Imperialism and War: Essays on Colonial Wars in Asia and Africa* (Leiden: Brill, 1989), pp. 22–49; Pradeep Barua, 'Military Developments in India, 1750–1850', *JMH* 58 (1994), 559–616; Jos Gommans, 'Indian Warfare and Afghan Innovation during the Eighteenth Century', *Studies in History* 11 (1995), 261–80; Stewart Gordon, 'The Limited Adoption of European-style Military Forces by Eighteenth Century Rulers in India', *Indian Economic and Social History Review* 35 (1998), 229–45; G. J. Bryant, 'Asymmetric Warfare: The British Experience in Eighteenth Century India', *JMH* 68 (2004), 431–69; Kaushik Roy, 'Military Synthesis in South Asia: Armies, Warfare and Indian Society, 1740–1849', *JMH* 69 (2005), 651–90.

The developing relationship between the East India Company and native sepoys has been examined by Seema Alavi, *The Sepoys and the Company: Tradition and Transition in Northern India, 1770–1830* (1995), which emphasises the flexibility of the Company in accommodating the different communities within India; by Channa Wickremesekera, *Best Black Troops in the World: British Perceptions and the Making of the Sepoy, 1746–1805* (2002); and in various articles.[24] So, too, have been British officers in the Company's service.[25] Erica Wald, *Vice in Barracks: Medicine, The Military and the Making of Colonial India, 1780–1868* (2014) demonstrates that military concerns with the health of the soldiery led to wider measures defining the Company's relationship with India generally. Older works include Amiya Barat, *The Bengal Native Infantry: Its Organisation and Discipline, 1796–1852* (1962). Attempts to restructure the officer corps met with opposition, as examined by Raymond Callahan, *The East India Company and Army Reform, 1783–98* (1972). Indeed, there was a 'white mutiny' in 1809. Indications of potential disciplinary problems with native armies were already evident with the mutiny at Vellore in 1806, caused by an order for sepoys to remove caste marks and shave beards, for which the best source is James Hoover, *Men Without Hats: Dialogue, Discipline and Discontent in the Madras Army, 1806–07* (2007). Presumably because of Vellore,

24 A. N. Gilbert, 'Recruitment and Reform in the East India Company Army, 1760–1800', *JBS* 15 (1975), 89–111; Seema Alavi, 'The Company Army and Rural Society: The Invalid Thana, 17680–1830', *MAS* 27 (1993), 147–78; James Hoover, 'The Recruitment of the Bengal Army: Beyond the Myth of Zemindar's Son', *Indo-British Review* 21 (1993), 144–56; G. J. Bryant, 'The Cavalry Problem in the Early British Indian Army, 1750–85', *WH* 2 (1995), 1–21; idem, 'Indigenous Mercenaries in the Service of European Imperialists: The Case of the Sepoys in the Early British Indian Army, 1750–1800', *WH* 7 (2000), 2–28.
25 G. J. Bryant, 'Officers of the East India Company's Army in the Days of Clive and Hastings', *JICH* 6 (1978), 203–27; Alan Guy, ' "People who will stick at nothing to make money": Officers' Income, Expenditure and Expectations in the Service of John Company, 1750–1840', in Alan Guy and Peter Boyden (eds), *Soldiers of the Raj: The Indian Army* (London: National Army Museum, 1999), pp. 39–56; Douglas Peers, 'Colonial Knowledge and the Military in India, 1780–1860', *JICH* 33 (2005), 157–80; idem, 'The Habitual Nobility of Being: British Officers and the Social Construction of the Bengal Army in the Early Nineteenth Century', *Modern Asian Studies* 25 (1991), 545–69; idem, 'Between Mars and Mammon: The East India Company and Efforts to Reform its Army, 1796–1832', *HJ* 25 (1991), 385–401; idem, 'Soldiers, Scholars and the Scottish Enlightenment: Militarism in Early Nineteenth Century India', *JICH* 16 (1994), 441–60.

the Madras army has attracted additional attention.[26] Indiscipline was partially a reflection of different military cultures.[27]

The standard history of the British conquest is Sir Penderel Moon, *The British Conquest and Dominion of India* (1989) but there are suggestive articles by Bryant, and a recent thesis by Manu Sehgal.[28] One early challenge for the Company in expanding British influence was the state of Mysore, presided over by first Haidar Ali and then his son, Tipu Sultan, and resulting in four wars (1767–9, 1780–4, 1790–2 and 1799), culminating in the taking of the fortress of Seringapatam. Aspects of the conflict are investigated in Anne Buddle (ed.), *The Tiger and the Thistle: Tipu Sultan and the Scots in India, 1760–1800* (1999), accompanying an exhibition at the National Gallery of Scotland.[29] Naturally enough, the exhibition focused on the artistic legacy of the conflict and, in passing, it is worth mentioning a shorter catalogue of an exhibition at the National Army Museum of Indian 'Company' images of the British and EIC armies, *Indian Armies, Indian Art: Soldiers, Collectors and Artists, 1780–1880* (2010). There is G. Kaliamurthy, *The Second Anglo-Mysore War, 1780–84* (1987) but the Mysore Wars as a whole seem ripe for a new study.

---

26 See also R. E. Frykenberg, 'New Light on the Vellore Mutiny', in Kenneth Ballhatchet and John Harrison (eds), *East India Company Studies: Papers presented to Professor Sir Cyril Philips* (Hong Kong: Asian Research Series, 1986), pp. 212–15; idem, 'Conflicting Norms and Political Integration in South India: The Case of the Vellore Mutiny', *Indo-British Review* 13 (1987), 51–63; Devadas Moodley, 'Vellore, 1806: The Meanings of Mutiny', in Jane Hathaway (ed.), *Rebellion, Repression and Reinvention: Mutiny in Comparative Perspective* (Westport, CT: Praeger, 2001), pp. 87–102; A. D. Cameron, 'The Vellore Mutiny', PhD dissertation, University of Edinburgh, 1984; C. A. Montgomery, 'The Sepoy Army and Colonial Madras, c.1806–57', DPhil dissertation, University of Oxford, 2002.

27 See Douglas Peers, 'Army Discipline, Military Cultures and State-Formation in Colonial India, c.1780–1860', in Bowen, Mancke and Reid (eds), *Britain's Oceanic Empire*, pp. 282–307.

28 G. J. Bryant, 'Pacification in the Early British Raj, 1755–86', *JICH* 14 (1985), 3–19; idem, 'The Military Imperative in Early British Expansion in India, 1750–85', *Indo-British Review* 21 (1993), 18–35; idem, 'British Logistics and the Conduct of the Carnatic Wars, 1746–83', *WH* 11 (2004), 278–306; Manu Sehgal, 'British Expansion and the East India Company, 1770–1815', PhD dissertation, University of Exeter, 2011.

29 See also Kaushik Roy, 'Rockets under Haidar Ali and Tipu Sultan', *Indian Journal of the History of Science* 40 (2005), 635–55.

A second challenge was that posed by the Marathas, against whom three wars were fought (1774–83, 1803–5, 1817–19). The background is provided by Stewart Gordon, *Marathas, Marauders and State Formation in Eighteenth Century India* (1994). General surveys are provided by K. G. Pitre, *The Second Anglo-Maratha War, 1802–05* (1990), and Randolf G. S. Cooper, *The Anglo-Maratha Campaigns and the Contest for India: The Struggle for Control of the South Asian Military Economy* (2005). It was in the Second Maratha War (1803–5) that Arthur Welles-ley, later Duke of Wellington, first made his mark. Jac Weller, *Wellington in India* (1972) was an early study but it can be supplemented by Anthony Bennell, *The Making of Arthur Wellesley* (1997), and Bennell's edition of *The Maratha War Papers of Arthur Wellesley, 1803* (1998). Cooper and Bennell contributed essays on Wellesley in India to Alan Guy (ed.), *The Road to Waterloo: The British Army and the Struggle against Revolutionary and Napoleonic France, 1793–1815* (1990), another fine National Army Museum catalogue. The often forgotten Gerard Lake, the British CinC in India during the Second Maratha War, is the subject of an unpublished thesis.[30]

Mention of Wellington is an appropriate point to turn to the British experi-ence of the French Revolutionary and Napoleonic Wars. Bruce Collins, *War and Empire: The Expansion of Britain, 1790–1830* (2010) provides a wide-ranging overview of the use of British military and naval power on a global scale although the impact of warfare is seen primarily in strategic terms. Equally impressive is Roger Knight, *Britain Against Napoleon: The Organisation of Victory, 1793–1815* (2013). Clive Emsley, *British Society and the French Wars, 1793–1815* (1979) remains a good survey. Emsley, however, was writing before the current concern with national identity. As suggested earlier, Linda Colley's *Britons* (1992) helped establish the debate. Colley's focus was only partly on the volunteer movement in the fashioning of national identity. She suggested patriotism transcended social divisions, although she also recognised some of the wider complexities of motivation and that the expansion of militia and volunteers had 'democratic

---

30 See also Kaushik Roy, 'Firepower-centric Warfare in India and the Military Mod-ernisation of the Marathas, 1740–1818', *Indian Journal of the History of Science* 40 (2005), 597–634; John Pemble, 'Resources and Techniques in the Second Maratha War', *HJ* 19 (1976), 375–404; Randolf G. S. Cooper, 'Beyond Beasts and Bullion: Economic Considerations in Bombay's Military Logistics, 1803', *MAS* 33 (1999), 159=83; Enid M. Fuhr, 'Strategy and Diplomacy in British India under Marquess Wellesley: The Second Maratha War, 1803–06', PhD dissertation, Simon Fraser University, 1994. For Lake, see R. Harris, 'General Gerard, Lord Lake, 1744–1808: A Military Life', PhD dissertation, University of Leicester, 2003.

implications'. In focusing more exclusively on the volunteer movement, J. E. Cookson expanded the debate in *The British Armed Nation, 1793–1815* (1997). This took the study of the auxiliary forces beyond the much earlier work of J. R. Western published in journals,[31] and Western's still important monograph, *The English Militia in the Eighteenth Century: The Story of a Political Issue, 1660–1802* (1965). Indeed, there had been little additional work on the eighteenth-century militia since Western, with the exception of John Robertson, *The Scottish Enlightenment and the Militia Issue* (1985) and two very different works focusing on the militia reforms of 1757. Eliga Gould suggested that reform was intended to integrate landed society more fully into armed service in support of the Hanoverians. By contrast, from the perspective of concepts of 'manliness' that reflects the current interest in military masculinity, Matthew McCormack situates reform as part of a wider crisis aimed at national regeneration after the early setbacks of the Seven Years War.[32]

Rather than Colley's identification of emerging centralisation, Cookson emphasised the extent of self-mobilisation and self-organisation upon which the British state depended, and also the wide regional differences in the nature of the response to the threat of invasion. Cookson concluded that patriotism was less significant than working class pragmatism, and what he characterised as the 'town-making' interests of the emerging urban elite. Similarly, Austin Gee, *The British Volunteer Movement, 1794–1814* (2003) viewed the volunteer movement, including the mounted yeomanry, as one rooted in local communities, which further stimulated localism, and afforded new opportunities for the respectable elements of the urban population. Despite the considerable autonomy granted volunteer corps, the growth of the movement was accomplished without concessions to popular reform and in ways designed to increase central control. In suggesting that the volunteer movement's lack of political activity was more significant than its loyalism, Gee's analysis did not bear out the apparent establishment fears identified by S. C. Smith as the primary reason for replacing the

---

31 See J. R. Western, 'The Formation of the Scottish Militia in 1797', *Scottish Historical Review* 34 (1955), 1–18; idem, 'The Volunteer Movement as an Anti-revolutionary Force, 1793–1801', *EHR* 71 (1956), 603–14; idem, 'The County Fencibles and the Militia Augmentation of 1794', *JSAHR* 34 (1956), 3–11

32 Eliga Gould, 'To Strengthen the King's Hands: Dynasty, Legitimacy, Militia Reform, and Ideas of National Unity in England, 1745–60', *HJ* 34 (1991), 329–48; Matthew McCormack, 'The New Militia: War, Politics and Gender in 1750s Britain', *Gender and History* 19 (2007), 483–500. See also Julia Banister, 'Military Masculinity and Public Opinion in the Eighteenth Century', PhD dissertation, University of Southampton, 2010.

volunteers with the local militia in 1808.³³ In a subsequent comparative article, Cookson suggested the militia soon adopted the 'apolitical' habits of the regular army while the emergence of the external threat from France 'levered volunteering away from local interests and loyalties', neutralising any potential internal political threat from the movement.³⁴

Cookson included Ireland in his study, the militia there being revived in 1793, and an Irish yeomanry raised in 1796 that continued to exist until 1834. The militia and yeomanry were intended to replace the earlier Irish volunteer movement, which had been suppressed in 1793 as tainted by its politicisation, with some elements demanding legislative independence for Ireland. All these elements of the Irish auxiliaries have attracted attention, but work on the volunteers remains largely in the academic journals. A related study is that of Roman Catholics in the British army.³⁵ In some ways the volunteer corps raised in Britain during the American War of Independence attracted similar middle class elements, and aroused similar political concerns although those formed in Britain had more of a local than a national focus, as demonstrated by Stephen Conway.³⁶ Padhraig Higgins, *A Nation of Politicians: Gender, Patriotism and Political Culture*

33 S. C. Smith, 'Loyalty and Opposition in the Napoleonic Wars: The Impact of the Local Militia, 1807–15', PhD dissertation, University of Oxford, 1984.
34 J. E. Cookson, 'Service Without Politics? Army, Militia and Volunteers in Britain during the American and Revolutionary Wars', *WH* 10 (2003), 381–97.
35 P. D. H. Smyth, 'The Volunteer Movement in Ulster: Background and Development, 1745–85', PhD dissertation, Queen's University, Belfast, 1974; idem, 'Our Cloudcap't Grenadiers: The Volunteers as a Military Force', *Irish Sword* 13 (1978–9), 185–207; idem, 'The Volunteers and Parliament, 1779–1784', in Thomas Bartlett and D. W. Hayton (eds), *Penal Era and Golden Age: Essays in Irish History, 1690–1850* (Belfast: Queen's University Institute of Irish Studies, 1979), pp. 113–36; K. P. Ferguson, 'The Volunteer Movement and the Government, 1778–1793', *Irish Sword* 13 (1978–9), 208–16; Pádraig Ó Snodaigh, 'Some Police and Military Aspects of the Irish Volunteers', *Irish Sword* 13 (1978–9), 217–29; idem, 'The Volunteers of '82: A Citizen Army or Armed Citizens? A Bicentennial Retrospect', *Irish Sword* 15 (1983), 177–88; idem, 'Class and the Irish Volunteers', *Irish Sword* 16 (1986), 165–84. For Catholics, see V. J. L. Fontana, 'Some Aspects of Roman Catholic Service in the Land Forces of the British Crown, c.1750–c.1820', PhD dissertation, University of Portsmouth, 2002.
36 Stephen Conway, '"Like the Irish"? Volunteer Corps and Volunteering in Britain during the American War', in Julie Flavell and Stephen Conway (eds), *Britain and America Go to War* (Gainesville, FL: University Press of Florida, 2004), pp. 143–69.

in Late Eighteenth Century Ireland (2010) offers a different view of the volunteers, echoing the new interest in concepts of masculinity, while Finton Cullen, *Visual Politics: The Representation of Ireland, 1750–1930* (1997) includes discussion of the visual imagery of the Irish volunteers.

For the Irish Militia, the older work of Sir Henry McAnally, *The Irish Militia, 1793–1816* (1949) is now supplemented by the partial reworking of Ivan Nelson, *The Irish Militia, 1793–1802: Ireland's Forgotten Army* (2007), and an important new work, Neal Garnham, *The Militia in Eighteenth-Century Ireland: In Defence of the Protestant Interest* (2012). On the Irish yeomanry, there is the excellent Allan Blackstock, *An Ascendancy Army: The Irish Yeomanry, 1796–1834* (1998), and his short study of Belfast, *Double Traitors? The Belfast Volunteers and Yeomen, 1778–1828* (2000).[37] Some of the earlier published work on the volunteers coincided with the bicentenary of their formation in 1778. Rather similarly, the bicentenary of the Irish rebellion of 1798 saw an impressive catalogue of the major exhibition at the Ulster Museum, including a section on militia, volunteers and yeomanry, W. A. Maguire (ed.), *Up in Arms: The 1798 Rebellion in Ireland: A Bicentenary Exhibition* (1998).

While the wider significance of the raising of local forces lies in the contrast between local autonomy and central control, the auxiliary forces have continued to result in local studies of value. Early examples from local County Record Office collections included M. Y. Ashcroft, *To Escape the Monster's Clutches* (1977) from North Yorkshire; R. G. E. Wood (ed.), *Essex and the French Wars, 1793–1815* (1977); and P. Bloomfield, *Kent and the Napoleonic Wars* (1987). Local studies have continued to appear in journals or in unpublished theses.[38] Equally, local record societies and local history societies have published a number of volumes dealing with the auxiliary forces. Often they are of primarily genealogical interest with the editorial content lacking in depth but there are exceptions such as Paul Morgan (ed.), *The Warwickshire Yeomanry in the Nineteenth Century: Some Fresh Aspects* (1994). In passing, it should be noted that, as

---

37 Blackstock has examined wider implications in 'The Union and the Military, 1801–c.1830', *Transactions of the Royal Historical Society* 10 (2000), 329–51. See also Neal Garnham, 'The Establishment of a Statutory Militia in Ireland, 1692–1716: Legislative Process and Protestant Mentalities', *Historical Research* 84 (2011), 266–87.

38 See Kevin Linch, 'A Geography of Loyalism? The Local Military Forces of the West Riding, 1794–1814', *W&S* 19 (2001), 1–22; and Michael Hales, 'Part-time Military Movements in Staffordshire, 1790–1870', PhD dissertation, University of Sheffield Hallam, 1997.

opposed to the militia and volunteers, the yeomanry lacks an academic monograph though there are two recent theses.[39]

The threat of invasion was a significant one. Richard Glover, *Britain at Bay: Defence Against Bonaparte, 1803–14* (1973) remains useful, while there are some important essays in Mark Philp (ed.), *Resisting Napoleon: The British Response to the Threat of Invasion, 1797–1815* (2006). The latter was part of a wider research project that also embraced an exhibition at the Bodleian Library in 2003, for which there is another excellent catalogue, Alexandra Franklin and Mark Philp (eds), *Napoleon and the Invasion of Britain* (2003). The emphasis was very much on the cultural legacy of the threat in terms of contemporary literary, artistic and pictorial outputs. Also relevant in this regard are sections of the catalogue of the Trafalgar bicentenary exhibition at the National Maritime Museum, Margarette Lincoln (ed.), *Nelson and Napoleon* (2005). Gillian Russell, *The Theatres of War: Performance, Politics and Society, 1793–1815* (1995) focuses on the role of theatre and spectacular in projecting military and naval themes. Russell has extended her work back to the American War.[40] It is important to see the cultural impact of warfare in a wider context extending back to the Seven Years War, for which Holger Hoock, *Empires of the Imagination: Politics, War, and the Arts in the British World, 1750–1850* (2010) is an important guide. It can be supplemented by the essays in John Bonehill and Geoffrey Quilley (eds), *Conflicting Visions: War and Visual Culture in Britain and France, c.1700–1830* (2005). A recent work, Catriona Kennedy, *Narratives of the Revolutionary and Napoleonic Wars: Military and Civilian Experience in Britain and Ireland* (2013) usefully focuses on how individuals interpreted their own experiences of war.

That the great struggle with Revolutionary and Napoleonic France should cement British global pre-eminence did not appear at all likely after initial setbacks, particularly in terms of operations in Flanders, massive losses of 97,000 seamen and soldiers from death, disease and discharge in the Caribbean in the 1790s, and the collapse of successive allied coalitions. The state of the army at the beginning of hostilities can be gauged from the unpublished work of the late John Pimlott.[41] The campaigns in Flanders still require a modern

---

39 Andrew D. Gilks, 'A History of Britain's Volunteer Cavalry, 1776–1908', PhD dissertation, University of Birmingham, 2005; and George M. Hay, 'The British Yeomanry Cavalry, 1794–1920', PhD dissertation, University of Kent, 2011.

40 Gillian Russell, 'Theatricality and Military Culture: British Army Camps in the 1770s', *Eighteenth Century Life* 183 (1994), 55–64.

41 J. L. Pimlott, 'The Administration of the British Army, 1783–93', PhD dissertation, University of Leicester, 1975.

re-assessment, as does the commander-in-chief, the Duke of York, for which there is still only Alfred Burne, *The Noble Duke of York: The Military Life of Frederick, Duke of York and Albany* (1949). The terrible cost of Caribbean warfare, however, is well covered in Michael Duffy, *Soldiers, Sugar and Seapower: The British Expeditions to the West Indies and the War Against Revolutionary France* (1987).[42] Other aspects of the campaigns have been covered by David Geggus, *Slavery, War and Revolution: The British Occupation of Saint Domingue, 1793–98* (1981). Ultimately, a solution to the problem of disease was to raise black troops in the Caribbean itself, as described by Roger Buckley, *Slaves in Redcoats: The British West India Regiments, 1795–1815* (1979), and his *The British Army in the West Indies: Society and the Military in the Revolutionary Age* (1998).

Evolving British strategy has been covered in two books by Piers Mackesy, *Statesmen at War: The Strategy of Overthrow, 1798–99* (1974); and *War without Victory: The Downfall of Pitt, 1799–1802* (1984). Mackesy also wrote an earlier study of Britain's Mediterranean strategy, *The War in the Mediterranean, 1803–10* (1957) that can be supplemented by two more specialised studies by Desmond Gregory, *The Ungovernable Rock: A History of the Anglo-Corsican Kingdom and its Role in Britain's Mediterranean Strategy during the Revolutionary War, 1793–97* (1985), and *The Insecure Base: A History of the British Occupation of Sicily, 1806–15* (1988). Napoleon's expedition to Egypt in 1798 rang alarms bells for the security of India and is the starting point for a number of studies of British grand strategy in the Middle East and South Asia including M. E. Yapp, *Strategies of British India: Britain, Iran and Afghanistan, 1798–1850* (1980); and three works by Edward Ingram, *Commitment to Empire: Prophecies of the Great Game in Asia, 1797–1800* (1981), *In Defence of British India: Great Britain in the Middle East, 1774–1842* (1984), and *Britain's Persian Connection, 1798–1828: Prelude to the Great Game in Asia* (1992).[43]

Often forgotten is the Anglo–American War of 1812–14. Not unexpectedly, this has attracted more attention in Canada and the United States than in Britain. Moreover, the most recent accounts from the British perspective have tended to concentrate on the role of the Royal Navy. General academic accounts are

---

42 See also Roger Buckley, 'The Destruction of the British Army in the West Indies, 1793–1815: A Medical History, *JSAHR* 56 (1978), 79–92; R. W. McCarter, 'Johnny Newcome's Poison: Alcohol Use and Abuse in the British West Indies Garrison, 1792–1815', PhD dissertation, Duke University, 1999.

43 See also G. J. Alder, 'Britain and the Defence of India: The Origins of the Problem, 1798–1815', *Journal of Asian History* 6 (1973), 14–44.

J Mackay Hitsman, *The Incredible War of 1812* (1965, reissued 1999); Donald Hickey, *The War of 1812: A Forgotten Conflict* (1989, reissued 2012)]; J. C. A. Stagg, *The War of 1812: Conflict for a Continent* (2012); and Jeremy Black, *The War of 1812: In the Age of Napoleon* (2009).[44] Ronald J. Dale, *The Invasion of Canada: Battles of the War of 1812* (2011) offers the Canadian perspective in a brief well-illustrated survey, while the production accompanying an exhibition by the Canadian War Museum, Peter Macleod, *Four Wars of 1812* (2012), is disappointing compared to other exhibition catalogues noted elsewhere in this volume.

British use of economic warfare is also covered in J. M. Sherwig, *Guineas and Gunpowder: British Foreign Aid in the Wars with France, 1793–1815* (1969). For the post-1803 period, there is also Christopher Hall, *British Strategy in the Napoleonic War, 1803–15* (1991), which evaluates the efforts of successive ministries to develop a coherent response to Napoleonic domination of the continent in the light of often-limited strategic options. How successful that proved is also analysed by Rory Muir, *Britain and the Defeat of Napoleon, 1807–15* (1996), which argues that Wellington's victories after 1808 shattered the myth of French battlefield invincibility irrespective of whether the war in the Spanish peninsula truly diverted French troops from the invasion of Russia.[45]

The means by which the army recovered from its early setbacks in the 1790s to emerge as capable of sustaining its effort in Portugal and Spain was the subject of Richard Glover, *Peninsular Preparation: The Reform of the British Army, 1795–1809* (1963). Piers Mackesy, *British Victory in Egypt, 1801* (1995) shows that the foundations of military reform had progressed sufficiently by 1801 to revive the army's reputation though trained light infantry was still lacking. Subsequent reform in the light infantry arm has been covered by David Gates, *The British Light Infantry Arm, c. 1790–1815: Its Creation, Training and Operational Role* (1987). There would still be failures as illustrated by Gordon C. Bond, *The Grand Expedition: The British Invasion of Holland in 1809* (1979) on

---

44 Black has also summarised his views on the wider strategic significance in 'The North American Theatre of the Napoleonic Wars, Or, as it is Sometimes Called, the War of 1812', *JMH* 76, 2012, 1053–66, part of a special issue of the journal devoted to the conflict. Another discussion of strategy is C. J. Bartlett, 'Gentlemen versus Democrats: Cultural Prejudice and Military Strategy in Britain in the War of 1812', *WH* 1 (1994), 140–59.

45 On the initial involvement in the Peninsula there is also Martin Robson, 'British Intervention in Portugal, 1793–1808' *HR* 76 (2003), 93–107; idem, 'British Intervention in Portugal, 1806–08', PhD dissertation, University of London, 2004.

the Walcheren expedition, and Ian Fletcher, *The Waters of Oblivion: The British Invasion of the River Plate, 1806–07* (1991). Curiously, there is no overall modern academic monograph dealing with the development of the army over the course of the period 1793 to 1815 as a whole.[46] However, three recent theses have now been published dealing with different aspects of the improved performance of the British army after 1807. Kevin Linch, *Britain and Wellington's Army: Recruitment, Society and Tradition, 1807–15* (2011) points to the importance of the militia as a source of recruits, but also to the efforts of the Duke of York and the Adjutant General, Sir Harry Calvert, to create the first real sense of regimental identity. Edward Coss, *All for the King's Shilling: The British Soldier under Wellington, 1808–14* (2010) draws on a substantial database to examine the social composition of the army, and upon modern military psychology to explain battlefield cohesiveness. Andrew Bamford, *Sickness, Suffering and the Sword: The British Regiment on Campaign, 1808–15* (2013) sees the regimental system as essentially decentralised.

Inevitably, Wellington and the Peninsular War have generated an enormous popular literature. Fortunately, there are two fine academic overviews in David Gates, *The Spanish Ulcer: A History of the Peninsular War* (1986), and Charles Esdaile, *The Peninsular War: A New History* (2002). There is a good range of essays in two works already mentioned, Ian Fletcher (ed.) *The Peninsular War* (1998), and Paddy Grifffith (ed.), *Modern Studies of the War in Spain and Portugal* (1999), and useful insights in Rory Muir, Robert Burnham, Howie Muir and Ron McGuigan, *Inside Wellington's Peninsular Army, 1808–14* (2006). Griffith also edited *Wellington, Commander: The Iron Duke's Generalship* (1985). Joshua Moon, *Wellington's Two-Front War: The Peninsular Campaigns, at Home and Abroad, 1808–14* (2011) sets the campaign against the background of Wellington's struggle for resources and domestic political support. Two recent solid studies of Wellington are Ian Robertson, *A Commanding Presence: Wellington on the Peninsula, 1808–14: Logistics, Strategy, Survival* (2008), and Huw Davies, *Wellington's Wars: The Making of a Military Genius* (2012). Davies has also covered the significance of operational intelligence for Wellington, and intelligence generally has attracted wider interest, including a useful account by the journalist, Mark Urban, *The Man Who Broke Napoleon's Codes* (2001), on George

---

46 See, however, K. J. Bartlett, 'The Development of the British Army during the Wars with France, 1793–1815' (PhD dissertation, University of Durham, 1997). Another important thesis is Zena Moore, 'Army Recruitment and the Uncertainties of the Fiscal-Military State in Britain, 1793–1815', PhD dissertation, University of London, 2006.

Scovell. Logistics, too, has also been covered, as has cavalry command in theses.[47] Two less familiar aspects of Wellington's campaigns are illuminated in Charles Esdaile, *The Duke of Wellington and the Command of the Spanish Army, 1812–14* (1990); and Christopher Hall, *Wellington's Navy: Sea Power and the Peninsular War, 1807–14* (2004). The latter demonstrates that Wellington's campaigns could not have succeeded without the navy's ability to supply the British army in the field, to contribute the heavy guns required for siege warfare, and to divert French resources by attacking coastal targets. An older but still valuable study is S. G. P. Ward, *Wellington's Headquarters: A Study of the Administrative Problems in the Peninsula, 1809–14* (1957). It might be added that Wellington's predecessor, Sir John Moore, killed at Corunna in 1809, deserves a reassessment for there is only Carola Oman, *Sir John Moore* (1953).

The culmination of Britain's war at Waterloo in June 1815 has generated probably even more popular accounts than the Peninsular War and has generated even more in the run up to the bicentenary in 2015. David Hamilton-Williams, *Waterloo: New Perspectives: The Great Battle Reappraised* (1993) is a reasonable summary. Jeremy Black, *The Battle of Waterloo: A New History* (2010) also sets the scene well and Black, as well as other academic historians, contributes an essay to Nick Lipscombe (ed.), *Waterloo: The Decisive Victory* (2014). One of the more interesting aspects has been the controversy generated by Peter Hofschröer, who has contended that Wellington not only deceived his Prussian allies but also concealed subsequently their role in his victory. Hofschröer has laid out his charges in two books, *1815 – The Waterloo Campaign: Wellington, his German Allies and the Battles of Ligny and Quatre Bras* (1998), and *1815 – The Waterloo Campaign: The German Victory* (1999). In addition, he has dealt with Wellington's antipathy towards the famous models of Waterloo completed by William Siborne in 1838 and 1844 in *Wellington's Smallest Victory: The Duke, the Model Maker and the Secret of Waterloo* (2004), Siborne being forced to

---

47 Huw Davies, 'Wellington's Use of Deception Tactics in the Peninsular War', *JSS* 29 (2006), 723–50; idem, 'Integration of Strategic and operational Intelligence during the Peninsular War', *Intelligence and National Security* 21 (2006), 202–23; idem, 'The Influence of Intelligence on Wellington's Art of Command', *Intelligence and National Security* 22 (2007), 619–43; idem, 'Diplomats as Spymasters: A Case Study of the Peninsular War, 1809–13', *JMH* 76 (2012), 37–68; Mark Romans, 'Professionalism and the Development of Military Intelligence in Wellington's Army, 1809–14', PhD dissertation, University of Southampton, 2005; T. M. O. Redgrave, 'Wellington's Logistical Arrangements in the Peninsular War', PhD dissertation, University of London, 1979; Mark T. Gerges, 'Command and Control in the Peninsula: The Role of the British Cavalry, 1808–14', PhD dissertation, Florida State University, 2005.

remove the representation of 40,000 Prussian troops from his first, larger model. There has been some response to Hofschröer's interpretation.[48] More significant as a consideration of Hofschröer's case as a whole is Christopher Bassford, Daniel Moran and Gregory Pedlow, *On Waterloo: Clausewitz, Wellington, and the Campaign of 1815* (2010).

The Siborne models call to mind the general cultural impact of Waterloo and of the Revolutionary and Napoleonic Wars in art, literature and memory in Britain. The Duchess of Richmond's Ball in Brussels on the eve of Waterloo caught both the contemporary and later imagination, as suggested by David Miller, *The Duchess of Richmond's Ball, 15 June 1815* (2004), and Nick Foulkes, *Dancing into Battle: A Social History of the Battle of Waterloo* (2006). Tourism to the field of Waterloo was a particular development. Among the better of the more recent general accounts are two which look at the cultural legacy, namely Paul O'Keefe, *Waterloo: The Aftermath* (2014), and R. E. Foster, *Wellington and Waterloo: The Duke, the Battle and Posterity, 1815–2015* (2014).[49] The Peninsular War and Waterloo also resulted in a plethora of servicemen's memoirs, discussed in part in Neil Ramsey, *The Military Memoir and Romantic Literary Culture, 1780–1835* (2012). Monuments to heroes of the conflict are covered in Alison Yarrington, *The Commemoration of the Hero, 1800–64: Monuments to the British Victors of the Napoleonic Wars* (1980).

---

48 John Hussey, 'At What Time on 15 June 1815 did Wellington Learn of Napoleon's Attack on the Prussians?', *WH* 6 (1996), 88–116. This generated Hofschröer's 'A Rely to John Hussey', *WH* 6 (1999), 468–78, and Hussey's rejoinder, 'Towards a Better Chronology for the Waterloo Campaign', *WH* 7 (2000), 463–80.

49 See A. V. Seaton, 'War and Thanatourism: Waterloo, 1815–1914', *Annals of Tourism Research* 26 (1999), 130–58; Stuart Semmel, 'Reading the Tangible Past: British Tourism, Collecting and Memory after Waterloo', *Representations* 69 (2000), 9–37; Elisa Milkes, 'A Battle's Legacy: Waterloo in Nineteenth Century Britain', PhD dissertation, Yale University, 2002; Timothy Fitzpatrick, 'Waterloo in Myth and Memory: The Battle of Waterloo, 1815–1915', PhD dissertation, Florida State University, 2013; and Susan Pearce, 'The Matérial of War: Waterloo and its Culture', in John Bonehill and Geoff Quilley (eds), *Conflicting Visions: War and Visual Culture in Britain and France, c.1700–1830* (Aldershot: Ashgate, 2005), pp. 207–26.

Chapter 6

1815–1914

As in the case of the 'long eighteenth century', it is appropriate to extend the concept of nineteenth-century warfare from 1815 up to the outbreak of the First World War in 1914. While this may appear to privilege the assumption of the Great War as marking profound discontinuity with conflicts prior to 1914, it offers the opportunity to interpret aspects of nineteenth-century conflict as an essential precursor of totality in the twentieth century. In addition, however, it may also be seen in the context of the British experience as an age of unparalleled imperial expansion.

As noted in the previous section, some general texts dealing with the nineteenth century begin with the French Revolutionary and Napoleonic Wars on the basis that the *levée en masse* introduced the concept of the mass citizen army and thus began the process of increasing totality in warfare. It might be argued, indeed, that the five essential steps on the road to 'total war' in the twentieth century were the impact of nationalism and democracy as expressed through the 'nation in arms'; the impact of industrialisation on the destructive capability of armies; a degree of misunderstanding by some soldiers as to the impact of new weapons on the battlefield; the greater willingness to accept war as an appropriate test of nationhood and national virility deriving from such influences as imperialism and crude Social Darwinism; and the lack of any universal readiness on the part of the international community to accept meaningful limitations on the future conduct of war. There is also logic, however, in unifying the analysis of the Napoleonic Wars with the succeeding period in that the two principal western military theorists of the nineteenth century – Jomini and Clausewitz – were essentially interpreters of the Napoleonic legacy to warfare. Those texts previously mentioned covering the longer period from the Revolutionary and Napoleonic Wars onwards to 1914 are Geoffrey Wawro, *Warfare and Society in Europe, 1792–1914* (2000), and David Gates, *Warfare in the Nineteenth Century* (2001). As also already noted, John Gooch, *Armies in Europe* (1980) and Hew Strachan, *European Armies and the Conduct of War* (1983) extend to 1945.

Just as Geoffrey Best, *War and Society in Revolutionary Europe, 1770–1870* (1982), opted to close with the Franco-Prussian War, the next volume in the

Fontana series, Brian Bond, *War and Society in Europe, 1870–1970* (1983) extended well beyond 1914. Though Wawro covers the period up to 1914, what might be regarded as the continuation volume in the 'Warfare and History' series, Michael Neiberg, *Warfare and Society in Europe: 1898 to the Present* (2004), backtracks to the Fashoda Incident in its first chapter. Similarly, the continuation of Jeremy Black, *Western Warfare, 1775–1882* (2001) is *Warfare in the Western World, 1882–1975* (2002). The indefatigable Black has also contributed *War in the Modern World since 1815* (2003), *The Age of Total War, 1860–1945* (2006), and more specific to this section, *War in the Nineteenth Century* (2009). Significantly, both Neiberg and Black take aspects of colonial rivalry as the starting point, Black beginning with the British intervention in Egypt in 1882. It will be recalled, too, that while Stig Förster and Jörg Nagler (eds), *The Road to Total War* (1997), concentrates on the American Civil War and the Franco-Prussian War, the second of the American and German collaborations on total war, Manfred Boemeke, Roger Chickering and Stig Förster (eds), *Anticipating Total War* (1999), points especially to colonial wars as equally significant in introducing greater totality into European warfare. In this regard, Bruce Vandervort, *Wars of Imperial Conquest in Africa, 1830–1914* (1998), is a useful summary, as is the entry in the Cassell series, Douglas Porch, *Wars of Empire* (2000), which carries its coverage into the post-1945 period. The other Cassell volume dealing with the nineteenth century is the more focused Brian Holden Reid, *The American Civil War and the Wars of the Industrial Revolution* (1999). Roger Chickering, Dennis Showalter and Hans van de Ven (eds), *The Cambridge History of War:* volume IV, *War and the Modern World* (2012), covers the period from 1850 to 2000 and, somewhat bizarrely, is the first volume to appear in the series. All provide some guidance on the large literature on European and other armies of the nineteenth century.

Perhaps inevitably, those conflicts thought to illustrate aspects of modernity have attracted most attention, notably the Crimean War (1854–6), the American Civil War (1861–5), and the German Wars of Unification (1864–71). General modern accounts of the Crimean War include Winfried Baumgart, *The Crimean War, 1853–56* (1999); Hugh Small, *The Crimean War* (2007); Orlando Figes, *Crimea: The Last Crusade* (2010); and the well-illustrated Paul Kerr (ed.), *The Crimean War* (1997), which accompanied a Channel Four television series. John S. Curtis, *Russia's Crimean War* (1979) provides an alternative to the usual preoccupation with the British and French armies.

The American Civil War has generated a huge literature. Good general histories include Peter Parrish, *The American Civil War* (1975); the two works by James McPherson, *Ordeal by Fire: The Civil War and Reconstruction* (1981), and *Battle Cry of Freedom: The Civil War Era* (1988); Herman Hattaway, *Shades of*

Blue and Gray: An Introductory Military History of the Civil War (1997); David Eicher, *The Longest Night: A Military History of the Civil War* (2001); and Susan-Mary Grant, *The War for a Nation: The American Civil War* (2006). For the German Wars of Unification, there is the fine overall study, Dennis Showalter, *The Wars of German Unification* (2004), which builds on his earlier *Railroads and Rifles: Soldiers, Technology and the Unification of Germany* (1975), as well as Arden Bucholz, *Moltke and the German Wars, 1864–71* (2001). The classic account of the Austro-Prussian War by Gordon Craig, *The Battle of Königgratz* (1964) can now be supplemented by Geoffrey Wawro, *The Austro-Prussian War: Austria's War with Prussia and Italy in 1866* (1996), which has the advantage over Craig of using Austrian as well as German sources. Wawro has also contributed *The Franco-Prussian War: Germany Conquers France in 1870–71* (2003), but Michael Howard, *The Franco-Prussian War* (1961) rightly retains its iconic status. A useful survey of one particular military development of lasting consequence is Nicholas Murray, *The Rocky Road to the Great War: The Evolution of Trench Warfare to 1914* (2013), which takes the Russo-Turkish War of 1877–8 as a starting point.

There is also the question of the development of military thought generally, such as soldiers' penchant for the late nineteenth-century 'cult of the offensive', which often figures in the more general surveys of European armies. Azar Gat, *The Development of Military Thought: The Nineteenth Century* (1992) covers the field. Jomini was better known than Clausewitz in the nineteenth century but it is the latter whose military thought has dominated the historiography, not least because of his perceived relevance to later warfare. Indeed, the only substantial work on Jomini's influence is Carol Reardon, *With a Sword in One Hand and Jomini in the Other: The Problem of Military Thought in the Civil War North* (2012), which looks at Jomini's influence in the United States up to and including the Civil War. Michael Howard and Peter Paret (eds), *Carl Von Clausewitz: On War* (1989) is usually regarded as the definitive English translation but they have acknowledged that their version is sometimes 'too clean'. Contributing to Hew Strachan and Andreas Herberg-Rothe (eds), *Clausewitz in the Twenty First Century* (2007), for example, Jan Willem Honig has raised doubts about the translation, pointing out that *politik* is consistently translated as policy rather than politics. Howard has also provided *Clausewitz: A Very Short Introduction* (2002), while Paret's works include *Clausewitz and the State* (1976) and *Understanding War: Essays on Clausewitz and the History of Military Power* (1992). Other treatments include Beatrice Heuser, *Reading Clausewitz* (2002); Hew Strachan, *Clausewitz's On War: A Biography* (2007); Jon Sumida, *Decoding Clausewitz: A New Approach to On War* (2008); and Andreas Herberg-Rothe, Jan Willem Honig and Daniel Moran (eds), *Clausewitz: The State and War*

(2011). Perhaps inevitably, Clausewitz also looms large in Hew Strachan, *The Direction of War: Contemporary Strategy in Historical Perspective* (2013). From the point of view of Britain, Christopher Bassford, *Clausewitz in English: The Reception of Clausewitz in Britain and America 1815–1945* (1994) suggests that Clausewitz had a little more impact than often supposed prior to the first English translation by J. J. Graham in 1873, and certainly influenced Henry Spenser Wilkinson after 1873. This is disputed, however, by Michael Handel, *Clausewitz and Modern Strategy* (1986).

Beyond Europe, the technology that was transforming the battlefield was also assisting European expansion, as examined in Donald Headrick, *The Tools of Empire: Technology and European Imperialism in the Nineteenth Century* (1981), and Philip Curtin, (1998) *Disease and Empire: The Heath of European Troops in the Conquest of Africa* (1998). J. A. de Moor and H. L. Wesseling (eds), *Imperialism and War* (1989) is a useful collection of essays on varying aspects of such expansion, with the merit of including the Dutch and Italian experiences. The imperial military experience generally is also the subject of a number of essays in David Killingray and David Omissi (eds), *Guardians of Empire: The Armed Forces of the Colonial Powers, c.1700–1964* (1999), while Karl Hack and Tobias Rettig (eds), *Colonial Armies in Southeast Asia* (2009) ranges from the 1880s to the 1940s.

The example of Europe was also significant for those non-European powers seeking to avoid European encroachment. Japan has attracted interest as in Stewart Lone, *Japan's First Modern War: Army and Society in the Conflict with China, 1894–95* (1994), and S. C. M. Paine, *The Sino-Japanese War of 1894–95: Perceptions, Power and Primacy* (2003). Of course, the Russo-Japanese War (1904–5) has been seen as providing particular military lessons for Europe that went unheeded. The classic narrative account is R. M. Connaughton, *The War of the Rising Sun and the Tumbling Bear* (1988), but this can now be supplemented by two rigorous academic collections, D. Wells and S. Wilson (eds), *The Russo-Japanese War in Cultural Perspective, 1904–05* (1999), and Rotem Kowner (ed.), *The Impact of the Russo-Japanese War* (2006). That other conflict immediately before the outbreak of the Great War, which provided at least some lessons, is investigated in Richard Hall, *The Balkan Wars: Prelude to the First World War* (2000). The Spanish-American War (1898) was the catalyst for far greater projection of American military power overseas and is examined in David Trask, *The War with Spain in 1898* (1981); Graham Cosmas, *An Army for Empire: The US Army in the Spanish-American War* (1994); and Joseph Smith, *The Spanish-American War: Conflict in the Caribbean and the Pacific, 1895–1902* (1994). What is generally regarded as the second most costly war in human history after the Second World War, the Taiping Rebellion in China between 1850 and 1864, is now the subject of S. Platt, *Autumn in the Heavenly Kingdom: China, the West and the Epic Story of the Taiping Civil War* (2012).

Turning to the British army, there is a still highly valuable overview in Edward Spiers, *The Army and Society, 1815–1914* (1980). Also covering the whole period are the eight volumes of the Marquess of Anglesey, *A History of the British Cavalry, 1816–1919* (1973–98), though they have a distinctly old-fashioned feel. Marion Harding (ed.), *The Victorian Soldier: Studies in the History of the British Army, 1816–1914* (1993), a series of essays published by the National Army Museum, ranges more widely than the Victorian period as its subtitle suggests. For the later period there is Edward Spiers, *The Late Victorian Army, 1868–1902* (1992), which provides a comprehensive survey of administration, officers and other ranks, civil-military relations, the army's role at home and abroad, its public image, and its operational and tactical methods. Ian F. W. Beckett, *The Victorians at War* (2003) covers a range of subjects between the Crimea and the South African War. In terms of coverage of wider periods, there is also the still useful Jay Luvaas, *The Education of An Army: British Military Thought, 1815–1940* (1964), and his *The Military Legacy of the Civil War: The European Inheritance* (1959).

Following the victory at Waterloo in 1815, it could be argued that British supremacy went effectively unchallenged for a century, to the extent that it was only the advent of the First World War that persuaded Britons that 'The Great War' no longer meant the great struggle against Revolutionary and Napoleonic France. In the whole period between 1815 and 1914, indeed, Britain was engaged in only one European war, namely that against Russia between 1854 and 1856. Even that relatively limited challenge, however, proved a severe shock, for the army had been comparatively slow to come to terms with the relentless pace of technological change. As Hew Strachan shows in *Wellington's Legacy: The Reform of the British Army, 1830–1854* (1984) and *From Waterloo to Balaclava: Tactics, Technology, and the British Army, 1815–1854* (1985), the army had not simply stagnated. There had been a lively professional debate and some reforms despite limited resources amid financial reductions and general public indifference.[1] Nonetheless, the army still had a certain public impact as suggested by Scott Hughes Myerly, *British Military Spectacle: From the Napoleonic Wars through the Crimea* (1996).

---

1 See also Hew Strachan, 'The Early Victorian Army and the Nineteenth Century Revolution in Government', *EHR* 95 (1980), 782–809; Peter Burroughs, 'The Human Cost of Imperial Defence in the Early Victorian Age', *VS* 24 (1980), 7–37; M. D. Welch, *Science and the British Officer: The Early Days of the Royal United Services Institute for Defence Studies, 1829–69* (London: RUSI Whitehall Papers, 1998).

Inevitably, current engagement in Afghanistan has seen many popular accounts of the first two Anglo-Afghan Wars of 1838–42 and 1878–81. The best academic treatment of the First Afghan War, however, remains J. A. Norris, *The First Afghan War, 1838–42* (1967), although Patrick Macrory, *Signal Catastrophe* (1966) runs it close. In fact, academic coverage of the army's other colonial campaigns prior to 1854 has been a little uneven. The Sikh Wars of 1845–9, and the Third China War were included in Brian Bond's edited collection, *Victorian Military Campaigns* (1967). The Sikh Wars, however, would certainly repay study, as would the Kandyan Wars of 1803–18, and the first two Burma Wars of 1824–6 and 1852–3. John Pemble, *The Invasion of Nepal: John Company at War* (1971) is exemplary and its recent reprinting is most welcome. The three China Wars of 1839–42, 1846–7, and 1856–60 have seen continuing popular interest, largely as a result of the issue of opium, but have also now attracted academic attention. Harry Gelber, *Opium, Soldiers and Evangelicals: England's 1840–42 War with China and its Aftermath* (2004) is a solid academic account of the first war. Chung Tan, *China and the Brave New World: A Study of the Origins of the Opium War, 1840–42* (1978), which draws on Chinese sources, suggests that the first war was neither a cultural nor a purely economic clash but arose from the nature of opium as a commodity. Julia Lovell, *The Opium War: Drug, Dreams and the Making of China* (2011) also draws on Chinese archives, concentrating largely on the first war. John Wong, *Deadly Dreams: Opium and the Arrow War (1856–60) in China* (1998), which also draws on Chinese sources, is primarily an analysis of economic imperialism, while James Hevia, *English Lessons: The Pedagogy of Imperialism in Nineteenth Century China* (2003) links the third war and the Boxer rebellion of 1900 together as exercises in cultural imperialism as well as military force. As will be noted later, the Maori Wars that extended from 1846 to 1872 have also been well covered. As for the third to eighth Cape Frontier Wars against the Xhosa of South Africa (1799–1803, 1811–12, 1818–19, 1834–5, 1846–7 and 1850–2), beyond the basic narratives by John Milton, *The Edges of War: A History of the Frontier Wars, 1702–78* (1983), and Noël Mostert, *Frontiers: The Epic of South Africa's Creation and the Tragedy of the Xhosa People* (1992), there is only an account of the eighth war by a gifted but non-academic historian, Keith Smith, *Harry Smith's Last Throw: The Eighth Cape Frontier War, 1850–53* (2013). Some primary sources are available in Michael Carver's Army Records Society edition, *Letters of a Victorian Army Officer: Edward Wellesley, 1840–54* (1995) for the seventh war, and Peter Boyden (ed.), *The British Army in Cape Colony: Soldiers' Letters and Diaries, 1806–58* (SAHR Special Publication 15, 2001). As suggested in a previous section, however, Peter Boyden,

Alan Guy and Marion Harding (eds), *Ashes and Blood: The British Army in South Africa, 1795–1914* (1999) covers the whole history of the army in South Africa to 1914.

Not for the first time in its history, the army was caught at a moment of transition in 1854, and the Crimea was not the limited colonial conflict for which the supporting services were prepared. Indeed, in a war in which new naval as well as military technologies were displayed, Andrew Lambert, *The Crimean War: British Grand Strategy against Russia, 1853–56* (1990) maintains that naval rather than military power was decisive in the war against Russia and, moreover, as deployed in the Baltic rather than the Black Sea. Certainly, naval consider-ations dictated the descent on Sebastopol.[2] M. S. Partridge, *Military Planning for the Defence of the United Kingdom, 1814–70* (1989) demonstrates that rail and steam technology could both assist, as well as hamper, home defence in the face of renewed fears of French invasion, although most reliance was placed on costly fortifications around key coastal ports and installations. The Crimean War had a distinct domestic impact, as suggested by Olive Anderson, *A Liberal State at War: English Politics and Economics during the Crimean War* (1967); C. C. Bayley, *Mercenaries for the Crimea: The German, Swiss and Italian Legions in British Service, 1854–56* (1977); and David Murphy, *Ireland and the Crimean War* (Dublin, 2002). Sympathy for the suffering of the soldier had an influence on the public perception of the army as reflected in popular representation, a subject explored by Matthew Paul Lalumia, *Realism and Politics in Victorian Art of the Crimean War* (1984); and Stefanie Markovits, *The Crimean War in the British Imagination* (2009). The Crimea is also central to general works on the military image such as J. W. M. Hichberger, *Images of the Army: The Military in British Art, 1815–1914* (1988); Paul Usherwood and Jenny Spencer-Smith, *Lady Butler: Battle Artists, 1846–1933* (1987), the catalogue of an exhibition at the National Army Museum; and Peter Harrington, *British Artists and War: The Face of Battle in Paintings and Prints, 1700–1914* (1993). One specialist area is covered in Stephen Harris, *British Military Intelligence in the Crimean War, 1854–56* (1999), while the well-known charge of the Light Brigade is debated in Mark Adkin, *The Charge: The Real Reason Why the Light Brigade Was Lost* (2000), and Terry Brighton, *Hell Riders: The Truth about the Charge of the Light Brigade* (2004), who disputes Adkin's theory that Captain Nolan deliberately misrepresented

---

2 Hew Strachan, 'Soldiers, Strategy and Sebastopol', *HJ* 21 (1978), 303–25. See also J. Warburton, 'A Medical History of the British Expeditionary Force in the East, 1854–56', PhD dissertation, University of Keele, 1982.

the order sent to the Light Brigade in order to prove that cavalry could charge guns successfully. Alastair Massie (ed.), *A Most Desperate Undertaking: The British Army in the Crimea, 1854–56* (2003) is the beautifully illustrated catalogue of a major National Army Museum exhibition. It might be added, generally, that most of the more prominent early Victorian commanders lack modern academic re-assessment including Charles Napier, Hugh Gough and Harry Smith.

In military organisational terms, the war brought a degree of further reform, although in some cases this actually predated the arrival of the army in the Crimea, as noted by John Sweetman, *War and Administration: The Significance of the Crimean War for the British Army* (1984). Sweetman has also published a serviceable biography of Raglan, *Raglan: From the Peninsula to the Crimea* (1993). Further reform was limited.[3] Much of the public interest was focused on the issue of flogging, a cause taken up by the radical Sir George de Lacy Evans, as explored by Edward Spiers, *Radical General: Sir George De Lacy Evans, 1787–1870* (1983).[4] As shown by Brian Bond, *The Victorian Army and the Staff College, 1854–1914* (1972), at least staff training was taken more seriously, though the Staff College had a long struggle for acceptance.

The shock of the Crimea was followed by that of the Indian Mutiny. Inevitably, perhaps, the coming of the Mutiny looms large in studies of the Indian army in the early nineteenth century. Of course, those general histories of the Indian army previously mentioned remain relevant, including several essays in Kaushik Roy (ed.), *War and Society in Colonial India* (2006). Though concentrating on the concept of the garrison state in an Indian context, Douglas Peers *Between Mars and Mammon: Colonial Armies and the Garrison State in Early Nineteenth Century India* (1995), emphasises the relative precariousness of Company and British rule. Military concerns thus fuelled the First Burma War (1824–6) and

---

3 Brian Bond, 'Prelude to the Cardwell Reforms, 1856–68', *JRUSI* 106 (1961), 229–36; R. L. Blanco, 'Education Reforms for the Enlisted Man in the Army of Victorian England', *History of Education Quarterly* 6 (1966), 61–72; idem, 'Army Recruiting Reforms, 1861–67', *JSAHR* 46 (1968), 217–24; Robert Welborn, 'The War Office during the Last Palmerston Administration, 1859–66', PhD dissertation, University of South Carolina, 1979; Peter Burroughs, 'Imperial Defence and the Victorian Army', *JICH* 15 (1986), 55–72.

4 See also R. L. Blanco, 'Attempts to Abolish Branding and Flogging in the Army of Victorian England before 1881', *JSAHR* 45 (1967), 137–45; J. R. Dinwiddy, 'The Early 19th Century Campaign against Flogging in the Army', *EHR* 97 (1982), 308–31; and Peter Burroughs, 'Crime and Punishment in the British Army, 1815–70', *EHR* 100 (1985), 545–71.

the seizure of Bharatpur (1825–6).[5] The theme of a garrison state has also been followed by Tan Tai Yong, *The Garrison State: The Military, Government and Society in Colonial Punjab, 1849–1947* (2005), who argues that the administration, political economy and society of the Punjab became highly militarised through the army's dependence on recruits from the area. Continuing unrest was illustrated by the mutiny at Barrackpore in 1824, covered by Premansu Kumar Bandyopadhyay, *Tulsi Leaves and the Ganges Water* (2003).

Interpretation of the Mutiny has varied widely, not least among Indian historians. Tapti Roy, *The Politics of a Popular Uprising: Bundelkhand, 1857* (1994), an example of the 'subaltern studies' approach, casts the Mutiny as a convergence of sepoy rebellion and wider revolt by 'lower' social groups. Erik Stokes (ed. Christopher Bayly), *The Peasant Armies: The Indian Revolt of 1857* (1986) sees the Mutiny as a peasant agrarian uprising. Stokes also rejects the idea of a widespread native conspiracy, but the idea of conspiracy is embraced by J. A. B. Palmer, *The Mutiny Outbreak at Meerut in 1857* (1966), and Saul David, *The Bengal Army and the Outbreak of the Indian Mutiny* (2009). John Pemble, *The Raj, The Indian Mutiny and the Kingdom of Oudh* (1977) situates the outbreak of mutiny specifically in the circumstances pertaining to Oudh. Contemporary historiography and literary aspects have been examined by Christopher Hibbert, *War of No Pity: The Indian Mutiny and Victorian Trauma* (2008), and by G. Chakravarty, both contrasting nicely with the pre-Mutiny image of the army as examined by Peers.[6]

Barbara English has rejected the theory of Rudrangshu Mukherjee that the massacre of the Europeans, including women and children, at Cawnpore replicated British violence, while Alison Blunt also looks at the issue of the treatment of

---

5 Douglas Peers, 'The Habitual Nobility of Being: British Officers and the Social Construction of the Bengal Army in the Early Nineteenth Century', *MAS* 25 (1991), 545–69; idem, 'Sepoys, Soldiers and the Lash: Race, Caste and Army Discipline in India, 1820–50', *JICH* 23 (1995), 211–47; idem, 'Gunpowder Empires and the Garrison State: Modernity, Hybridity and the Political Economy of Colonial India, c. 1750–1860', *Comparative Studies of South Asia, Africa and the Middle East* 27 (2007), 245–58. See also L. M. Crowell, 'The Madras Army in the Northern Circars, 1832–33: Pacification and Professionalism', PhD dissertation, Duke University, 1982; idem, 'Military Professionalism in a Colonial Context: The Madras Army, circa 1832', *MAS* 24 (1990), 249–73.

6 G. Chakravarty, 'Imagining Resistance: British Historiograohy and Popular Fiction on the Indian Rebellion, 1857–59', PhD, University of Cambridge, 1999; Douglas Peers, 'Those Noble Exemplars of the True Military Tradition: Constructions of the Indian Army in the Mid Victorian Press', *MAS* 31 (1997), 109–42.

British women.[7] Mukherjee clings to his argument in *Spectre of Violence: The 1857 Kanpur Massacres* (1998) but then, in *Awadh in Revolt, 1857–58: A Study of Popular Resistance* (2001), modifies it to some extent by suggesting that perceived British intent was the spur. However, he still sees the relationship between British officers and sepoys as resting on racial violence.[8] In a different kind of revisionism, Mukherjee's *Mangal Pandey: Brave Martyr or Accidental Hero?* (2005) attempts to recover the mindset of the sepoy at the time of the Mutiny, downplaying later nationalist interpretations, but this is questioned by Richard Forster, who argues that Pandey's actions were not isolated from proto-nationalism.[9]

Kim Wagner, *The Great Fear of 1857: Rumours, Conspiracies and the Making of the Indian Uprising* (2010) turns attention back to the sepoys themselves, and to contingency in the context of their long-standing grievances. Recent collections include Sabyasadhi Bhattacharya (ed), *Rethinking 1857* (2007); and Biswamoy Pati (ed.), *The Great Rebellion of 1857: Exploring Transgressions, Contexts and Diversities* (2010), while Rosie Llewellyn-Jones, *The Great Uprising in India, 1857–58: Untold Stories, Indian and British* (2007) presents a number of specific case studies on lesser known aspects. One lesser known aspect of the aftermath so far as the general public is concerned is the 'white mutiny' by European regiments of the East India Company when they were incorporated into the British army in 1859. Peter Stanley, *White Mutiny: British Military Culture in India, 1825–75* (1998) examines the events, interpreting it as part of a reshaping of social relationships in British society between 'masters and men'.[10] Particular mention should also be made of the four-volume *Mutiny on the Margins: New Perspectives on the Indian Uprising of 1857* series (2013), deriving from an AHRC-funded project at the

---

7 Rudrangshu Mukherjee, 'Satan Let Loose upon the Earth: The Kanpur Massacres in India in the Revolt of 1857', *P&P* 128 (1990), 92–116; Barbara English, 'The Kanpur Massacres in India and the Revolt of 1857', *P&P* 142 (1994), 169–78; Alison Blunt, 'Embodying War: British Women and Domestic Defilement in the Indian Mutiny', *Journal of Historical Geography* 26 (2000), 403–28.

8 See also Rudrangshu Mukherjee, 'The Sepoy Mutinies Revisited', in Mushirul Hasan and Narayani Gupta (eds), *India's Colonial Encounter: Essays in Memory of Eric Stokes* (Delhi: Manohar, 1993), pp. 193–204 but reproduced in Roy (ed.), *War and Society in Colonial India*, pp. 114–25.

9 Richard Forster, 'Mangal Pandey: Drug-Crazed Fanatic or Canny Revolutionary?' *Columbia Undergraduate Journal of South Asian Studies* 1 (2009), 3–23.

10 See also Peter Stanley, 'Military Culture and Military Protest: The Bengal Europeans and the White Mutiny of 1859', in Jane Hathaway (ed.), *Rebellion, Repression, Reinvention* (Santa Barbara, CA: ABC-Clio, 2001), pp. 103–18; idem, '"Dear Comrades": Barrack Room Culture and the White Mutiny of 1859–60', *Indo-British Review* 21 (1996), 165–75.

University of Edinburgh for the 150th anniversary of the Mutiny. The fourth volume edited by Crispin Bates and Gavin Rand deals with 'Military Aspects of the Indian Uprising'. As with earlier Victorian commanders, mutiny figures such as Henry Havelock, John Nicholson, Colin Campbell and James Outram would all benefit from modern academic re-assessment.

So far as the new Indian army is concerned, as suggested in an earlier section, the issue of the martial races has drawn attention as in David Omissi, *The Sepoy and the Raj: The Indian Army, 1860–1940* (1994); Lionel Caplan, *Warrior Gentleman: Gurkhas in Western Imagination* (1995); and Heather Streets, *Martial Races: The Military, Race and Masculinity in British Imperial Culture, 1857–1914* (2004), which encompasses Scottish Highlanders as well as Sikhs and Gurkhas; and Kaushik Roy, *Brown Warriors of the Raj: Recruitment and the Mechanics of Command in the Sepoy Army, 1859–1913* (2008). A fine and important study of the army's relationship with the post-1857 Punjab is Rajit Mazumder, *The Indian Army and the Making of the Punjab* (2003). Others including Omissi, Caplan and Roy have also contributed to the martial races debate in chapters and articles.[11]

Kaushik Roy has investigated aspects of discipline, as well as logistics and its contribution to both sepoy welfare and military strength.[12] A different

---

11 See also David Omissi, 'Martial Races: Ethnicity and Security in Colonial India, 1858–1939', *W&S* 9 (1991), 1–27; Lionel Caplan, 'Bravest of the Brave: Representations of the Gurkha in British Military Writings', *MAS* 25 (1991), 571–98; Mary Des Chene, 'Military Ethnology in British India', *South Asia Research* 19 (1999), 122–35; Philip Constable, 'The Marginalisation of a Dalit Martial Race in Late Nineteenth and Early Twentieth Century Western India', *Journal of Asian Studies* 609 (2001), 439–78; Kaushik Roy, 'Beyond the Martial Race Theory: A Historiographical Assessment of Recruitment in the British-Indian Army', *Calcutta Historical Review* 21–2 (1999–2000), 139–54; idem, 'The Construction of Regiments in the Indian Army, 1859–1913', *WH* 8 (2001), 127–48; idem, 'Recruiting for the Leviathan: Regimental Recruitment in the British Indian Army, 1859–1913', *Calcutta Historical Review* 23–4 (2001–4), 59–81; and Thomas Metcalf, 'Sikh Recruitment for Colonial Military and Police Forces, 1874–1914', in Thomas Metcalf, *Forging the Raj: Essays on British India in the Heyday of Empire* (Oxford: Oxford University Press, 2005), pp. 250–81.

12 Kaushik Roy, 'Coercion through Leniency: British Manipulation of the Courts Martial System in the Post-Mutiny Indian Army, 1859–1913', *JMH* 65 (2001), 937–64'; idem, 'Spare the Rod, Spoil and Soldier? Crime and Punishment in the Army of India, 1860–1913', *JSAHR* 84 (2006), 9–23; Kaushik Roy, 'Feeding the Leviathan: Supplying the British-Indian Army, 1859–1913', *JSAHR* 80 (2002), 144–61; idem, 'Equipping Leviathan: Ordnance Factories of British India, 1859–1913', *WH* 10 (2003), 398–423. For an earlier period, see Lorenzo Crowell, 'Logistics in the Madras Army, c.1830', *W&S* 10 (1992), 1–33.

perspective is that of Nile Green, *Islam and the Army of Colonial India: Sepoy Religion in the Service of Empire* (2009), examining the Hyderabad Contingent between 1850 and 1930. Indianisation of the officer corps was to become much more of an issue in the twentieth century, but Pradeep Barua, *Gentlemen of the Raj: The Indian Officer Corps, 1817–1949* (2003) sets it in the context of an idea first raised by Sir Thomas Munro at Madras in 1817. Chandar Sundaram examines the longer perspective in a thesis and articles, and there is also Michael Creese's 2007 thesis on Indian officers in the Indian cavalry between 1858 and 1918.[13]

As suggested previously, there are several studies of nineteenth-century British garrisons in Australia, Britain, Canada, Ireland, New Zealand and South Africa. By contrast, the British soldier in India has been generally neglected other than by reference to his vices. European volunteers in India, however, have been covered by Chris Kempton, *The Regiments and Corps of the HIEC and Indian Army Volunteer Forces* (2012), and by Kaushik Roy.[14] Other non-European colonial forces within the British Empire have not fared as well. Apart from Timothy Parsons, *The African Rank and File: Social Implications of Colonial Military Service in the King's African Rifles, 1902–64* (1999), modern studies have been confined to journal articles and theses although Paul Ubaeyi, *British*

---

13 Chandar Sundaram, 'A Grudging Concession: The Indianisation of the Indian Army's Officer Corps, 1817–1917', PhD, McGill University, 1996; Michael Creese, 'Swords Trembling in Their Scabbards: A Study of Indian Officers in the Indian Cavalry, 1858–1918', PhD, University of Leicester, 2007. See also Chandar Sundaram, ' "Martial" Indian Aristocrats and the Military System of the Raj: The Imperial Cadet Corps, 1900–14', *Journal of Imperial and Commonwealth History* 25 (1997), 415–39; idem, 'Preventing "Idleness": The Maharajah of Cooch Behar's Proposal for Officer Commissions in the British Army for the Sons of Indian Princes and Gentlemen, 1897–98', *South Asia* 18 (1995), 115–30.

14 See Douglas Peers, 'Imperial Vice: Sex, Drink and the Health of British Troops in North Indian Cantonments, 1800–58', in David Killingray and David Omissi (eds), *Guardians of Empire: The Armed Forces of the Colonial Powers, 1700–1964* (Manchester: Manchester University Press, 1999), 25–52; Erica Wald, 'Vice, Medicine, the Military and the Making of Colonial; India, 1780–1880', PhD dissertation, University of Cambridge, 2009; Kaushik Roy, 'India', in Ian F. W. Beckett (ed.), *Citizen Soldiers and the British Empire, 1837–1902* (London: Pickering & Chatto, 2012), pp. 101–20. For a rare study of the rank and file in India, see J. H. Rumsby, 'The 16th Lancers, 1822–46: The Experience of Regimental Soldiering in India', PhD dissertation, University of Leeds, 2004.

Military and Naval Forces in West African History, 1807–74 (1978) covers the West India Regiments.[15]

Crises of imperial defence at this time also included the possibility of war with the Union during the American Civil War, given the perception that British sympathies lay with the Confederacy. The defence of Canada is examined by Kenneth Bourne, *Britain and the Balance of Power in North America, 1815–1908* (1967). In addition, and notwithstanding the Crimean alliance, there was the hostility of France, leading to the three invasion 'panics' of 1846–7, 1851–2, and 1859–60. The second panic resulted in the revival of the militia, and the third in the revival of the volunteer force. Apart from the overview in Ian F. W. Beckett, *The Amateur Military Tradition, 1558–1945* (1991), and the coverage of the auxiliaries in Britain and the militia in Ireland in Ian F. W. Beckett (ed.), *Citizen Soldiers and the British Empire, 1837–1902* (2012), there are two specialist works on the volunteers, Ian F. W. Beckett, *Riflemen Form: A Study of the Rifle Volunteer Movement, 1859–1908* (1982), and Hugh Cunningham, *The Volunteer Force* (1975). Specialist studies on the Victorian militia and yeomanry remain confined to theses.[16] The popularity of volunteering suggested the continuing

---

15 S. C. Ukpabi, 'West Indian Troops and the Defence of British West Africa in the Nineteenth Century', *African Studies Review* 18 (1974), 33–50; David Killingray, 'The Mutiny of the West African Regiment in the Gold Coast, 1901', *International Journal of African Historical Studies* 16 (1983), 441–54; idem, 'The Rod of Empire: The Debate over Corporal Punishment in the British African Colonial Forces, 1888–1946', *JAH* 35 (1994), 201–16; idem, The Colonial Army in the Gold Coast: Official Policy and Local Response, 1890–1947', PhD dissertation, University of London, 1982; Risto Marjomaa, 'The Martial Spirit: Yao Soldiers in British Service in Nyasaland (Malawi), 1895–1939', *JAH* 44 (2003), 413–32; A. E. Ekoko, 'British Defence Policy in Western Africa, 1878–1914', PhD dissertation, University of Aberdeen, 1976; T. J. Lovering, 'Authority and Identity: Malawian Soldiers in Britain's Colonial Army, 1891–1964', PhD dissertation, University of Stirling, 2002; Ronald Lamothe, 'Slaves of Fortune: Sudanese Soldiers and the River War, 1896–98', PhD dissertation, University of Boston, 2010.

16 See also Patricia Morton, 'Another Victorian Paradox: Anti-Militarism in a Jingoistic Society', *Historical Reflections* 5 (1981), 169–89; eadem, 'A Military Irony: The Victorian Volunteer Movement', *JRUSI* 131 (1986), 63–9. In addition to the two theses on the yeomanry mentioned in an earlier section, there is Duncan Anderson, 'The English Militia in the Mid-Nineteenth Century: A Study of its Military, Social and Political Significance', DPhil dissertation, University of Oxford, 1982, and Will Butler, 'The Irish Amateur Military Tradition in the British Army, c.1854–1945', PhD dissertation, University of Kent, 2013. Another thesis on the later British militia is also being undertaken currently at the University of Kent.

re-appraisal of the soldier following the Crimea and the Mutiny, not least through the prominence accorded to figures such as Henry Havelock. The latter also contributed to the growth of 'Christian militarism', this being identified as another factor in the rehabilitation of the soldier.[17]

The far-reaching army reforms associated with Edward Cardwell between 1868 and 1872, including abolition of purchase, and the introduction of short service, however, were primary motivated by economic considerations. Though there has been no biography of Cardwell since the 1950s, the reforms and their longer-term impact have been the subject of considerable study in articles, chapters and theses, as well as in the works by Edward Spiers mentioned previously.[18] While Anthony Bruce, *The Purchase System in the British Army, 1660–1871* (1980) naturally covers abolition in a wider survey, the pre-purchase officer corps is also examined in Gwyn Harries-Jenkins, *The Army in Victorian Society* (1977). The longer-term development of the officer corps has been examined in theses.[19] David French, *Military Identities: the Regimental System, the British Army, and the British People, c. 1870–2000* (2005) dissects the construction of 'county' regiments through Cardwell's 'localisation' and the 'territorialisation' of High Childers in 1881.

---

17 Olive Anderson, 'The Growth of Christian Militarism in Mid Victorian Britain', *EHR* 89 (1971), 46–72; Geoffrey Best, 'Militarism and the Victorian Public School' in B. Simon and I. Bradley (eds), *The Victorian Public School* (London: Gill & Macmillan, 1975), pp. 129–46.

18 See also Brian Bond, 'The Effect of the Cardwell Reforms in Army Organisation, 1874–1904', *JRUSI* 105 (1960), 515–24; A. V. Tucker, 'Army and Society in England, 1870–1900: A Reassessment of the Cardwell Reforms', *JBS* 2 (1963), 110–41; N. H. Moses, 'Cardwell's Abolition of the Purchase System in the British Army, 1868–74: A Study in Administrative and Legislative Processes', PhD dissertation, University of London, 1969; T. F. Gallagher, Cardwellian Mysteries: The Fate of the British Army Regulation Bill, 1871', *HJ* 18 (1975), 327–48; Anthony Bruce, 'Edward Cardwell and the Abolition of Purchase', in Ian F. W. Beckett and John Gooch (eds), *Politicians and Defence: Studies in the Formulation of British Defence Policy* (Manchester: Manchester University Press, 1981), pp. 24–46.

19 Ian Worthington, 'Antecedent Education and Officer Recruitment: The Origins and Early Development of the Public Schools-Army Nexus, 1849–1908', PhD dissertation, University of Lancaster, 1982; D. Huffer, 'The Infantry Officers of the Line of the British Army, 1815–68', PhD dissertation, University of Birmingham, 1995; Corinne L. Mahaffey, 'The Fighting Profession: The Professionalisation of the British Line Infantry Officer Corps, 1870–1902', PhD dissertation, University of Glasgow, 2004. See also Ian F. W. Beckett, 'The Annual Confidential Report and Promotion in the Late Victorian Army', *BJMH* 1 (2014), 12–43.

Recruiting remained a difficulty and there were certainly examples of 'Pimlico' and 'Whitechapel' Highlanders. The equation made between Indian 'martial races' and the Scots and Irish, as in the work of Heather Streets, has already been noted but reference should also be made to Edward Spiers, *The Scottish Soldier and Empire, 1854–1902* (2006), and Diana Henderson, *Highland Soldier, 1820–1920* (1989), though the latter has a rather antiquarian air.[20]

A. R. Skelley, *The Victorian Army at Home* (1977) is still an indispensable source for such issues as recruitment and retention, pay and rewards, discipline and crime, health, and educational provision.[21] Similarly, Myna Trustram, *Women of the Regiment: Marriage and the Victorian Army* (1984) is an important source for service life, including prostitution and venereal disease, which became a matter of wider social contention.[22] The role of women as military nurses, emerging from the Crimean War, is covered in Anne Summers, *Angels and Citizens: British Women as Military Nurses, 1854–1914* (1988). Florence Nightingale,

---

20 See also Harry Hanham, 'Religion and Nationality in the Mid-Victorian Army', in M. R. D. Foot (ed.), *War and Society* (London: Paul Elek, 1973), pp. 159–82; Terence Denman, 'Ethnic Soldiers Pure and Simple: The Irish in the Late Victorian Army', *WH* 3 (1996), 253–73; Heather Streets, 'Identity in the Highland Regiments in the Nineteenth Century: Soldier, Region, Nation', in Steve Murdoch and Andrew Mackillop (eds), *Fighting for Identity: Scottish Military Experience, c. 1550–1900* (Leiden: Brill, 2002), pp. 213–38; Ian Kelly, 'Echoes of Success: Identity in the Highland Regiments', PhD dissertation, University of Aberdeen, 2007; idem, 'The Highland Brigade at Tel-el-Kebir: A Jumping-off Point for Big Military History', in Ian F. W. Beckett (ed.), *Victorians at War: New Perspectives*, Society for Army Historical Research Special Publication 16 (London, 2007), pp. 47–58; Neal Garnham, The Only Thing that Everybody Likes: Military-Civilian Relations in Late Victorian Ulster', *Eire-Ireland* 41 (2006), 59–79; and Nick Perry, 'The Irish Landed Class and the British Army, 1850–1950', *WH* 18 (2011), 304–32.

21 See also Brian Bond, 'Recruiting the Victorian Army, 1870–92', *VS* 5 (1962) 331–38.

22 See also R. L. Blanco, 'The Attempted Control of Venereal Disease in the Army of Mid-Victorian England', *JSAHR* 45 (1967), 234–41; Myna Trustram, 'Distasteful and Derogatory? Examining Victorian Soldiers for Venereal Disease', in London Feminist History Group, *The Sexual Dynamics of History: Men's Power, Women's Resistance* (1983), 154–64; J. G. Gamble, 'The Origins, Administration and Impact of the Contagious Diseases Acts from a Military Perspective', PhD dissertation, University of Southern Mississippi, 1983; Ken Hendrickson, 'A Kinder, Gentler British Army: Mid Victorian Experiments in the Management of Army Vice at Gibraltar and Aldershot', *W&S* 14 (1996), 21–33. For a different aspect of the influence of women, see Ian F. W. Beckett, 'Women and Patronage in the Late Victorian Army', *History* 85 (2000), 463–80.

of course, was very much involved albeit a controversial figure. Sue M. Goldie (ed.), *I Have Done My Duty: Florence Nightingale in the Crimean War, 1854–56* (1987), is a scholarly edition of her wartime correspondence. Recreation is considered by Tony Mason and Eliza Riedl, *Sport and the Military: The British Armed Forces, 1880–1960* (2010); and James Campbell, *The Army Isn't All Work: Physical Culture and the Evolution of the British Army, 1860–1920* (2012)

Cardwell's organisational reforms did not ease relations between soldiers and politicians, as indicated by W. S. Hamer, *The British Army: Civil-Military Relations, 1885–1905* (1970), which deals with later administrative tinkering. There are relevant essays, too, in Paul Smith (ed.), *Government and the Armed Forces in Britain, 1856–1990* (1996). Like Cardwell, Childers lacks a modern biographer, although the role of Edward Stanhope as Secretary of State has been re-evaluated.[23] In part, friction centred upon the formulation of strategic policy, which has been considered in some of the essays in Greg Kennedy (ed.), *Imperial Defence: The Old World Order, 1856–1956* (2007). Within the army itself, however, there were distinct differences between those who favoured emulating continental military theories, and those who acknowledged the realities of imperial engagement, as well as between those associated with the 'home' army and those associated with the Indian army. Both these areas have been extensively studied.

Martin Samuels, *Command or Control? Command, Training and Tactics in the British and German Armies, 1888–1918* (1995), and Michael Ramsay, *Command or Cohesion: The Citizen Soldier and Minor Tactics in the British Army, 1870–1918* (2002) address tactical issues. In strategic terms, the security of India was increasingly seen in the context of the perceived Russian threat in Central Asia. To those works mentioned in a previous section on the defence of India by historians such as Edward Ingram and Malcolm Yapp can be added G. J. Alder, *British India's Northern Frontier, 1865–95* (1963); D. R. Gillard, *The Struggle for Asia, 1828–1914* (1977); Robert Blyth, *The Empire of the Raj: India, Eastern Africa and the Middle East, 1858–1947* (2003); Evgeny Sergeev, *The Great Game, 1856–1907: Russo-British Relations in Central and East Asia* (2013); and in those parts of his earlier thesis appearing in Robert Johnson, *The Afghan Way of War: Culture and Pragmatism – A Critical History* (2011). Much of the debate has also been carried in academic journals and theses. Adrian Preston invariably exaggerates his case as to the influence of Indian perspectives on the actual

---

23 Ian F. W. Beckett, 'Edward Stanhope at the War Office, 1887–92', *JSS* 5 (1982), 278–307; idem, 'The Stanhope Memorandum of 1888: A Re-interpretation', *BIHR* 57 (1984), 240–7.

strategic priorities of the British government, which remained home defence.[24] The Intelligence Department at the War Office played no small part in the debate on strategic options, a slightly updated version of William Beaver's 1976 PhD dissertation now being more widely available as *Under Every Leaf: How Britain Played the Greater Game from Afghanistan to Africa* (2012). It supplements the older work by T. G. Ferguson, *British Military Intelligence, 1870–1914* (1984). Aspects of the 'Great Game', however, are also the subject of C. A. Bayly, *Empire and Information: Intelligence-Gathering and Social Communication in India, 1780–1870* (1996); Richard Popplewell, *Intelligence and Imperial Defence: British Intelligence and the Defence of the Indian Empire, 1904–24* (1995) and, most

---

24 For a tactical command focus, see Ian McLeod, 'Operational Infantry Brigade Command in the Victorian Army', PhD dissertation, University of Buckingham, 2011. For strategy, see T. F. Gallagher, 'British Military Thinking and the Coming of the Franco-Prussian War', *Military Affairs* 39 (1975), 19–22; Adrian Preston, 'The Eastern Question in British Strategic Policy during the Franco-Prussian War', *Canadian Historical Association Historical Papers* 5 (1972), 55–88; idem, 'Sir Charles MacGregor and the Defence of India, 1857–77', *HJ* 12 (1969), 58–77; Keith Jeffery, 'The Eastern Arc of Empire: A Strategic View, 1850–1950', *JSS* 5 (1982), 531–45; Robert Johnson, 'Russians at the Gates of India? Planning the Defence of India, 1885–1900', *JMH* 67 (2003), 697–744; idem, 'The Penjdeh Crisis and its Impact on the Great Game and the Defence of India, 1885–97', PhD dissertation, University of Exeter, 2000; Ian F. W. Beckett, 'The Road from Kandahar: The Politics of Retention and Withdrawal in Afghanistan, 1880–81', *JMH* 78 (2014), 1263–94; Anthony Hampshire, 'Continental Warfare and British Military Thought, 1859–80', PhD dissertation, University of London, 2006; T. A. Heathcote, 'British Policy and Baluchistan, 1854–76', PhD dissertation, University of London, 1969; A. Bali, 'The Russo-Afghan Boundary Demarcation, 1884–95: Britain and the Russian Threat to the Security of India', PhD dissertation, University of Ulster, 1986; G. Tealakh, 'The Russian Advance in Central Asia and the British Response, 1834–84', PhD dissertation, University of Durham, 1991; S. Dutta, 'Strategy and Structure: A Case Study of Imperial Policy and Tribal Society in British Baluchistan, 1876–1905', PhD dissertation, University of London, 1991; M. D. Welch, *Science in a Pickelhaube: British Military Lesson Learning at the RUSI, 1870–1900* (London: Royal United Services Institute for Defence Studies Whitehall Papers series, 1999); Ian F. W. Beckett, 'The Compulsion of Destitution: The British Army and the Dilemma of Imperial Defence, 1870–1914', in Peter Dennis and Jeffrey Grey (eds), *Raise, Train and Sustain: Delivering Land Combat Power* (Canberra; Australian Military History Publications, 2010), pp. 30–52. For invasion, see H. R. Moon, 'The Invasion of the United Kingdom: Public Controversy and Official Planning, 1888–1914', PhD dissertation, University of London, 1968.

recently, James Hevia, *The Imperial Security State: British Colonial Knowledge and Empire-Building in Asia* (2012).

The two soldiers who were most taken to represent the home and Indian armies were Garnet Wolseley and Frederick Roberts. Wolseley has been especially well served with Joseph Lehmann, *All Sir Garnet: A Life of Field Marshal Lord Wolseley* (1964), and Halik Kochanski, *Sir Garnet Wolseley: Victorian Hero* (1999). In addition, there are also additions of all Wolseley's surviving campaign journals: Adrian Preston (ed.), *In Relief of Gordon: Lord Wolseley's Campaign Journal of the Khartoum Relief Expedition, 1884–85* (1967); idem, *Sir Garnet Wolseley's South African Diaries (Natal), 1875* (1971); idem, *Sir Garnet Wolseley's South African Journal, 1879–80* (1973); Anne Cavendish (ed.), *Cyprus, 1878: The Journal of Sir Garnet Wolseley* (1991); and Ian F. W. Beckett (ed.), *Wolseley and Ashanti: The Asante War Journal and Correspondence of Major General Sir Garnet Wolseley, 1873–74* (2009).[25] David James, *Lord Roberts* (1954) badly needs updating but centring on Roberts are two works by Rodney Atwood, *The March to Kandahar: Roberts in Afghanistan* (2008), and *Roberts and Kitchener in South Africa, 1900–02* (2011).[26] There are also editions of Roberts's papers by Brian Robson (ed.), *Roberts in India: The Military Papers of Field Marshal Lord Roberts, 1876–93* (1993); and André Wessels, *Lord Roberts and the War in South Africa, 1899–1902* (2000).

The other great imperial figures of Herbert Kitchener and Charles Gordon have been the subject of several biographies. For Kitchener, Philip Magnus, *Kitchener: Portrait of an Imperialist* (1958) can be supplemented by John Pollock,

---

25 See also Adrian Preston, 'Wolseley, the Khartoum Relief Expedition and the Defence of India, 1885–1900', in Adrian Preston and Peter Dennis (eds), *Swords and Covenants* (London: Croom Helm, 1976); idem, 'Frustrated Great Gamesmanship: Sir Garnet Wolseley's Plans for War against Russia, 1873–80', *IHR* 2 (1980), 239–65; Ian Harvie, 'The Wolseley Ring: A Case Study in the Exercise of Patronage in the Late Victorian Army', MA dissertation, University of Buckingham, 1993.

26 See also Rodney Atwood, ' "So Single-minded a Man and So Noble-hearted a Soldier": Field Marshal Earl Roberts of Kandahar, Waterford and Pretoria', in Ian F. W. Beckett (ed.), *Victorians at War: New Perspectives* (Society for Army Historical Research Special Publication 16, 2007), pp. 59–74; Ian F. W. Beckett, 'Soldiers, the Frontier and the Politics of Command in British India', *SWI* 16 (2005), 280–92; Heather Streets, 'Military Influence in the Late Victorian and Edwardian Popular Media: The Case of Frederick Roberts', *Journal of Victorian Culture* 8 (2003), 231–56.

Kitchener (2002).[27] Pollock has also provided the best recent biography of Gordon, *Gordon: The Man Behind the Legend* (1993).[28] André Wessels (ed.), *Lord Kitchener and the War in South Africa, 1899–1902* (2006) is an edition of Kitchener's South African War papers.

Wolseley, Roberts, Kitchener and Gordon all figure in essays in Steven J. Corvi and Ian F. W. Beckett (eds), *Victoria's Generals* (2009), as do Redvers Buller, Lord Chelmsford, George Colley and Evelyn Wood. Among other serviceable modern biographies are Geoffrey Powell, *Buller: A Scapegoat* (1994); Stephen Manning, *Evelyn Wood VC: Pillar of Empire* (2007); and Christopher Brice, *The Thinking Man's Soldier: The Life and Career of General Sir Henry Brackenbury, 1837–1914* (2012).[29] The only full biography of the Duke of Cambridge, who dominated the army as commander-in-chief from 1856 to 1895, remains Giles St Aubyn, *The Royal George: The Life of Prince George, Duke of Cambridge, 1819–1904* (1963) since, a little oddly, Kevin Farrell, *The Military and the Monarchy: The Case of the Career of the Duke of Cambridge in an Age of Reform* (2011) carries the story only to 1874.[30]

Of course, it was colonial campaigning that made military reputations. Bond's *Victorian Military Campaigns* was a pioneering collection of essays at a time when there was little academic interest in Victorian colonial warfare. A number of the eight campaigns considered have since been the subject of monographs, but this is still a useful summary. Such is the volume of work on later colonial campaigns – much of it popular and stimulated in good part by what amounts almost to a British obsession with the Anglo-Zulu War of 1879 – that only a selection of the academic titles can be considered.

Despite the concentration on the Zulu, some other later campaigns have attracted attention. James Belich, *The New Zealand Wars and the Victorian*

27 See also Keith Surridge, 'More than a Great Poster: Lord Kitchener and the Image of the Military Hero', *HR* 74 (2001), 298–313.
28 See also Douglas Johnson, 'The Death of Gordon: A Victorian Myth', *JICH* 10 (1982), 285–310; Stephanie Laffer, 'Gordon's Ghosts: Major General Charles George Gordon and His Legacies, 1885–1960', PhD dissertation, Florida State University, 2010.
29 See also James Thomas, 'Sir Redvers Buller in the Post-Cardwellian Army: A Study of the Rise and Fall of a Military Reputation', PhD dissertation, Texas A & M University, 1993; Jeff Mathews, 'Lord Chelmsford: British General in Southern Africa, 1878–79', PhD dissertation, University of South Africa, 1986.
30 See also Brian Bond, 'The Retirement of the Duke of Cambridge', *JRUSI* 106 (1961), 544–53.

Interpretation of Racial Conflict (1986), for example, claims that the Maori 'invented' trench warfare during the three Maori Wars of 1846–7, 1860–1 and 1863–6. Other historians have contested Belich's claims with regard to the origins of trench warfare and the uniqueness of Maori warfare including Christopher Pugsley, John M. Gates, Peter Maxwell, *Frontier: The Battle for the North Island of New Zealand* (2000), and Matthew Wright, *Two Peoples, One Land: The New Zealand Wars* (2006).[31] Despite its flaws, however, Belich, who also revisited the last phase of the third Maori War in *I Shall Die: Titokowaru's War, New Zealand, 1868–69* (1989), usefully points to the difficulties in accepting Victorian accounts at face value. The Maori Wars need to be set in the context of earlier inter-tribal conflict as analysed by R. D. Crosby, *The Musket Wars: A History of Inter-Iwi Conflict, 1806–45* (1999), which shows the impact of imported firearms.

Similarly, study of the Anglo-Zulu War itself has been marked by the contributions of academic historians like John Laband and Paul Thompson who are thoroughly conversant with the Zulu polity. Laband's work includes *Kingdom in Crisis: The Zulu Response to the British Invasion of 1879* (1992); *Rope of Sand: The Rise and Fall of the Zulu Kingdom in the Nineteenth Century* (1995); and *The Transvaal Rebellion: The First Boer War, 1880–81* (2005). Thompson's *The Natal Native Contingent in the Anglo-Zulu War, 1879* (1997) has been reprinted as *Black Soldiers of the Queen: The Natal Native Contingent in the Anglo-Zulu War* (2006). Laband and Thompson together have also published *The Buffalo Border, 1879: The Anglo-Zulu War in Northern Natal* (1983); *Kingdom and Colony at War: Sixteen Studies of the Anglo-Zulu War of 1879* (1990); and *The Illustrated Guide to the Anglo-Zulu War* (2000). New research was also presented in Andrew Dominy and Charles Ballard (eds), *The Anglo-Zulu War: New Perspectives* (1981). Some accounts by non-academic authors, however, are worthy of mention for their rigorous approach to sources such as F. W. D. Jackson, *Hill of the Sphinx: The Battle of Isandlwana* (2002); Adrian Greaves, *Rorke's Drift* (2002); Huw M. Jones, *The Boiling Cauldron: Utrecht District and the Anglo-Zulu War, 1879* (2006); and Keith Smith, *Studies in the Anglo-Zulu War* (2008). Jackson was one of the first authors to challenge the traditional idea that a shortage of ammunition in

---

31 See Chris Pugsley, 'Maori Did Not Invent Trench Warfare', *New Zealand Defence Quarterly* 22 (1998), 33–37; John M Gates, 'James Belich and the Modern Maori Pa: Revisionist History Revised', *W&S* 19 (2001), 49–70; Paul D'Arcy, 'Maori and Muskets from a Pan-Polynesian Perspective', *New Zealand History* 34 (2000), 117–32.

the firing line led to the British defeat at Isandlwana.[32] Special recognition should be accorded to Ian Knight, whose many works include *Zulu Rising* (2010). The Anglo-Zulu War has also seen the publication of a range of primary sources such as Sonia Clark (ed.), *Zululand at War, 1879* (1984); John Laband (ed.), *Lord Chelmsford's Zululand Campaign, 1878–79* (1994); John Laband and Ian Knight (eds), *Archives of Zululand: The Anglo-Zulu War, 1879*, 2 vols (2000); and Keith Smith (ed.), *Select Documents: A Zulu War Sourcebook* (2006). The Ninth Cape Frontier War (1877–8) has also received attention as the immediate precursor to the Zulu War, as in Philip Gon, *The Road to Isandlwana* (1979). Tying in with the increasing academic interest in masculinity, R. Morrell, *From Boys to Gentlemen: Settler Masculinity in Colonial Natal, 1880–1920* (2001), devotes some attention to the colonial volunteer forces.

Inevitably, current engagement in Afghanistan has seen many popular accounts of the first two Anglo-Afghan Wars of 1838–42 and 1878–81. The best academic treatment of the First Afghan War remains J. A. Norris, *The First Afghan War, 1838–42* (1967), while the Second Afghan War is well served in Brian Robson, *The Road to Kabul: The Second Afghan War, 1878–81* (1986). Robson has also produced a good account of the two expeditions to Suakin in the Eastern Sudan in *Fuzzy Wuzzy: The Campaigns in the Eastern Sudan, 1884–85* (1993). Suakin was the scene of a brief involvement by a New South Wales contingent as outlined in Peter Stanley (ed.), *But Little Glory: The New South Wales Contingent to the Sudan, 1885* (1985). Based on his University of Reading thesis, Fergus Nicoll has also covered aspects of the British involvement in the Sudan in *The Mahdi of Sudan and the Death of General Gordon* (2004) and *Gladstone, Gordon and the Sudan Wars: The Battle over Imperial Intervention in the Victorian Age* (2013). The earlier Red River expedition of 1870 is well analysed in J. M. Bumsted, *The Red River Rebellion* (1996) and the Abyssinian expedition equally so in Darrell Bates, *The Abyssinian Difficulty: The Emperor Theodorus and the Magdala*

---

32 See F. W. D. Jackson, 'Isandlwana, 1879: The Sources Re-examined', *JSAHR* 43 (1965), 30–43, 113–32, 169–83; Edmund Yorke, 'Isandlwana, 1879: Reflections on the Ammunition Controversy', *JSAHR* 72 (1994), 205–18; Ian Knight, 'Ammunition and Isandlwana: A Reply', *JSAHR* 73 (1995), 237–50. For the impact of the Zulu War in Britain, see Jonathan Hicks, 'The Anglo-Zulu War of 1879: The Myth and the Reality', PhD dissertation, University of Wales, 2003; and Stephen Manning, 'Foreign News Gathering and Reporting in the London and the Devon Press: The Anglo-Zulu War, 1879: A Case Study', PhD dissertation, University of Exeter, 2005.

Campaign, 1867–68 (1979). The Kandyan, Burma and Persian Wars all have popular accounts but would repay academic study although A. T. Q. Stewart, *The Pagoda War: Lord Dufferin and the Fall of the Kingdom of Ava, 1885–86* (1972) is an account for the general reader by an academic historian. Stafford Glass, *The Matabele War* (1968) and, an especially good analysis, Arthur Keppel-Jones, *Rhodes and Rhodesia: The White Conquest of Zimbabwe, 1884–1902* (1983) cover the extension of British rule through the auspices of the British South Africa Company.

An emphasis upon the excesses of British campaigning has emerged in recent years, including such examples as the Australian Frontier Wars, expertly examined in John Connor, *The Australian Frontier Wars, 1788–1838* (2002); the Cape Frontier Wars; the pursuit of the Zulu after the battles of Khambula and Ulundi; and the executions carried out by Roberts in Kabul in 1880.[33] African perspectives on colonial warfare also feature in Stephen M. Miller (ed.), *Soldiers and Settlers in Africa, 1850–1918* (2009).

Ultimately, despite occasional setbacks such as Isandlwana and Maiwand, the British enjoyed the advantages of superior firepower and technology. Tim Moreman, *The Army in India and the Development of Frontier Warfare, 1849–1947* (1998) provides a particularly useful guide to the learning process on the North West Frontier, for which techniques of political pacification have also been assessed, as in Hugh Beattie, *Imperial Frontier: Tribe and State in Waziristan* (2002); Martin Ewans, *Securing the Indian Frontier in Central Asia: Confrontation and Negotiation, 1865–95* (2010); Christopher Wyatt, *Afghanistan and the Defence of Empire: Diplomacy and Strategy during the Great Game* (2011); and Christian

---

33 See Edward Spiers, 'The Use of Dum Dum Bullets in Colonial Warfare', *JICH* 4 (1973), 3–14; Charles Townshend, 'Martial Law: Legal and Administrative Problems of Civil Emergency in Britain and the Empire, 1800–1940', *HJ* 25 (1982), 167–95; Michael Lieven, 'Butchering the Brutes All Over the Place: Total War and Massacre in Zululand, 1879', *History* (1999), 614–32; Craig Wilcox, 'The Culture of Restrained Force in British Australia', in Carl Bridge (ed.), *Ranging Shots: New Directions in Australian Military History* (London: Sir Robert Menzies Centre, 1998), pp. 7–18; Edward Spiers, 'Dervishes and Fanaticism: Perception and Impact', in Matthew Hughes and Gaynor Johnson (eds), *Fanaticism and Conflict in the Modern Age* (London: Frank Cass, 2005), pp. 19–32; Joachen Arndt, 'Treacherous Savages and Merciless Barbarians: Knowledge, Discourse and Violence during the Cape Frontier Wars, 1834–53', *JMH* 74 (2010), 709–36; Rob Johnson, 'General Roberts, the Occupation of Kabul, and the Problems of Transition, 1879–80', *WH* 20 (2013), 300–22.

Tripodi, *Edge of Empire: The British Political Officer and Tribal Administration on the North West Frontier, 1877–1947* (2011).[34]

It did not make campaigning necessarily easier, and the experience of ordinary soldiers has proved a fruitful avenue. A geographer rather than an historian, Frank Emery, pioneered the use of soldiers' letters to local newspapers in *The Red Soldier: The Zulu War, 1879* (1977), and *Marching Over Africa: Letters from Victorian Soldiers* (1986). Popular authors have followed the trend but Edward Spiers has subjected newspaper sources to academic scrutiny in *The Victorian Soldier in Africa* (2004); *The Scottish Soldier and Empire, 1854–1902* (2006); and *Letters from Ladysmith: Eyewitness Accounts from the South African War* (2010).

Attention on the press is appropriate for the reputation of such figures as Wolseley and Roberts was built by the press, often with the assiduous help of the soldiers themselves. Not unexpectedly, British successes and even defeats were viewed in heroic terms, the projection of heroism being seen as an aspect of masculinity in Graham Dawson, *Soldier Heroes: British Adventure, Empire*

---

34 See Howard Bailes, 'Technology and Imperialism: A Case Study of the Victorian Army in Africa', *VS* 24 (1980), 83–104; Ian F. W. Beckett, 'Victorians at War: War, Technology and Change', *JSAHR* 81 (2003), 330–39; idem, 'Retrospective Icon: The Martini-Henry', in Karen Jones, Giacomo Macola and David Welch (eds), *A Cultural History of Firearms in the Age of Empire* (Farnham: Ashgate, 2013), pp. 233–50; Matthew Ford, 'Towards a Revolution in Firepower? Logistics, Lethality and the Lee Metford', *WH* 20 (2013), 273–99; Tim Moreman, 'The British and Indian Armies and North West Frontier Warfare, 1849–1914', *JICH* 20 91992), 35–64; idem, 'The Arms Trade and the North West Frontier Pathan Tribes, 1890–1914', *JICH* 22 (1994), 187–216; idem, The Army in India and the Military Periodical Press, 1830–98', in David Finkelstein and Douglas Peers (eds), *Negotiating India in the Nineteenth Century Media* (Basingstoke: Palgrave, 2000), pp. 210–32; W. Murray Hogben, 'British Civil-Military Relations on the North West Frontier of India', in Adrian Preston and Peter Dennis (eds), *Swords and Covenants* (London: Croom Helm, 1976), pp. 123–46; R. O. Christensen, 'Conflict and Change among the Afridis and Tribal Policy, 1839–1947', PhD dissertation, University of Leicester, 1987; idem, 'Tribesmen, Government and Political Economy on the North West Frontier', in Barbara Ingham and Colin Simmons (eds), *Development Studies and Colonial Policies* (London: Frank Cass, 1987), pp. 175–93; idem, 'Tradition and Change on the North West Frontier', *Modern Asian Studies* 16 (1982), 159–66; Christian Tripodi, 'Good for One But Not the Other: The Sandeman System of Pacification as Applied to Baluchistan and the North West Frontier, 1871–1947', *JMH* 73 (2009), 767–802.

and the Imagining of Masculinities (1994).[35] The development of the Victoria Cross has been analysed by M. J. Crook, *The Evolution of the Victoria Cross* (1975), and Melvin C. Smith, *Awarded for Valour: A History of the Victoria Cross and the Evolution of British Heroism* (2008). Colonial warfare clearly contributed to an increasing militaristic popular mood, as suggested by C. D. Eby, *The Road to Armageddon: The Martial Spirit in English Popular Literature, 1870–1914* (1988); and Steve Attridge, *Nationalism, Imperialism and Identity in Late Victorian Culture: Civil and Military Worlds* (2003), who covers the music hall as well as literature and poetry.[36]

The essays in two collections edited by John M. Mackenzie (ed.), *Propaganda and Empire: The Manipulation of British Public Opinion, 1880–1960* (1986) and especially *Popular Imperialism and the Military, 17850–1950* (1992), provide general overviews. The press is also one of the many subjects covered in two centenary commemorative collections, Edward Spiers (ed.), *Sudan: The Reconquest Reappraised* (1998), and John Gooch (ed.), *The Boer War: Direction, Experience and Image* (2000).[37] The press similarly figures in Peter Harrington and Frederic Sharf (eds), *Omdurmann 1898: The Eyewitnesses Speak* (1998), and the same authors' *The Boxer Rebellion: China 1900 – The Artists' Perspective* (2000). It might be added that, with regard to the Boxer Rebellion, the classic Peter Fleming, *The Siege of Peking* (1959), can now be supplemented with Diana Preston, *The Boxer Rebellion* (2001). Glenn Wilkinson, *Depictions and Images of*

---

35 See also Michael Lieven, 'Heroism, Heroics and the Making of Heroes: The Anglo-Zulu War of 1879', *Albion* 30 (1998), 419–38; and Michael Silvestri, 'Lord and Master Nikkai Seyn: The Construction of John Nicholson as a British Imperial Hero', in Michael Silvestri, *Ireland and India: Nationalism, Empire and Memory* (Basingstoke: Palgrave Macmillan, 2009), pp. 76–112.

36 See also Anne Summers, 'Militarism in Britain before the Great War', *History Workshop Journal* 2 (1976), 104–23.

37 See also Roger Stearn, 'G. W. Steevens and the Message of Empire', *JICH* 17 (1989), 210–31'; idem, 'Bennet Burleigh, Victorian War Correspondent', *SOTQ* 65 (1991), 5–10; idem, 'War Images and Image Makers in the Victorian Era: Aspects of the British Visual and Written Portrayal of War, c.1865–1906', PhD dissertation, University of London, 1987; Jacqueline Beaumont Hughes, 'The Press and the Public during the Boer War, 1899–1902', *The Historian* 61 (1999), 10–15; Nora Hoover, 'Victorian War Correspondents G. A. Henty and H. M. Stanley: The Abyssinian Campaign, 1867–68', PhD dissertation, Florida State University, 2005; Glenn Wilkinson, 'There is No More Stirring Story: The Press Depiction and Images of War during the Tibet Expedition, 1903–04', *W&S* 9 (1991), 1–16.

War in Edwardian Newspapers, 1899–1914 (2002), takes the story through the Edwardian period.

It was the early defeats of the South African War (1899–1902), coupled with a growing perception that German continental ambitions rather than French and Russian colonial ambitions would be the mostly likely future challenge to Britain, that proved the catalyst for reform intended to fit the army for a continuing global role. Though intended for a general readership, Thomas Pakenham, *The Boer War* (1993) was an intelligent reassessment while there were important essays in Peter Warwick (ed.), *The South African War: The Anglo-Boer 1899–1902* (1980). The latter reflected emerging interest in Black African perspectives, also evident in Peter Warwick, *Black People and the South African War, 1899–1902* (1983), and Bill Nasson, *Black Participation in the Anglo-Boer War, 1899–1902* (1999). Other pre-centenary reassessments included S. B. Spies, *Methods of Barbarism? Roberts and Kitchener and Civilians in the Boer Republics, 1900–1902* (1977), dealing with British concentration camps; Jay Stone and Erwin Schmidl, *The Boer War and Military Reform* (1988), dealing with Austro-Hungarian as well as British military perspectives; and Keith Surridge, *Managing the South African War, 1899–1902: Politicians versus Generals* (1998), an important study of relations between the British High Commissioner, Milner, and the three successive commanders-in-chief, Buller, Roberts and Kitchener.[38]

The centenary then resulted in a valuable new general history, Bill Nasson, *The South African War* (1999), the collection edited by Gooch referred to above, and three more edited collections, Peter Dennis and Jeffery Grey (eds), *The Boer War: Army, Nation and Empire* (2000); Donal Lowry (ed.), *The South African War Reappraised* (2000); and David Omissi and Andrew Thompson (eds), *The Impact of the South African War* (2002). All cover not just Britain and South Africa, but the Empire as a whole and, in the case of Omissi and Thompson, European reactions. In addition, the South African Journal for Contemporary History, *Joernaal vir Eietydse Geskiedenis*, produced a special number in 2000

---

38 See also Keith Surridge, 'All You Soldiers Are What We Call Pro-Boer: The Military Critique of the South African War', *History* 82 (1997), 582–600; idem, 'Rebellion, Martial Law and British Civil-Military Relations: The War in Cape Colony, 1899–1902', *SWI* 8 (1997), 35–60; Stephen Miller, 'The British Way of War: Cultural Assumptions and Practices in the South African War, 1899–1902', *JMH* 77 (2013), 1329–48; Joseph Vergolina, 'Methods of Barbarism or Western Tradition: Britain, South Africa, and the Evolution of Escalatory Violence as Policy', *JMH* 77 (2013), 1303–28.

based on papers at the major centenary conference at Bloemfontein in 1999, the majority of which were delivered in English rather than Afrikaans.[39]

One particular issue has been the army's learning process in South Africa. Pakenham sought to rehabilitate the reputation of Buller, which was savaged by Leo Amery in *The Times History of the War in South Africa* (1900–9), and which was largely followed by later popular accounts. Pakenham, indeed, suggests Buller had been a major tactical innovator in the latter stages of his advance on Ladysmith. Equally, Stephen M. Miller, *Lord Methuen and the British Army: Failure and Redemption in South Africa* (1999) argues that Methuen adapted to the changing conditions of war. Howard Bailes, too, saw much improvement in the army by the 1890s and that the early failings in 1899 were a result of officers not adhering to the new methods being pioneered at Aldershot.[40] In *The Late Victorian Army*, Spiers casts some doubt on this revisionism, and D. M. Leeson also questions the amount of pre-war progress. Clearly there were major failures in areas such as logistics and medical arrangements.[41]

As suggested by reference to Amery, the early historiography of the war itself was contested, a useful survey being Craig Wilcox (ed.), *Recording the South African War: Journalism and Official History, 1899–1914* (1999). In many ways

---

39 'The Anglo-Boer War, 1899–1902: A Reappraisal', *Joernaal vir Eietydse Geskiedenis* 25:2 (2000).

40 Howard Bailes, 'Patterns of Thought in the Late Victorian Army', *JSS* 4 (1981), 29–45; idem, 'Technology and Tactics in the British Army, 1866–1900', in Ronald Haycock and Keith Neilson (eds), *Men, Machines and War* (Waterloo, ON: Wilfred Laurier University Press, 1988), pp. 23–47.

41 D. M. Leeson, 'Playing at War: The British Military Manoeuvres of 1898', *WH* 15 (2008), 432–61; Spencer Jones, 'Shooting Power: A Study of the Effectiveness of Boer and British Rifle Fire, 1899–1914' *BJMH* 1 (2014), 29–44; idem, 'The Thin Khaki Line: The Evolution of Infantry Attack Formations in the British Army, 1899–1914', in Michael Locicero, Ross Mahoney and Stuart Mitchell (eds), *A Military Transformed? Adaptation and Innovation in the British Military, 1792–1945* (Solihull: Helion & Co, 2014), pp. 83–96; idem, 'The Shooting of the Boers was Extraordinary: British Views of Boer Marksmanship in the Second Anglo-Boer war, 1899–1902', in Karen Jones, Giacomo Macola and David Welch (eds), *A Cultural History of Firearms in the Age of Empire* (Farnham: Ashgate, 2013), pp. 251–66. See also A. H. Page, 'The Supply Services of the British Army in the South African War, 1899–1902', DPhil dissertation, University of Oxford, 1976; M. S. Stone, 'Medical Care and the Victorian Army: Health, Hospitals and Social Conditions Encountered by British Troops during the South African War', PhD dissertation, University of London, 1993. See also Maureen O'Connor, 'The Vision of Soldiers: Britain, France, Germany and the United States Observe the Russo-Turkish War', *WH* 4 (1997), 264–95.

this has certainly continued into modern South Africa as several of the centenary collections indicated.[42]

A contemporary debate, which has enjoyed continuing currency, is that over the performance of the British cavalry in South Africa, the cavalry invariably being depicted in popular accounts as conservative and wedded to cold steel. Stephen Badsey, *Doctrine and Reform in the British Cavalry, 1880–1918* (2008) has particularly revised the traditional image, suggesting the British cavalry was sufficiently trained for both mounted and dismounted action by 1914. Jean Bou, *Light Horse: A History of Australia's Mounted Arm* (2009), is also revisionist. The actual procurement of the army's horses is the subject of Graham Winton, *Theirs Not to Reason Why: Horsing the British Army, 1875–1925* (2013).[43]

The war resulted in a significant response from the British public that was very much a precursor to the response in 1914. The earlier attempt in Richard Price, *An Imperial War and the British Working Class: Working Class Attitudes and Reactions to the Boer War, 1899–1902* (1972), to pass off the recruitment for the Imperial Yeomanry as primarily the result of unemployment has been thoroughly discredited by Stephen Miller, *Volunteers on the Veld: Britain's Citizen Soldiers and the South African War, 1899–1902* (2007), and the less academic Will Bennett, *Absent-Minded Beggars: Yeomanry and Volunteers in the Boer War* (1999).[44]

---

42 See also Ian F. W. Beckett, 'The Historiography of Small Wars: Early Historians and the South African War', *SWI* 2 (1991), 276–89; idem, 'Military Historians and the South African War: A Review of Recent Literature', *SOTQ* 54 (1978), 12–14.

43 See also Brian Bond, 'Doctrine and Training in the British Cavalry, 1870–1914', in Michael Howard (ed.), *The Theory and Practice of War* (London: Cassell, 1965), pp. 97–125; Edward Spiers, 'The British Cavalry, 1902–14', *JSAHR* 57 (1977), 71–79; Stephen Badsey, 'Mounted Cavalry in the Second Boer War', *Sandhurst Journal of Military History* 2 (1991), 11–27; idem, 'The Boer War and British Cavalry Doctrine: A Re-consideration', *JMH* 71 (2007), 75–98; Sandra Swart, 'Horses in the South African War, 1899–1903', *Society and Animals* 18 (2010), 348–56; Spencer Jones, 'Scouting for Soldiers: Reconnaissance and the British Cavalry', *WH* 18 (2011), 495–524.

44 See also Michael Blanch, 'Imperialism, Nationalism and Organised Youth', in J. Clarke, C. Critcher and R. Johnson (eds), *Working Class Culture* (New York: St Martin's Press, 1979), pp. 103–20; Stephen Miller, 'In Support of the Imperial Mission? Volunteering for the South African War, 1899–1902', *JMH* 69 (2005), 691–712; idem, 'Slogging across the Veld: British Volunteers and the Guerrilla Phase of the South African War', *JSAHR* 84 (2006), 158–74; E. W. McFarland, 'Empire-Enlarging Genius: Scottish Imperial Yeomanry Volunteers in the Boer War', *WH* 13 (2006), 299–328.

The domestic social impact of the war in South Africa was considerable, fuelling the tentative beginnings of the welfare state.[45] Other impacts were seen in contemporary poetry, art and commemoration, as depicted in Martin Van Wyk Smith, *Drummer Hodge: The Poetry of the Anglo-Boer War, 1899–1902* (1978), and Ryno Greenwall, *Artists and Illustrators of the Anglo-Boer War* (1992).[46]

Beyond Britain, the war also had a decided impact on the white dominions as suggested by essays in the edited collections as well as those works dealing with the military contributions of Australia, Canada and New Zealand, namely Carman Miller, *Painting the Map Red: Canada and the South African War. 1899–1902* (1993); Craig Wilcox, *Australia's Boer War: The War in South Africa, 1899–1902* (2002); and John Crawford and Ian McGibbon (eds), *One Flag, One Queen, One Tongue: New Zealand, the British Empire and the South African War* (2003). In Australia in particular there has been a debate on how far British officers serving as colonial commandants manipulated the offers of foreign service in 1899.[47]

---

45 See Ian F. W. Beckett, 'Britain's Imperial War: A Question of Totality?', *Joernaal vir Eietydse Geskiedenis* 25 (2000), 1–22; Clive Trebilcock, 'War and the Failure of Industrial Mobilisation, 1899 and 1914', in Jay Winter (ed.), *War and Economic Development* (Cambridge: Cambridge University Press, 1975), pp. 139–64; Marc Yakutiel, 'Treasury Control and the South African War, 1899–1905', DPhil dissertation, University of Oxford, 1989.

46 See also Mark Connelly and Peter Donaldson, 'South African War Memorials in Britain: A Case Study of Memorialisation in London and Kent', *W&S* 29 (2010), 20–46.

47 See also Carman Miller, 'The Unhappy Warriors: Conflict and Nationality among the Canadian Troops during the South African War', *JICH* 23 (1995), 77–104; idem, 'Loyalty, Patriotism and Resistance: Canada's Response to the Anglo-Boer War, 18991–902', *South Africa Historical Review* 41 (2000), 312–23; Katharine McGowan, 'A Finger in the Fire: Canadian Volunteer Soldiers and their Perceptions of Canada's Collective Identity through their Experience of the Boer War', *W&S* 28 (2009), 89–114; C. N. Connelly, 'Manufacturing Spontaneity: The Australian Offers of Troops for the Boer War', *Historical Studies* 18 (1978), 106–17; S. J. Clarke, 'Marching to their Own Drum: Military Commandants in the Australian Colonies and New Zealand, 1870–1901', PhD dissertation, University of New South Wales, 1999. Clarke has contributed chapters on this issue to Dennis and Grey (eds), *Boer War*, pp. 129–50; and to Crawford and McGibbon (eds), *One Flag*, pp. 12–27; as has Luke Trainor in a chapter in Omissi and Thompson (eds), *Impact of South African War*, pp. 251–67.

Perceived military failings, of course, led to largely unsuccessful reforms in Britain by St John Brodrick and H. O. Arnold-Forster between 1902 and 1905 and then to the reforms implemented by R. B. Haldane after 1906. For the general post-1902 period there is now Timothy Bowman and Mark Connelly, *The Edwardian Army: Recruiting, Training and Deploying the British Army, 1902–14* (2012) and, with particular respect to tactical reform, Spencer Jones, *From Boer War to World War: Tactical Reform of the British Army, 1902–14* (2012).[48] Some of the lessons absorbed in South Africa were seemingly modified by those derived from the Russo-Japanese War.[49]

The Brodrick and Arnold-Forster periods are examined by Rhodri Williams, *Defending the Empire: The Conservative Party and British Defence Policy, 1899–1915* (1991).[50] A 'managerial revolution' in higher defence organisation was achieved, however, prior to 1906 with the emergence of the Committee of Imperial Defence (CID) and the creation of a General Staff. John Gooch, *The Plans of War: The General Staff and British Military Strategy, 1900–1916* (1974) is a detailed study of the evolution of the General Staff from the deliberations

---

48 See also Edward Spiers, 'Rearming the Edwardian Artillery', *JSAHR* 57 (1979), 162–76; idem, 'Reforming the Infantry of the Line, 1900–14', *JSAHR* 59 (1981), 82–94; Andrew Whitmarsh, 'British Army Manoeuvres and the Development of Military Aviation, 1910–12', *WH* 14 (2007), 325–46; Brian Hall, 'The Life Blood of Communication? The British Army, Communications and the Telephone, 1877–1914', *W&S* 27 (2008), 43–65; idem, 'The British Army and Wireless Communications, 1896–1918', *WH* 19 (2012), 290–321; Nicholas Evans, 'From Drill to Doctrine: Forging the British Army's Tactics, 1897–1909', PhD dissertation, University of London, 2007.

49 See Philip Towle, 'The Russo-Japanese War and British Military Thought', *JRUSI* 116 (1971), 64–8; Tim Travers, 'Technology, Tactics and Morale: Jean de Bloch, the Boer War and British Military Thought, 1900–14', *Journal of Modern History* 51 (1979), 264–86; Keith Neilson, 'That Dangerous and Difficult Enterprise: British Military Thinking and the Russo-Japanese War', *W&S* 9 (1991), 17–37; Gary Cox, 'Of Aphorisms, Lessons and Paradigms: Comparing the British and German Official Histories of the Russo-Japanese War', *JMH* 56 (1992), 389–401; Maureen O'Connor, 'The Vision of Soldiers: Britain, France, Germany and the United States observe the Russo-Japanese War', *WH* 4 (1997), 264–95; and Patrick Porter, 'Military Orientalism? British Observers of the Japanese Way of War, 1904–10', *W&S* 26 (2007), 1–25.

50 See also A. V. Tucker, 'The Issue of Army Reform in the Unionist Government, 1903–05', *HJ* 9 (1966), 90–100, J. Bertie, 'H.O. Arnold-Forster at the War Office, 1903–05', PhD dissertation, University of Liverpool, 1974; and L. J. Satre, 'St John Brodrick and Army Reform, 1901–03', *JBS* 15 (1976), 117–39.

of the Esher Committee to the Great War, with a number of case studies of the resulting strategic planning for war with different potential enemies. It can be supplemented by John Gooch (ed.), *The Prospect of War: Studies in British Defence Policy, 1847–1942* (1981); and in David French and Brian Holden Reid (eds), *The British General Staff: Reform and Innovation, 1890–1939* (2002). The CID is examined by Nicholas d'Ombrain, *War Machinery and High Policy: Defence Administration in Peacetime Britain, 1902–14* (1973), which built on the earlier study, Franklyn Johnson, *Defence by Committee: The British Committee of Imperial Defence, 1885–1959* (1960). Reform also extended to India where Kitchener attempted to reorganise the Indian army for a modern war.[51]

The General Staff oversaw a re-orientation of British strategy, which has been covered in a number of works besides Gooch, including J. E. Tyler, *The British Army and the Continent, 1904–14* (1938); Samuel Williamson, *The Politics of Grand Strategy: Britain and France Prepare for War, 1904–14* (1969); Michael Howard, *The Continental Commitment: The Dilemma of British Defence Policy in the Era of Two World Wars* (1972); and Aaron Friedberg, *The Weary Titan: Britain and the Experience of Relative Decline, 1895–1905* (1988).[52] On the very eve of war, however, the degree of consensus that had emerged between the military leadership and some of the political leadership was thrown into disarray by the breach in civil-military relations resulting from the Curragh Incident, for which there is Ian Beckett (ed.), *The Army and the Curragh Incident, 1914*

---

51 J. P. Mackintosh, 'The Role of the Committee of Imperial Defence before 1914', *EHR* 77 (1962), 490–503; John Gooch, 'Sir George Clarke's Career at the Committee of Imperial Defence, 1904–07', *HJ* 18 (1975), 555–69; John W. Coogan and Peter F. Coogan, 'The British Cabinet and the Anglo-French Staff Talks, 1905–15: Who Knew What and When Did He Know It?', *Journal of British Studies* 24 (1985), 110–31; Tim Moreman, 'Lord Kitchener, the General Staff and the Army in India, 1902–14', in David French and Brian Holden Reid (eds), *The British General Staff: Reform and Innovation, 1890–1939* (London: Frank Cass, 2002), pp. 57–74; Benjamin Gillon, 'British Planning for the Defence of India and the Reorganisation of the Indian Army, 1902–15', PhD dissertation, University of Glasgow, 2008. For West Africa, see A. Edho Ekoko, 'British Military Planning against France in West Africa, 1898–1906', *JSS* 4 (1981), 285–95; idem, 'British War Plans against Germany in West Africa, 1903–14', *JSS* 7 (1984), 441–56.

52 See also N. W. Summerton, 'The Development of British Military Planning for War against Germany, 1904–14', PhD dissertation, University of London, 1970; John McDermott, 'The Revolution in British Military Planning from the Boer War to the Moroccan Crisis', in Paul Kennedy (ed.), *The War Plans of the Great Powers, 1880–1914* (London: Allen & Unwin, 1979), pp. 99–117.

(1986).[53] Reference should also be made to Timothy Bowman, *Carson's Army: The Ulster Volunteer Force, 1910–22* (2007) for the militarisation that had occurred in Ireland itself during the Home Rule Crisis.

Haldane is the subject of the major reassessment by Edward Spiers, *Haldane: An Army Reformer* (1980). One particular aspect of the reforms, namely Haldane's creation of the Territorial Force has resulted in some welcome academic interest in the auxiliary forces including Peter Dennis, *The Territorial Army* (1987), and two works by K. W. Mitchinson tracing both the Territorial Force and the National Reserve, *Defending Albion: Britain's Home Army, 1908–19* (2005), and *England's Last Hope: The Territorial Force, 1908–14* (2008). Mitchinson focuses on the work of the County Territorial Associations, and fills an important gap in the understanding of the difficulties and heavy administrative workload of the associations in such areas as recruiting, training, equipment, finance and mobilisation amid the general indifference of the War Office.[54] Part of the background debate was agitation for the introduction of some form of conscription, for which the early chapters of R. J. Q. Adams and R. Poirier, *The Conscription Controversy in Britain, 1900–18* (1987) are relevant.[55]

As it happened, colonial auxiliary forces were also reformed after the South African War, for which reference can be made to Craig Wilcox, *For Hearths and Homes: Citizen Soldiering in Australia, 1854–1945* (1988); John Mordike, *An Army for a Nation: A History of Australian Military Developments, 1880–1914* (1992); James Wood, *Militia Myths: Ideas of the Canadian Citizen Soldier, 1896–1921* (2010); Peter Cooke and John Crawford, *The Territorials: The History of the Territorial and Volunteer Forces of New Zealand* (2011); and John Connor, *Anzac and Empire: George Foster Pearce and the Foundations of Australian Defence* (2011). Mordike, it should be said, is something of a polemicist regarding alleged British machinations to utilise Australian manpower, and Wilcox is far more

53 See also Ian F. W. Beckett, "A Note on Government Intelligence and Surveillance during the Curragh Incident, March 1914', *INS* 1 (1986), 435–440; idem, 'Some Further Correspondence Relating to the Curragh Incident of March 1914', *JSAHR* 69 (1991), 98–116; Mark Connelly, 'The Army, the Press and the Curragh Incident, March 1914', *HR* 84 (2011), 535–57.
54 See also A. J. A. Morris, 'Haldane's Army Reforms, 1906–08: The Deception of the Radicals', *History* 156 (1971), 17–34; Edward Spiers, 'Haldane's Reform of the Regular Army: Scope for Revision', *British Journal of International Studies* 6 (1980), 69–81; Kristopher Gies, 'Amateur Soldiering in Industrial Britain: The Early Territorial Force in Glasgow, 1908–14', PhD dissertation, University of Guelph, 2010.
55 See also Michael Allison, 'The National Service Issue, 1900–14', PhD dissertation, University of London, 1975.

measured. As suggested in an earlier section, general military developments in the white dominions over the wider timescale have been usefully covered in C. D. Coulthard-Clark, *Soldiers in Politics: The Impact of the Military on Australian Political Life and Institutions* (1996); Albert Palazzo, *The Australian Army: A History of its Organisation, 1901–2001* (2001); J. L. Granatstein, *Canada's Army: Waging War and Keeping the Peace* (2002); Jeffrey Grey's *The Australian Army: A History* (2006), and *A Military History of Australia* (2008); Desmond Morton, *A Military History of Canada* (2001); and Bernd Horn (ed.), *Forging a Nation: Perspectives on the Canadian Military Experience* (2002). Among older studies for Canada are Richard Preston, *Canada and Imperial Defence: A Study of the Origins of the British Commonwealth's Defence Organisation, 1867–1919* (1967); Desmond Morton, *Ministers and Generals: Politics and the Canadian Militia, 1868–1904* (1970); Richard Preston, *The Defence of the Undefended Border: Planning for War in North America, 1867–1939* (1977), Stephen J. Harris, *Canadian Brass: The Making of a Professional Army, 1860–1939* (1988); and, as previously mentioned, George Stanley's *Canada's Soldiers* (1954). For Australia, there is Neville Meaney, *The Search for Security in the Pacific, 1901–14* (1981), and also the valuable essays in Michael McKernan and M. Browne (eds), *Australia: Two Centuries of War and Peace* (1988). For New Zealand, Ian McGibbon, *The Path to Gallipoli: Defending New Zealand, 1840–1915* (1981), is also an important study.[56] Dominion attitudes to defence on the eve of world war are also covered in the essays in the latest publication from the Army Chief of Staff historical conferences in Australia, Peter Dennis and Jeffrey Grey (eds), *1911: Preliminary Moves* (2011).

---

56 See also G. J. Clayton, 'Defence Not Defiance: The Shaping of New Zealand's Volunteer Force', PhD dissertation, University of Waikato, 1990.

Chapter 7
From 1914

From previous sections, it will be apparent that some texts cover varying periods between the French Revolution and the Second World War. As also previously noted, Brian Bond, *War and Society in Europe, 1870–1970* (1983); Michael Neiberg, *Warfare and Society in Europe: 1898 to the Present* (2004); and Jeremy Black, *Warfare in the Western World, 1882–1975* (2002), as well as Black's *The Age of Total War, 1860–1945* (2006), bring the story to 1945 or, indeed, beyond. It will be noted, too, that three of the American and German collaborative volumes on the nature of total war are concerned with conflict between 1914 and 1945. Moreover, Arthur Marwick's influential interpretations of total war embraced both world wars. As also mentioned previously, Roger Chickering, Dennis Showalter and Hans van de Ven (eds), *The Cambridge History of War:* volume IV, *War and the Modern World* (2012), covers the period from 1850 to 2000. A series of volumes with a unifying theme are those edited by Allan Millett and Williamson Murray, namely *Military Effectiveness: The First World War*; *Military Effectiveness: The Interwar Period*, and *Military Effectiveness: The Second World War*, all published in 1988. For the post-1945 period there is Jeremy Black, *War since 1945* (2010), while Robert Citino, *Blitzkrieg to Desert Storm: The Evolution of Operational Warfare* (2004) looks at the period from 1940 to the First Gulf War.

For perspectives on war in the twenty-first century, works include Jan Angstrom and Isabelle Duyvesteyn (eds), *Rethinking the Nature of Modern War* (2005); David Jordan, James D. Kiras, David J. Lonsdale, Ian Speller, Christopher Tuck and C. Dale Walton (eds), *Understanding Modern Warfare* (2008); Hew Strachan and Sibylle Scheipers (eds), *The Changing Character of War* (2011); Karl Erik Haug and Ole Jørgen Maaø (eds), *Conceptualising Modern War* (2011); Julian Lindley-French and Yves Boyer (eds), *The Oxford Handbook of War* (2012); and Paul B. Rich and Isabelle Duyvesteyn (eds), *The Routledge Handbook of Insurgency and Counterinsurgency* (2012); and Hew Strachan, *The Direction of War: Contemporary Strategy in Historical Perspective* (2013).

For Britain, Hew Strachan (ed.) *Big Wars and Small Wars: The British Army and the Conduct of War in the Twentieth Century* (2006) embraces the aftermath of the South African War, the two world wars and the post-1945 contrast between the conventional concerns of those serving in the British Army of the Rhine, and those soldiers confronting low-intensity conflict around the globe. F. W. Perry, *The Commonwealth Armies: Manpower and Organisation in Two World Wars* (1988) surveys the development of the British and Dominion forces as a whole. Most of the post-1945 British counter-insurgency campaigns are included in Daniel Marston and Carter Malkasian (eds), *Counterinsurgency in Modern Warfare*, 2nd edn. (2008). Two invaluable compilations from official statistics are *Statistics of the Military Effort of the British Empire during the Great War* (1922), and *Fighting with Figures: A Statistical Digest of the Second World War* (1995).

Not unexpectedly, there are substantial numbers of histories of both world wars ranging from popular narratives of varying quality to more thematic and analytical academic texts. Only the latter will be considered. Moreover, the literature on the world wars is now so vast that all parts of this section will necessarily be highly selective.

For the First World War, the best short survey is Michael Howard, *The First World War* (2002), which is to be preferred to the idiosyncratic Norman Stone, *World War One: A Short History* (2007). Hew Strachan (ed.) *The Oxford Illustrated History of the First World War* (1998) is an accessible account covering most aspects. Strachan himself has also published *The First World War: A New Illustrated History* (2003), and the first massive volume of a trilogy, *The First World War: To Arms* (2001), although it does not seem that the second volume will appear for some years. Two contrasting accounts are Ian F. W. Beckett, *The Great War, 1914–18*, 2nd edn. (2007), which is thematic, and David Stevenson, *1914–18: The First World War* (2004), which combines a thematic and chronological approach. General accounts with a more specific focus include Gerd Hardach, *The First World War, 1914–18* (1973), which is essentially about economics; David Stevenson, *The First World War and International Politics* (1988), which is self-explanatory; and Michael Neiberg, *Fighting the Great War: A Global History* (2005), which concentrates on military aspects. Jay Winter and Antoine Prost, *The Great War in History, Debates and Controversies, 1914 to the Present* (2005) is concerned with the historical memory of the war. Ian F. W. Beckett, *The Making of the First World War* (2012) attempts to assess the long-term significance of the war, as does Jeremy Black, *The Great War and the Making of the Modern World* (2011). Hugh Cecil and Peter Liddle (eds), *Facing Armageddon: The First World War Experienced* (1996), has a wide range of essays. All these have full bibliographies.

Britain has been especially well served in terms of general surveys of the First World War. Following on from the venerable Sir Llewellyn Woodward, *Great Britain and the First World War* (1967), Trevor Wilson, *The Myriad Faces of War* (1986), and John Bourne, *Britain and the Great War, 1914–18* (1989), presented more analytical narratives though Bourne is far more detailed on military than other matters. Niall Ferguson, *The Pity of War* (1998) is somewhat discursive with some bold assertions, sometimes of a counter-factual nature, underpinned by his belief that Britain should not have entered the war. On the other hand, as an economic historian, Ferguson is expectedly sound on economic issues, and also raises interesting questions in areas such as the risks of surrender, and the taste for killing.[1] Stephen Constantine, Maurice Kirby and Mary Rose (eds), *The First World War in British History* (1995), retains its value in terms of its wide coverage of all aspects of the war effort to a greater extent than John Turner (ed.), *Britain and the First World War* (1988). British society has been a particular focus from Arthur Marwick, *The Deluge: British Society and the First World War* (1965), to Gerard de Groot, *Blighty: British Society in the Era of the Great War* (1996); the strangely titled Adrian Gregory, *The Last Great War: British Society and the First World War* (2008); and to the most recent and up to date study, Alan Simmonds, *Britain and World War One* (2012), which is rather better suited to an undergraduate text than Gregory. For a wider perspective there is Geoffrey Searle, *A New England? Peace and War, 1886–1918* (2004), while Peter Dewey, *War and Progress: Britain, 1914–45* (1997) links both world wars.

Again, the bibliographies of all these general studies on Britain will point to the wealth of work on various aspects such as the growth of the state, the role of women, cultural impacts, memory and commemoration, and so on. A few general studies should be mentioned in these areas, however, such as Kathleen Burk (ed.), *War and the State: The Transformation of British Government, 1914–18* (1982); Tony Howard and John Stokes (eds), *Acts of War: Representations of Military Conflict on the British Stage and Television since 1945* (1996); Susan Grayzel, *Women and the First World War* (2002); George Robb, *British Culture and the First World War* (2002); and Jessica Meyer (ed.), *British Popular Culture and the First World War* (2008). A valuable regional study is Keith Grieves (ed.), *Sussex in the First World War* (2004), an approach that should be more widely emulated. Brian Bond (ed.), *The First World War and British Military History* (1991) offers a range of historiographical essays from the earliest patriotic depictions of the war through the 'battle of the memoirs' in the 1920s and 1930s, the controversies of the Official History, and the iconoclasm of the 1960s, to the beginnings of modern re-assessments.

Ireland has been covered in David Fitzpatrick (ed.), *Ireland and the First World War* (1986); Keith Jeffery, *Ireland and the Great War* (2000), based on his 1998 Lees Knowles lectures; and Adrian Gregory and Sonia Pašeta (eds),

---

1 See also Niall Ferguson, 'Prisoner Taking and Prisoner Killing in the Age of Total War: Towards a Political Economy of Military Defeat', *WH* 11 (2004), 148–92.

Ireland and the Great War: A War to Unite Us All (2002). For Scotland there is also an edited collection, Catriona Macdonald and E. W. McFarland (eds), *Scotland and the Great War* (1999). Among many studies of the component parts of the British Empire, there are D. C. Ellinwood and S. D. Pradhan (eds), *India and World War I* (1978); Michael McKernan, *The Australian People and the Great War* (1980); Joan Beaumont, *Broken Nation: Australians in the Great War* (2013); Peter McLaughlin, *Ragtime Soldiers: The Rhodesian Experience in the First World War* (1980); Desmond Morton and J. L. Granatstein, *Marching to Armageddon: Canadians and the Great War, 1914–19* (1989); Joan Beaumont (ed.), *Australia's War, 1914–18* (1995); Craig Wilcox and Janice Aldridge (eds), *The Great War: Gains and Losses – Anzac and Empire* (1995); Glenford Howe, *Race, War and Nationalism: A Social History of West Indians in the First World War* (2002); Daniel Marc Segesser, *Empire und Totaler Krieg: Australien, 1905–18* (2002); Richard Smith, *Jamaica and the Great War: Race, Masculinity and the Development of National Consciousness* (2004); Christopher Pugsley, *The Anzac Experience: New Zealand, Australia and Empire in the First World War* (2004); David Clark Mackenzie (ed.), *Canada and the First World War: Essays in Honour of Robert Craig Brown* (2005); John Crawford and Ian McGibbon (eds), *New Zealand's Great War: New Zealand, the Allies and the First World War* (2007); Timothy Winegard, *Indigenous Peoples of the British Dominions and the First World War* (2011); Bill Nasson, *Springboks on the Somme: South Africa in the Great War, 1914–25* (2012); and imperial experiences generally are covered in Richard Fogarty and Andrew Jarboe (eds), *Empires in World War I: Shifting Frontiers and Imperial Dynamics in a Global Conflict* (2012).[2] Again all such studies have full bibliographies relating to dominion and colonial participation.

Consideration of purely military aspects of the war must begin with the formulation of strategy and civil-military relations. The tortured story of British war aims, strategy and the struggle between politicians and soldiers have been covered in a number of works including the outstanding trilogy by David French, *British Economic and Strategic Planning, 1905–15* (1982); *British Strategy and War Aims, 1914–16* (1986); and *The Strategy of the Lloyd George Coalition,*

---

2 See also C. L. Joseph, 'The British West Indies Regiment, 1914–18', *Journal of Caribbean History* 2 (1971), 94–124; David Killingray, 'All the King's Men: Blacks in the British Army in the First World War, 1914–18', in Rainer Lotz and Ian Pegg (eds), *Under the Imperial Carpet: Essays in Black History, 1780–1950* (1986), pp. 164–81; Michael Heely, 'Empire, Race and War: Black Participation in British Military Efforts during the 20th Century', PhD dissertation, Loyola University, 1998.

1916–18 (1995). French challenges the traditional views of military 'westerners' opposed by political 'easterners', suggesting instead that the main players shared the same basic aims, and that the few politicians who advocated a strategy of limited liability had been eclipsed at an early stage. He further demonstrates that the original intention to allow the French and Russians to take the brunt of the war effort on land had to be abandoned. Once Britain became, albeit briefly, the major partner in the alliance in 1917, it was determined to prevent the political balance shifting entirely in the United States of America's favour through husbanding sufficient resources to retain diplomatic leverage at the war's close. French has also written on specific strategic decisions and issues, including an especially important article on the acceptance of military attrition as a strategy.[3]

Britain was initially the junior partner of France and Russia, and the realities of coalition warfare are seen from different perspectives by William Philpott, *Anglo-French Relations and Strategy on the Western Front, 1914–18* (1996), and Elizabeth Greenhalgh, *Victory Through Coalition: Britain and France during the First World* War (2005), since the former is based primarily on British archives, and the latter on French archives.[4] In particular, they have duelled over the purposes of the Somme offensive in 1916.[5] The debate continues in Philpott's *Bloody Victory: The Sacrifice on the Somme and the Making of the Twentieth*

---

3 David French, 'The Military Background to the "Shell Crisis" of May 1915', *JSS* 2 (1979), 192–205; idem, 'The Origins of the Dardanelles Campaign Reconsidered', *History* 68 (1983), 210–24; idem, 'The Dardanelles, Mecca and Kut: Prestige as a Factor in British Eastern Strategy, 1914–16', *W&S* 5 (1987), 45–61; idem, 'The Meaning of Attrition, 1914–16', *EHR* 103 (1988), 385–405.

4 See also William Philpott, 'The Strategic Ideas of Sir John French', *JSS* 12 (1989), 455–78; idem, 'Kitchener and the 29th Division: A Study in Anglo-French Strategic Relations, 1914–15', *JSS* 16 (1993), 375–407; idem, 'Britain and France Go to War: Anglo-French Relations on the Western Front, 1914–18', *WH* 23 (1995), 43–64; Elizabeth Greenhalgh, 'The Experience of Fighting with Allies: The Case of the Capture of Falfemont Farm during the Battle of the Somme, 1916', *WH* 10 (2003), 157–83.

5 Elizabeth Greenhalgh, 'Why the British were on the Somme in 1916', *WH* 6 (1999), 147–73; eadem, 'Parade-Ground Soldiers: French Army Assessments of the British on the Somme', *Journal of Military History* 63 (1999), 283–312; eadem, 'Flames over the Somme: A Retort to William Philpott', *WH* 10 (2003), 335–42; William Philpott, 'Why the British were Really on the Somme: A Reply to Elizabeth Greenhalgh', *WH*, 9 (2002), 446–71. See also Hew Strachan, 'The Battle of the Somme and British Strategy', *JSS* 21 (1998), 79–95.

Century (2009). They are broadly in agreement, however, on the centrality of the Anglo-French alliance to allied victory, and Greenhalgh has further argued for the importance of Ferdinand Foch to eventual victory in the West in *Foch in Command: The Forging of a First World War General* (2011).[6] Anglo-French relations in 1914 are also the subject of Roy A. Prete, *Strategy and Command: The Anglo-French Coalition on the Western Front 1914* (2012).[7] One aspect of the later Anglo-American alliance is the British role in training US troops, and some Americans came under British control, as recounted by Mitch Yockelson, *Borrowed Soldiers: Americans under British Command, 1918* (2008).

In addition to the works by David French, wider strategic issues are also covered in a number of older studies including Paul Guinn, *British Strategy and Politics, 1914–18* (1965); V. H. Rothwell, *British War Aims and Peace Diplomacy* (1971); Cameron Hazlehurst, *Politicians at War, July 1914 to May 1915: A Prologue to the Triumph of Lloyd George* (1971); and Barry Hunt and Adrian Preston (eds), *War Aims and Strategic Policy in the Great War* (1977). More modern studies include John Turner, *British Politics and the Great War: Coalition and Conflict, 1915–18* (1992); P. K. Davis, *Ends and Means: The British Mesopotamia Campaign and Commission* (1994); David Dutton, *The Politics of Diplomacy: Britain and France in the Balkans in the First World War* (1998); and Matthew Hughes, *Allenby and British Strategy in the Middle East* (1999), which can be supplemented by his edition for the Army Records Society, *Allenby in Palestine: The Middle East Correspondence of Field Marshal Viscount Allenby* (2004).[8]

Both Kitchener and Robertson are central to the discussion of strategy. Kitchener's insights as strategist if not his skills of military organisation have been re-assessed, as in George Cassar, *Kitchener: Architect of Victory* (1977).[9] Robertson also has a fine modern biography in David Woodward, *Field Marshal*

---

6 See also Elizabeth Greenhalgh, 'Myth and Memory: Sir Douglas Haig and the Imposition of Allied Unified Command in March 1918', *JMH* 68 (2004), 771–820.

7 See also Roy A. Prete, 'French Strategic Planning and the Deployment of the BEF in France in 1914', *Canadian Journal of History* 24 (1989), 42–62.

8 See also David Dutton, 'The Calais Conference of December 1915', *HJ* 21 (1978), 143–56; idem, 'The "Robertson Dictatorship" and the Balkan Campaign in 1916', *JSS* 9 (1986), 64–78; Brock Millman, '"A Counsel of Despair": British Strategy and War Aims, 1917–18', *JCH* 36 (2001), 241–70. For more on Allenby as field commander, see Jonathan Newell, 'Learning the Hard Way: Allenby in Egypt and Palestine, 1917–18', *JSS* 14 (1991), 363–87.

9 See also Keith Neilson, 'Kitchener: A Reputation Refurbished?' *Canadian Journal of History* 15 (1980), 207–27.

Sir William Robertson: Chief of the Imperial General Staff in the Great War (1998), and Woodward earlier published an Army Records Society edition of *The Military Correspondence of Field Marshal Sir William Robertson, Chief of the Imperial General Staff, 1915–18* (1989). Woodward remains the best overall guide to the troubled relationship between Lloyd George on the one hand and Haig and Robertson on the other in *Lloyd George and the Generals* (1983).[10]

The conduct of operations, particularly with regard to the British army on the Western Front, has become a major matter for debate amongst historians. The popular British image of a war mired in the mud of Passchendaele, and by the belief that men were condemned to walk slowly across No Man's Land into a hail of machine gun fire by callous and reactionary generals on the Somme, contrasts markedly with the academic image of an army transformed by late 1917 into a modern combined-arms force that had fully embraced modern technology. The academic debate on the so-called 'learning curve' on the Western Front, however, remains a lively one, interpretations varying on how quickly, and how evenly, lessons were disseminated and applied, and whether the imperative to change was directed by General Headquarters (GHQ) from above, or was generated by initiatives at lower levels. While German strategy often took little account of political realities, it is generally suggested that German operational concepts were in advance of those of the allies. Direct comparison between Germany and Britain is made by Martin Samuels in *Command or Control? Command, Training and Tactics in the British and German Armies, 1888–1918* (1995), and *Doctrine and Dogma: German and British Infantry Tactics in the First World War* (1992). Overall, however, the study of British doctrine has been confined to articles.[11]

The controversies surrounding the leadership of Sir Douglas Haig are central to the debate on the learning curve in the British army. The mantle of Haig's principal defender in the 1960s, John Terraine, has been taken up by Gary Sheffield in *Forgotten Victory: The First World War - Myths and Realities* (2002), and *The Chief: Douglas Haig and the British Army* (2011), Sheffield arguing that

---

10 See also David Woodward, 'Britain in a Continental War: The Civil-Military Debate over the Strategic Direction of the War of 1914–18', *Albion* 12 (1980), 37–65; idem, 'Did Lloyd George Starve the British Army of Men prior to the German Offensive of 21 March 1918?', *HJ* 27 (1984), 241–52.
11 See Jim Beach, 'Inspired by the General Staff: Doctrine Writing at British GHQ, 1917–18', *WH* 19 (2012), 464–91; Mike Berchtold, 'Command, Leadership and Doctrine on the Great War Battlefield: The Australian, British and Canadian Experience at the Battle of Arras, May 1917', *W&S* 32 (2013), 116–37.

change was generated from the top. Paddy Griffith, *Battle Tactics of the Western Front: The British Army's Art of Attack, 1916–1918* (1994); the essays in Paddy Griffith (ed.), *British Fighting Methods in the Great War* (1996); and those in Gary Sheffield and Dan Todman (eds), *Command and Control on the Western Front: the British Army's Experience, 1914–1918* (2005), make the case for marked improvement of British operational methods and a fairly uniform progression to improved operational planning. Emphasis is placed on doctrinal manuals produced in 1916 and 1917, which are seen as equal to those produced by the Germans. Of course, it is a matter of how far the manuals were followed in practice. Despite the qualified re-assessment of Haig and GHQ, however, the balance of the debate remains highly critical, casting the learning curve as distinctly uneven, and progress emanating as a result of pressures from below rather than from above. Peter Simkins, *From the Somme to Victory: The British Army's Experience on the Western Front, 1916–18* (2014) is a considered restatement of the 'learning curve', a phrase largely originated by Simkins himself.

The case against Haig is strongly made by Tim Travers, *The Killing Ground: The British Army, the Western Front and the Emergence of Modern Warfare, 1900–1918* (1987), and *How the War was Won: Command and Technology in the British Army on the Western Front, 1917–1918* (1992).[12] Travers emphasises inconsistencies in the way commanders veered between over-control and lack of guidance, and suggests subordinate commanders were capable of exercising more initiative in 1918 from the necessity of improvisation, and the sheer weight of allied material resources.

Travers has been supported by Robin Prior and Trevor Wilson in *Command on the Western Front: The Military Career of Sir Henry Rawlinson, 1914–18* (1992), *The Somme* (2005), and *Passchendaele: The Untold Story* (1996). They argue that the perceived improvement detected by other historians in artillery techniques and in tactical methods generally was highly uneven in its application through the army as a whole. J. Paul Harris, *Douglas Haig and the First World War* (2008), is

---

12 See also Tim Travers, 'The Offensive and the Problem of Innovation in British Military Thought, 1870–1915', *JCH* 13 (1978), 531–53; idem, 'The Hidden Army: Structural Problems in the British Officer Corps, 1900–18', *JCH* 17 (1982), 523–44; idem, 'Learning and Decision-Making on the Western Front, 1915–16: The British Example', *Canadian Journal of History* 18 (1983), 87–97; idem, 'A Particular Style of Command: Haig and GHQ, 1916–18', *JSS* 10 (1987), 363–76; idem, 'The Evolution of British Strategy and Tactics on the Western Front in 1981: GHQ, Manpower and Technology', *JMH* 54 (1990), 173–200; idem, 'Command and Leadership Styles in the British Army: The 1915 Gallipoli Model', *JCH* 29 (1994), 403–42.

a finely balanced and persuasive critique of Haig, and undoubtedly the best biography available, superseding Gerard De Groot, *Douglas Haig 1861–1928* (1988), which was not always sound on purely military aspects. Together with Sanders Marble, Harris has also examined the intelligent alternative to Haig's obsession with a technologically unobtainable breakthrough.[13] Jonathan Boff, *Wining and Losing on the Western Front: The British Third Army and the Defeat of Germany in 1918* (2012), again suggests the patchy nature of progress.[14] Both sides of the then emerging debate were put in Brian Bond and Terry Cave (eds), *Haig: A Reappraisal 70 Years On* (1999), but Haig's critics have the academic upper hand.

Assessment of the learning curve at different levels of command is offered by Brian Bond (ed.), *Look to your Front: Studies in the First World War* (1999); Nikolas Gardner, *Trial by Fire: Command and the BEF in 1914* (2003); Simon Robbins, *British Generalship on the Western Front, 1914–1918: Defeat into Victory* (2005); Andy Simpson, *Directing Operations: British Corps Commanders on the Western Front, 1914–18* (2006); and Mark Connelly, *Steady the Buffs: A Regiment, a Region and the Great War* (2006). Not withstanding the title, the latter is actually most concerned with the application of the learning curve at the lowest tactical level. The latest valuable contribution looking at all command levels from Sir John French down to battalion commanders in 1914 are the essays in Spencer Jones (ed.), *Stemming the Tide: Officers and Leadership in the British Expeditionary Force, 1914* (2013).[15]

Other than Haig, and Prior and Wilson's study of Rawlinson, particular leading figures have also been covered. Ian F. W. Beckett and Steven Corvi (eds), *Haig's Generals* (2006), provides an overview of the work done on Edmund Allenby, William Birdwood, Julian Byng, Hubert Gough, Henry Horne, Charles Monro, Herbert Plumer and Horace Smith-Dorrien. Since its publication, there have been some further studies of British generals including Simon Robbins, *The Silent General: Horne of the First Army - A Biography of Haig's Trusted Great War Comrade at Arms* (2007), supplementing his Army Records Society edition,

---

13 J. Paul Harris and Sanders Marble, 'The Step-by-Step Approach: British Military Thought and Operational Method on the Western Front, 1915–17', *WH* 15 (2008), 17–42.

14 See also Jonathan Boff, 'Combined Arms during the Hundred Days Campaign, August–November 1918', *WH* 17 (2010), 459–78.

15 See also Nik Gardner, 'Command in Crisis: The BEF and the Forest of Mormal, August 1914', *W&S* 16 (1998), 13–32; Nick Lloyd, 'With Faith and Without Fear: Sir Douglas Haig's Command of First Army during 1914', *JMH* 71 (2007), 1051–76.

The First World War Letters of General Lord Horne (2009); Andrew Syk (ed.), *The Military Papers of Lieutenant General Frederick Stanley Maude, 1914–17* (2012); and Mike Senior, *Lieutenant General Sir Richard Haking, XI Corps Commander, 1915–18: A Study in Corps Command* (2012). P. A. Pedersen, *Monash as Military Commander* (1985), and A. M. J. Hyatt, *General Sir Arthur Currie: A Military Biography* (1988), remain the best studies of the leading dominion commanders. There are also excellent studies of Sir John French and Sir Henry Wilson respectively in Richard Holmes, *The Little Field Marshal: A Life of Sir John French* (1981); and Keith Jeffery, *Field Marshal Sir Henry Wilson: A Political Soldier* (2006). The latter suggests that, while an intriguer, Wilson successfully oiled the wheels of the Anglo-French alliance at crucial moments although, as CIGS, he was compelled to match limited resources with widening commitments. Slightly older are Ian F. W. Beckett, *Johnnie Gough VC: A Biography of Brigadier-General Sir John Edmund Gough* (1989); Ian F. W. Beckett, *The Judgement of History: Sir Horace Smith-Dorrien, Lord French and 1914* (1993); and John Baynes, *Far from a Donkey: The Life of General Sir Ivor Maxse* (1995). Pushing the study of leadership down to the lower levels Christopher Moore-Blick, *Playing the Game: The British Junior Infantry Officer on the Western Front, 1914–18* (2011), based on a thesis, can be supplemented by another on NCOs.[16]

Of course, there are significant numbers of studies of campaigns and battles, many popular rather than academic. Academic studies on the Somme and Passchendaele by Prior and Wilson, and on the Somme by Philpott, have already been mentioned. In addition, there are Gary Sheffield, *The Somme* (2003), and Peter Liddle (ed.), *Passchendaele in Perspective: The Third Battle of Ypres* (1997), which needs to be treated with some caution as a result of unilateral editorial interventions that changed aspects of some contributors' essays. Among other academic studies of Western Front actions can be numbered Ian F. W. Beckett, *Ypres: The First Battle, 1914* (2004); Nicholas Lloyd, *Loos 1915* (2008); and Bryn Hammond, *Cambrai 1917: The Myth of the First Great Tank Battle* (2008). Much has been made of the often unacknowledged military successes of the British army between August and November 1918 and, in addition to those studies already cited, there is a useful summary in J. Paul Harris and Niall Barr, *Amiens to the Armistice: The BEF in the Hundred Days Campaign, 8 August to 11 November 1918* (1998). While it is also important for the issue of German morale, David Stevenson, *With Our Backs to the Wall: Victory and Defeat in 1918* (2011) is a major re-assessment of the military factors of account in the

---

16 Stephen Penny, 'Discipline and Morale: The British NCO on the Western Front, 1914–18', PhD dissertation, De Montfort University, 2004.

last phase of the war. Mention should be made of the proceedings of two of the annual Chief of Army Staff conferences in Australia, Peter Dennis and Jeffrey Grey (eds), *Defining Victory, 1918* (1999), and Dennis and Grey (eds), *1917. Tactics, Training and Technology* (2007), which contain important essays on operational issues, including the contribution of the Dominion corps. They can be read in parallel to the studies of evolving practice in Bill Rawling, *Surviving Trench Warfare: Technology and the Canadian Corps, 1914–18* (1992); Shane Schreiber, *Shock Army of the British Empire: The Canadian Corps in the Last Hundred Days of the Great War* (1997), and Kenneth Radley, *Get Tough, Stay Tough: Shaping the Canadian Corps, 1914–18* (2014), though it should be emphasised that progress was general by 1917–18 and not confined to the Dominion formations as sometimes suggested.[17]

Looking beyond the Western Front, there are fine modern studies of the Gallipoli campaign by Tim Travers, *Gallipoli, 1915* (2002), and Robin Prior, *Gallipoli: The End of the Myth* (2009), which both draw upon recently available Ottoman archives. Cultural as well as historiographical aspects of Gallipoli are among the topics considered in Jenny Macleod (ed.) *Gallipoli: Making History* (2004), and Macleod's own monograph, *Reconsidering Gallipoli* (2004).[18] Ross Anderson, *The Forgotten Front 1914–1918: The East African Campaign* (2004), is a good example of new interest in the 'side shows'. Alan Wakefield and Simon Moody, *Under the Devil's Eye: Britain's Forgotten Army at Salonika, 1915–18* (2004), is a solid study by two museum professionals albeit more intended for general readers. There are also popular works on the British campaign in Italy but this would benefit from some academic attention, and there is now a doctoral thesis on the British army in Italy.[19] The campaign in Mesopotamia now has Charles Townshend, *When God Made Hell: The British Invasion of Mesopotamia and the Creation of Modern Iraq, 1914–21* (2010).[20] The Palestine campaign tends to be dominated by popular accounts, including many related to T. E. Lawrence,

---

17 See also Ian M. Brown, '"Not Glamorous, But Effective": The Canadian Corps and the Set-Piece Attack, 1917–1918', *JMH* 58 (1994), 421–44.

18 See also Jenny Macleod, 'General Sir Ian Hamilton and the Dardanelles Commission', *WH* 8 (2001), 418–41.

19 John Dillon, 'The Experience of the British Army in Italy in World War One', PhD dissertation, University of Reading, 2013. See also Ross Anderson, 'The Battle of Tanga, 2–5 November 1914', *WH* 8 (2001), 294–32; Anne Samson, 'Britain, South Africa and the East African Campaign, 1914–18: The Union Comes of Age', PhD dissertation, University of London, 2004.

20 See also Nik Gardner, 'Charles Townshend's Advance on Baghdad: The British Offensive in Mesopotamia, September-November 1915', *WH* 20 (2013), 182–200.

the best study of whom being Jeremy Wilson, *Lawrence of Arabia: The Authorised Biography* (1989). There are, however, the studies of Allenby mentioned above, and also Jonathan Newell's unpublished thesis on the period prior to Allenby taking command, as well as a welcome new study of morale in James Kitchen, *The British Imperial Army in the Middle East: Morale and Military Identity in the Sinai and Palestine Campaigns, 1916–18* (2014), which adds to Kristian Ulrichsen, *Logistics and Politics of the British Campaigns in the Middle East, 1914–22* (2011), and Edward Woodfin, *Camp and Combat on the Sinai and Palestine Front: The Experience of the British Empire Soldier, 1916–18* (2012).[21]

Turning to the operational level of war, Sanders Marble, *British Artillery on the Western Front in the First World War* (2013), is an important study of the key to relative operational success. It adds to Hubert C. Johnson, *Breakthrough: Tactics, Technology and the Search for Victory on the Western Front* (1994), and the pioneering work by Shelford Bidwell and Dominick Graham, *Firepower: British Army Weapons and Theories of War, 1904–45* (1982), which concentrated on artillery developments.[22] J. Paul Harris, *Men, Ideas and Tanks: British Military Thought and Armoured Forces, 1903–39* (1995), examines the concepts behind what was decidedly not a breakthrough weapon in practice, and is especially critical of the developing theories of J. F. C. Fuller. David Childs, *A Peripheral Weapon? The Production and Employment of British Tanks in the First World War* (1999), has a focus on the War Office Tank Board as playing a significant role in the evolution of a more effective weapon by 1918.[23] Works relevant to the Great War on the only actual breakthrough weapon, cavalry, have been previously mentioned. To these can be added David Kenyon, *Horsemen in No Man's Land: British Cavalry and Trench Warfare, 1914–1918* (2011), which arguably pushes revisionism too far.

Another weapon of limited potential was gas, since all armies were able increasingly to operate in a gas environment. For the British and Dominion armies it is covered by Albert Palazzo, *Seeking Victory on the Western Front: The British Army and Chemical Warfare in World War I* (2000), which suggests that the British were more innovative than the Germans in gas development overall. Tim Cook, *No Place to Run: The Canadian Corps and Gas Warfare in the First World War* (1999), emphasises the ability of troops to work in a gas environment

---

21 Jonathan Newell, 'British Military Policy in Egypt and Palestine, August 1914–June 1917', PhD dissertation, University of London, 1990.

22 See also Albert Palazzo, 'The British Army's Counter Battery Staff Office and Control of the Enemy in World War I', *JMH* 63 (1999), 55–74.

23 See also Tim Travers, 'Could the Tanks of 1918 have been War-winners for the British Expeditionary Force?' *JCH* 27 (1992), 389–406.

by 1917–18.[24] Technical developments are covered in Anthony Saunders, *Reinventing Warfare, 1914–18: Novel Munitions and Tactics of Trench Warfare* (2012), and Saunders has also looked at a controversial British practice, *Raiding on the Western Front* (2012).[25] The Royal Flying Corps, of course, began the war as part of the army and, as well as its primary roles in reconnaissance and observation, air fighting, and, later, in strategic bombing, it eventually developed a ground attack role.[26] Brian Hall's articles on pre-war experiments in wireless have been noted in a previous section, but his thesis is actually on the Great War, and an article has recently appeared.[27]

Other specialised monographs include Ian M. Brown, *British Logistics on the Western Front, 1914–18* (1998), which emphasises the vital contribution of logistics to the final victory in 1918, and Mark Harrison, *The Medical War: British Military Medicine in the First World War* (2010), both of which deservedly won the Templer Medal of the Society for Army Historical Research as the best books on British military history in their respective years of publication. Harrison in particular is a sure guide to the wider range of studies undertaken on medical aspects of the war.[28]

---

24 See also Simon Jones, 'Gas Warfare: The British Defensive Measures – The Second Battle of Ypres', *Stand To* 14 (1985), 15–23; idem, 'Under a Green Sea: The Defensive British Response to Gas Warfare', *The Great War* 1–2 (1989–90), 126–32, 14–21; Tim Cook, 'Against God-Inspired Conscience: The Perception of Gas Warfare as a Weapon of Mass Destruction, 1915–39', *W&S* 18 (2000), 49–69; Yigal Sheffy, 'The Chemical Dimension of the Gallipoli Campaign: Introducing Chemical Warfare in the Middle East', *WH* 12 (2005), 278–317.

25 See also D. M. Leeson, 'The British Army's Percussion Hand Grenades, 1914–16', *First World War Studies* 1 (2010), 81–102. By contrast, see Paul Hodges, 'They don't like it up them: Bayonet Fetishisation in the British Army during the First World War', *Journal of War and Cultural Studies* 1 (2008), 123–38.

26 See David Jordan, 'The Army Co-operation Missions of the Royal Flying Corps/ RAF, 1914–18', PhD dissertation, University of Birmingham, 1997.

27 Brian Hall, 'The BEF and Communications on the Western Front, 1914–18', PhD dissertation, University of Salford, 2009; idem, 'Technical Adaptation in a Global Conflict: The British Army and Communications beyond the Western Front', *JMH* 78 (2014), 37–71; idem, 'Technological Adaptation in a Global Conflict: the British Army and Communications Beyond the Western Front, 1914–18', *JMH* 78 (2014), 37=72.

28 See also Suzann Buckley, 'The Failure to Resolve the Problem of Venereal Disease among the Troops in Britain during World War One', in Brian Bond and Ian Roy (eds), *War and Society: A Yearbook of Military History* (London: Croom Helm, 1975), pp. 65–85; Robert L. Atenstaedt, 'The Trench Disease: The British Medical Response to the Great War', DPhil dissertation, University of Oxford, 2005.

Military intelligence is increasingly an evolving area for study. As noted in a previous section, Jim Beach, *Haig's Intelligence: GHQ and the German Army, 1916–1918* (2013) is particularly important.[29] Previously, there was the not altogether satisfactory Michael Occleshaw, *Armour Against Fate: British Military Intelligence in the First World War* (1989) and the densely technical selection of documents edited for the Army Records Society in John Ferris (ed.), *The British Army and Signals Intelligence during the First World War* (1992).[30] Michael Dockrill and David French (eds), *Strategy and Intelligence: British Policy during the First World War* (1996), has rather less on intelligence than might be supposed from the title. Perhaps surprisingly, there has been quite full coverage of British military intelligence in the Middle East through Yigal Sheffy, *British Military Intelligence in the Palestine Campaign, 1914–18* (1998), and chapters in Michael Handel (ed.), *Intelligence and Military Operations* (1990).[31]

There has also been a spate of doctoral dissertations on the operations of various divisions to supplement Andrew Iarocci, *Shoestring Soldiers: The 1st Canadian Division at War, 1914–15* (2008); and Robert Stevenson, *To Win the Battle: The 1st Australian Division in the Great War, 1914–18* (2013). While offering considerably more than many of the 'Pals' battalion histories produced for the popular market, the problem is that such theses need to be incorporated into a wider tactical study that can draw their conclusions together.[32]

---

29 See also Jim Beach, 'British Intelligence and German Tanks, 1916–18', *WH* 14 (2007), 454–75; idem, 'Intelligent Civilians in Uniform: The BEF's Intelligence Corps Officers, 1914–18', *W&S* 27 (2008), 1–22.

30 See also David French, 'Sir John French's Secret Service on the Western Front, 1914–15', *JSS* 7 (1984), 423–40; John Ferris, 'The British Army and Signals Intelligence in the Field during the First World War', *INS* 3 (1988), 23–48.

31 See also Richard Popplewell, 'British Intelligence in Mesopotamia, 1914–16', *INS* 5 (1990), 139–72; Andrekos Varnava, 'British Military Intelligence in Cyprus during the Great War' *WH* 19 (2012), 353–78.

32 Simon Peaple, 'The 46th (North Midland) Division TF on the Western Front, 1915–18', PhD dissertation, University of Birmingham, 2003; J. Roberts, 'Killer Butterflies: Infantry Combat Behaviour and Morale in the 19th (Western) Division during the Great War', PhD dissertation, University of Coventry, 2004; Craig French, 'The 51st Highland Division in the First World War', PhD dissertation, University of Glasgow, 2006; Stephen Sandford, 'The 10th (Irish) Division in the First World War', PhD dissertation, Queen's Belfast, 2008; Chris Forrest, 'The 52nd (Lowland) Division in the Great War, 1914–18', PhD dissertation, University of Salford, 2010; Alan Thomas, 'British 8th Infantry Division on the Western Front, 1914–18', PhD dissertation, University of Birmingham, 2010. See also Andrew Whitmarsh, 'The Development of Infantry Tactics in the British 12th (Eastern) Division, 1915–1918', *Stand To* 48 (Jan. 1997), 28–32.

As already suggested in relation to the learning curve, the Dominion perspective is significant and the historiography of the military experience of the Dominions and Colonies reflects the same wide coverage accorded to aspects of the Great War in Britain. Those general and more specialised texts mentioned previously are guides to the wider literature. The wider Indian army context is covered in Anirudh Deshpande, *British Military Policy in India, 1900–45: Colonial Constraints and Declining Power* (2005); and Kaushik Roy, (ed.), *The Indian Army in the Two World Wars* (2011).[33] The problematic performance of the Indian army on the Western Front is the subject of a popular account, Gordon Corrigan, *Sepoys in the Trenches: The Indian Corps on the Western Front, 1914–15* (1999), which is now supplanted by the academic study, George Morton Jack, *The Indian Army on the Western Front: India's Expeditionary Force to France and Belgium in the First World War* (2014). Jeffrey Greenhut, whose thesis remains unpublished, undertook some pioneering work on the Indian Corps and there is also another useful thesis on wartime expansion.[34]

David Omissi, *Indian Voices of the Great War: Soldiers' Letters, 1914–18* (1999) is an important source for the experience of ordinary Indian soldiers, albeit that the censors' reports used are as recorded by regimental scribes and then translated for the benefit of the censors. Those from Punjabi soldiers and the Punjab experience have also been examined.[35] An American thesis, which has only just been completed, extends the study of the Indian soldier abroad from the Western Front to hospitals in Britain and France and to POW camps in Germany, while there is also another American thesis exploring concepts of masculinity within

---

33 See also DeWitt Ellinwood, 'Ethnicity in a Colonial Asian Army: British Policy, War and the Indian Army, 1914–18', in DeWitt Ellinwood and Cynthia Enloe (eds), *Ethnicity and the Military in Asia* (London: Transaction Books, 1981), pp. 89–143.

34 Jeffery Greenhut, 'Race, Sex and War: The Impact of Race and Sex on Morale and Health Services for the Indian Corps on the Western Front, 1914', *Military Affairs* 45 (1981), 71–4; idem, 'The Imperial Reserve: The Indian Corps on the Western Front, 1914–15', *JICH* 12 (1983), 54–73; idem, 'The Imperial Reserve: The Indian Infantry on the Western Front, 1914–18', PhD dissertation, University of Kansas, 1978; I. D. Leask, 'The Expansion of the Indian Army during the Great War', PhD dissertation, University of London, 1989. See also Mark Harrison, 'Disease, Discipline and Dissent: The Indian Army in France and England, 1914–15', in Mark Harrison, Roger Cooter and Steve Sturdy (eds), *Medicine and Modern Warfare* (Amsterdam: Rodopi, 1999), pp. 185–203.

35 Susan VanKoski, 'Letters Home 1915–16: Punjabi Soldiers Reflect on War and Life in Europe and Their Meanings for Home and Self', *International Journal of Punjab Studies* 2 (1995), 43–63; Tan Tai-Yong, 'An Imperial Home Front: Punjab and the First World War', *JMH* 64 (2000), 371–410.

the Indian army.[36] Equally Nikolas Gardner and Kaushik Roy cover difficult experiences in Mesopotamia.[37]

The Singapore Mutiny of 1915 involving the 5th (Native) Light Infantry has been the subject of perhaps excessive interest, with more recent studies such as Tilak Raj Sareen (ed.), *Secret Documents on the Singapore Mutiny, 1915* (1995), and Kuwajima Sho, *Mutiny in Singapore: War, Anti-War and the War for India's Independence* (2006), tending to give it an external and political context it lacked, since familiar internal issues were at its root.[38] Nonetheless, the Indian army did not break in either world war.[39]

By contrast, one aspect of the contribution of Indian manpower to the Great War that has been neglected is the question of the Indian labour contingents on the Western Front and elsewhere. These deserve far more attention than they have received thus far, work on the Chinese Labour Corps being far more prominent as explored by one popular title, Michael Summerskill, *China on the Western Front: Britain's Chinese Workforce in the First World War* (1982); and the recent academic work, Xu Guoqi, *Strangers on the Western Front: Chinese Workers*

---

36 Andrew Tait Jarboe, 'Soldiers of Empire: Indian Sepoys in and beyond the Imperial Metropole during the First World War, 1914–19', PhD, North-eastern University, 2013; R. A. McLain, 'The Body Politic: Imperial Masculinity, the Great War and the Struggle for the Indian Self, 1914–18', PhD, University of Illinois at Urbana-Champaign, 2002.

37 See also Nikolas Gardner, 'Sepoys and the Siege of Kut-al-Amara, 1915–16', *WH* 11 (2004), 307–26; Kaushik Roy, 'The Army in India in Mesopotamia from 1916 to 1918: Tactics, Technology and Logistics Reconsidered', in Ian F. W. Beckett (ed.), *1917: Beyond the Western Front* (Leiden: Brill, 2009), pp. 131–58; idem, 'From Defeat to Victory: Logistics of the Campaign in Mesopotamia, 1914–18', *First World War Studies* 1 (2010), 35–55.

38 Nicholas Tarling, 'The Singapore Mutiny, 1915', *Journal of the Malaysian Branch of the Royal Asiatic Society* 55 (1982), 26–59; R. W. E. Harper and H. Miller, *Singapore Mutiny* (1984); Ian F. W. Beckett, 'The Singapore Mutiny of February 1915', *JSAHR* 62 (1984), 132–55; Christine Doran, 'Gender Matters in the Singapore Mutiny, 1915', *Sojurn* 17 (2002), 76–93; Kuwajima Sho, 'Indian Mutiny in Singapore, 1915: People Who Observed the Scene and People Who Heard the News', *New Zealand Journal of Asian Studies* 11 (2009), 375–84; Leon Comber, 'The Singapore Mutiny (1915) and the Genesis of Political Intelligence in Singapore', *INS* 24 (2009), 529–41; Tim Harper, 'Singapore 1915 and the Birth of the Asian Underground', *MAS: First View* [online content] (August 2013), 1–30.

39 See Raymond Callahan, 'The Indian Army, Total War and the Dog That Didn't Bark in the Night', in Jane Hathaway (ed.), *Rebellion, Repression, Reinvention: Mutiny in Comparative Perspective* (Westport, CT: Greenwood, 2001), pp. 119–30.

in the Great War (2011). African carrier corps in British pay have also been examined by Geoffrey Hodges, *The Carrier Corps: Military Labor in the East African Campaign, 1914–18* (1986), and in essays in Melvin E Page (ed.), *Africa and the First World War* (1987). Albert Grundlingh, *Fighting Their Own War: South African Blacks in the First World War* (1987), should also be consulted for the impact of war in southern Africa.[40]

Armies' effective functioning depended upon reliable manpower. Institutional studies have cast some revealing light on the social and psychological aspects of the soldier's wartime experience, with significant consequences for the understanding of nations at war. In the case of Britain, as casualties mounted, the challenge of war resulted in the imposition of conscription, a major break with all pre-war expectations with enormous social implications. General manpower problems and the slow evolution of a coherent manpower policy have been examined by Keith Grieves, *The Politics of Manpower, 1914–1918* (1988).[41] Ian F. W. Beckett and Keith Simpson (eds), *A Nation in Arms: A Social Study of the British Army in the First World War* (1985), established the parameters for the study of the 'nation in arms', including the need to take account of regulars, Territorials, the New Armies and conscripts, though the latter were not accorded a separate essay. It was further illuminated by the outstanding study of the raising and training of the 'New Armies', Peter Simkins, *Kitchener's Army: The Raising of the New Armies, 1914–1916* (1988). Both incorporated the first studies into local recruitment such as J. M. Osborne, *The Voluntary Recruiting Movement in Britain, 1914–16* (1982), which concentrated largely on Bristol, and, therefore, shed light on the supposed 'rush to the colours' in 1914.[42]

---

40 See also Donald Savage and J. Forbes Munro, 'Carrier Corps Recruitment in the British East African Protectorate, 1914–18', *JAH* 7 (1966), 313–432.; B. P. Willan, 'The South African Native Labour Contingent in France, 1916–18', *JAH* 19 (1978), 61–86; Geoffrey Hodges, 'African Manpower Statistics for British Forces in East Africa, 1914–18', *JAH* 19 (1978), 101–16; David Killingray and James Matthews, 'Beasts of Burden: British West African Carriers in the First World War', *Canadian Journal of African Studies* 13 (1979), 6–23.

41 See also Keith Grieves, 'Total War: The Quest for a British Manpower Policy, 1917–18', *JSS* 9 (1986), 79–95.

42 See also Peter Dewey, 'Military Recruiting and the British Labour Force during the First World War', *HJ* 27 (1984), 199–224; Adrian Gregory, 'British War Enthusiasm in 1914: A Reassessment', in Gail Braybon (ed.), *Evidence, History and the Great War: Historians and the Impact of 1914–18* (Oxford: Berghahn Books, 2003), pp. 67–85.

Subsequent work on British reactions to the outbreak of war and the impact on recruitment have included David Silbey, *The British Working Class and Enthusiasm for War, 1914–16* (2005), and Catriona Pennell, *A Kingdom United: Popular Responses to the Outbreak of the First World War in Britain and Ireland* (2012). Subsequently, a whole series of important doctoral dissertations and journal articles has illuminated aspects of local recruitment in various regions.[43] As with the divisional studies, however, it really now requires an over-reaching synopsis to draw this material together, and to relate it to the other existing published case studies. As already indicated, studies of individual units of a popular nature - especially 'Pals' battalions - have been numerous. Academic studies that add materially to the examination of local responses to war, however, include K. W. Mitchinson, *Gentlemen and Officers: The Impact and Experience of War on a Territorial Regiment* (1994); and Helen McCartney, *Citizen Soldiers: The Liverpool Territorials in the First World War* (2005).

Recruitment in Ireland has been a particular interest, not least the extent to which either the rival pre-war paramilitaries, the Ulster Volunteer Force and the Irish Volunteers, enlisted into the wartime army. Apart from Timothy Bowman, *Carson's Army: The Ulster Volunteer Force, 1910–22* (2007); Nick Perry (ed.), *Major General Oliver Nugent and the Ulster Division, 1915–1918* (2007); and Terry Denman, *Ireland's Unknown Soldiers: the 16th (Irish) Division in the Great War, 1914–1918* (1992), much of the literature takes the form of articles. It should be noted, however, that David Fitzpatrick's analysis of recruitment figures

---

43 Keith Grieves, 'Lowther's Lambs: Rural Paternalism and Voluntary Recruitment in the First World War', *Rural History* 4 (1993), 55–75; John Hartigan, 'Volunteering in the First World War: The Birmingham Experience, August 1914–May 1915', *Midland History* 24 (1999), 167–86; Bonnie White, 'Volunteerism and Early Recruitment Efforts in Devonshire, 1914–15', *HJ* 52 (2009), 641–66; M. D. Blanch, 'Nation, Empire and the Birmingham Working Class, 1899–1914', PhD dissertation, University of Birmingham, 1975; Patricia Morris, 'Leeds and the Amateur Military Tradition: The Leeds Rifles and Their Antecedents, 1859–1918', PhD dissertation, University of Leeds, 1983; Kit Good, 'England Goes to War, 1914–15', PhD dissertation, University of Liverpool, 2002; Helen Townsley, 'The First World War and Voluntary Recruitment: A Forum for Regional Identity? An Analysis of the Nature, Expression and Significance of Regional Identity in Hull, 1900–18', PhD dissertation, University of Sussex, 2008; Andrew Gale, 'The West Country and the First World War', PhD dissertation, University of Lancaster, 2008; and Stuart Hallifax, 'Citizens at War: The Experience of the Great War in Essex, 1914–18', DPhil dissertation, University of Oxford, 2010.

is flawed.[44] Among many studies of the greatest internal threat posed to British government during the war, namely the Easter Rising, the best are Michael Foy and Brian Barton, *The Easter Rising* (1999), and Charles Townshend, *Easter 1916: The Irish Rebellion* (2006).

Scotland is well covered in general works and two divisional studies mentioned previously as well as a specific study of recruitment.[45] For Wales, however, there is no general academic study, and only a few suggestive additional works, all but one unpublished.[46]

---

44 Patrick Callan, 'Recruiting for the British Army in Ireland during the First World War', *Irish Sword* 17 (1987–8), 42–56; Terry Denman, 'The Catholic Irish Soldier in the First World War: The Racial Environment', *Irish Historical Studies* 27 (1991), 352–65; David Fitzpatrick, 'The Logic of Collective Sacrifice: Ireland and the British Army, 1914–1918', *HJ* 38 (1995), 1017–30; Nick Perry, 'Nationality in the Irish Infantry Regiments in the First World War', *W&S* 12 (1994), 65–95; idem, 'Maintaining Regimental Identity in the Great War: The Case of Irish Infantry Regiments', *Stand To* 54 (1998), 5–11; Timothy Bowman, 'Composing Divisions: The Recruitment of Ulster and National Volunteers into the British Army in 1914', *Causeway* 2 (1995), 24–27; idem, 'The Irish Recruiting and Anti-Recruiting Campaigns, 1914–1916', in Bertrand Taithe and Tim Thornton (eds), *Propaganda, Political Rhetoric and Identity, 1300–2000* (Stroud: Sutton Publishing, 1999), pp. 223–38; idem, 'The Ulster Volunteer Force and the Formation of the 36th (Ulster) Division', *Irish Historical Studies* 32 (2001), 498–518; idem, 'Officering Kitchener's Armies: A Case Study of the 36th (Ulster) Division', *WH* 16 (2009), 189–212; James McConel, 'Recruiting Sergeants for John Bull? Irish Nationalist MPs and Enlistment during the Early Months of the Great War', *WH* 14 (2007), 408–38; Richard Grayson, 'Military History from the Street: New Methods for Researching First World War Service in the British Military', *WH* 21 (2004), 465–95; idem, 'Ireland's National Memory of the First World War: Forgotten Aspects of the Battle of Messines, June 1917', *BJMH* 1 (2014), 48–65; S. G. M. Hughes, 'Northern Irish Regiments in the Great War: Culture, Mythology, Politics and National Identity', PhD dissertation, University of Wales, 1999.

45 Derek Rutherford Young, 'Voluntary Recruitment in Scotland, 1914–16', PhD dissertation, University of Glasgow, 2001.

46 Clive Hughes, 'Army Recruiting in Gwynedd, 1914–16', MA dissertation, University of Wales, 1983; Gervase Phillips, 'Dai Bach Y Soldiwr: Welsh Soldiers in the British Army, 1914–18', *Llafur* 6 (1993), 94–105; Richard Wood, 'The South Wales Miners' Contribution to the Tunnelling Companies on the Western Front during the Great War', PhD dissertation, University of Swansea, 2012.

Conscripts have been largely neglected beyond the wholly inadequate Ilana Bet-el, *Conscripts* (2003), which betrays little understanding of the British army, or of the differences between 'Derbyites' and true conscripts.[47] Initially, most attention on conscription itself focused on the small minority of conscientious objectors when only 16,500 claims for exemption were made on such grounds. Older studies of conscientious objection include John Rae, *Conscience and Politics: The British Government and the Conscientious Objector to Military Service, 1916–19* (1970), and T. C. Kennedy, *The Hound of Conscience: A History of the No-Conscription Fellowship* (1981).[48] Detailed analysis of the military tribunal system - traditionally portrayed as passive instruments of the military authorities - has been bedevilled by the haphazard survival of archives but, based on the wealth remaining for Northamptonshire, James McDermott, *British Military Service Tribunals, 1916–18* (2011), shows tribunals responsive to local needs, and that it was occupation that most determined exemption. His transformational work can be supplemented with some other local studies, but there are substantial unexploited archives for Cardiganshire, Middlesex, Peebles and part of Warwickshire.[49]

One factor explaining the uneven application of conscription is the simple fact that large numbers of men in working class Britain were physically unfit for military

---

47 See, however, Ian F. W. Beckett, 'The Real Unknown Army: British Conscripts, 1916–19', *The Great War* 2 (1989), 4–13.

48 See James McDermott, 'Conscience and the Military Service Tribunals in the First World War: Experiences in Northamptonshire', *WH* 17 (2010), 60–85; A. R. Mack, 'Conscription and Conscientious Objection in Leeds and York during the First World War', MPhil dissertation, University of York, 1983.

49 Peter Ashley-Smith, 'Kineton and the Military Tribunals, 1915–1918', *Warwickshire History* 13 (2005), 15–24; Keith Grieves, 'Military Tribunal Papers: The Case of Leek Tribunal in the First World War', *Archives* 16 (1983), 145–50; idem, 'Mobilising Manpower: Ardenshaw Tribunal in the First World War', *Manchester Region History Review* 3 (1989–90), 21–29; Adrian Gregory, 'Military Service Tribunals, Civil Society in Action, 1916–18', in Jose Harris (ed.), *Civil Society in British History: Ideas, Identities, Institutions* (Oxford: Oxford University Press, 2003), pp. 177–90; C. Housden, 'Kingston's Military Tribunal, 1916–18', *Occasional Papers in Local History* 2/04 (Centre for Local History Studies, Kingston University, 2004); Ivor Slocombe, 'Recruitment into the Armed Forces during the First World War: The Work of Military Tribunals in Wiltshire', *The Local Historian* 30 (2000), 105–23; and Peter Spinks, 'The War Courts: The Stratford-upon-Avon Borough Tribunal, 1916–18', *The Local Historian* 32 (2002), 377–92.

service. Before becoming associated with studies of commemoration, Jay Winter undertook some important early studies on social aspects of the impact of wartime recruitment that made this clear, the fruits appearing in Jay Winter, *The Great War and the British People* (1986).[50] One manifestation of pre-war deprivation was the appearance of the 'Bantam' battalions comprising men enlisted below the normal minimum height, previously tackled only in a popular account but now examined by Peter Simkins.[51] Health tended to be equated with stature and there was also a certain bias shown towards those who were manifestly not Anglo-Saxon, such as Russian and East European Jews, paradoxically also often castigated for declining to come forward voluntarily to enlist. Martin Watts, *The Jewish Legion and the First World War* (2004) provides an analysis of those, mostly from Palestine, enlisted into Jewish units of the British army.

Those who enlisted despite being too young to do so have attracted some popular interest but the subject would benefit from an academic approach. Those over military age, however, who joined a revived volunteer force in the form of the Volunteer Training Corps and the other reserve formation for home defence, are well covered in K. W. Mitchinson, *Defending Albion: Britain's Home Army, 1908–19* (2005).[52]

Women were another additional resource and, of course, the wartime role of women has been extensively investigated. Given the general studies previously mentioned in this and earlier sections on women's war work, it is only work on those women employed directly by the army that will be covered here. The general field is surveyed by Lucy Noakes, *Women in the British Army: War and*

---

50 See also Jay Winter, 'Britain's Lost Generation of the First World War', *Population Studies* 31 (1977), 449–66; idem, 'Some Aspects of the Demographic Consequences of the First World War in Britain', *Population Studies* 30 (1976), 539-62; idem, 'Military Fitness and Civilian Health in Britain during the First World War', *JCH* 15 (1980), 211–44.

51 Peter Simkins, '"Each One a Pocket Hercules": The Bantam Experiment and the Case of the 35th Division', in Sanders Marble (ed.), *Scraping the Barrel: The Military Use of Substandard Manpower, 1860–1969* (New York: Fordham University Press, 2012), pp. 79–104.

52 See also Ian F. W. Beckett, 'Aspects of a Nation in Arms: Britain's Volunteer Training Corps in the Great War', *Revue Internationale d'Histoire Militaire* 63 (1985), 27–39; J. M. Osborne, 'Defining Their Own Patriotism: British Volunteer Training Corps in the First World War', *JCH* 23 (1988), 59–75; Brock Millman, 'British Home Defence Planning and Civil Dissent, 1917–18', *WH* 5 (1998), 204–32.

the Gentle Sex, 1907–48 (2006).[53] To those studies of gender issues previously mentioned may be added Janet Watson, *Fighting Different Wars: Experience, Memory and the First World War in Britain* (2004), which examines different male and female perspectives on war experience. Masculinity itself is addressed by Joanna Bourke, *Dismembering the Male: Men's Bodies, Britain and the Great War* (1996); Jessica Meyer, *Men of War: Masculinity and the First World War in Britain* (2012); and by Michael Roper, *The Secret Battle: Emotional Survival in the Great War* (2009), who re-interprets the perceived paternalism between officers and men as more akin to 'maternalism'.[54]

The issue of how the morale of British citizen soldiers was sustained in the face of modern industrialised warfare when other armies collapsed has also attracted a great deal of interest. A pioneering study was John Fuller, *Troop Morale and Popular Culture in the British and Dominion Armies, 1914–18* (1991), which used contemporary trench newspapers to suggest that the effective recreation of British popular culture behind the lines played a significant role. Any idea that there was either a distinct 'war generation' or any real separation between the citizen soldier and civilian society has long been disproved. Graham Seal, *The Soldiers' Press: Trench Journals in the First World War* (2013) greatly expands knowledge of the number of British trench journals but strives too hard to say something that differs from Fuller's analysis. It is also clear that those 'at home' were far from uninformed as to the conditions at the front.[55] Gary Sheffield, *Leadership in the Trenches: Officer-Man Relations, Morale and Discipline in the British Army in the Era of the First World War* (2000) turns the

---

53 See also Jenny Gould, 'Women's Military Service in First World War Britain', in Margaret Higonet, Jane Jenson, Sonya Michel and Margaret Collins Weitz (eds), *Behind the Lines: Gender and the Two World Wars* (New Haven, CT: Yale University Press, 1987), pp. 114–25; Elizabeth Crosthwait, 'The Girl Behind the Man Behind the Gun: The Women's Army Auxiliary Corps, 1914–18', in Leonore Davidoff and Belinda Westover (eds), *Our Work, Our Lives, Our Words* (Basingstoke: Palgrave, 1986), pp. 161–81; Doron Lamm, 'Emily Goes to War: Explaining the Recruitment to the Women's Army Auxiliary Corps', in B. Melman (ed.), *Borderlines: Gender and Identities in War and Peace* (London: Routledge, 1998), pp. 377–95; Krisztina Robert, 'Gender, Class and Patriotism: Women's Paramilitary Units in First World War Britain', *IHR* 19 (1997), 52–65.

54 See also Margaret Millman, 'In the Shadow of War: Continuities and Discontinuities in the Construction of the Masculine Identities of British Soldiers, 1914–24', PhD dissertation, University of Greenwich, 2003.

55 See Eric F. Schneider, 'The British Red Cross Wounded and Missing Enquiry Bureau: A Case of Truth-Telling in the Great War', *WH* 4 (1997), 296–315.

spotlight on the paternalism expected of the British officer that created a culture of dependency, but also mitigated harsher aspects of discipline. Timothy Bowman, *Irish Regiments in the Great War: Discipline and Morale* (2003) engages with the more general debates on wartime morale and discipline in the British and other armies, and on the impact of ethnicity on military prowess, demonstrating that breaches of discipline in Irish regiments were relatively minor and certainly not politicised. The most recent study is the impressive Alex Watson, *Enduring the Great War: Combat, Morale and Collapse in the German and British Armies, 1914–18* (2008), which finds similar 'coping strategies' in the British and German armies, concluding that British confidence in their ability to win and growing material superiority proved the stronger.[56] Clive Emsley, *Soldier, Sailor, Beggarman, Thief: Crime and the British Armed Services since 1914* (2013), considers criminal offences committed by servicemen during, and also immediately after, both world wars.

Discipline and morale has also figured largely in studies of the Anzac Corps and the relationship of Australians and, to a far lesser extent, New Zealanders, to British disciplinary norms. Paul Baker, *King and Country Call: New Zealanders, Conscription and the Great War* (1988), and Christopher Pugsley, *On the Fringe of Hell: New Zealanders and Military Discipline in the First World War* (1991), are important studies, New Zealanders being subject to the British Army Act in terms of the potential for being executed when Australians were not. The 'Anzac myth' is certainly examined by all those general texts on Australia at war mentioned previously, which also have a full bibliography of journal literature. There has been a great deal of popular material published in Australia that perpetuates the Anzac myth of colonial 'supermen' imbued by a 'bush ethos' of egalitarian 'mateship', and which invariably portrays Australians as victims of British military incompetence. It was a process effectively begun by the Australian official historian, C. E. W. Bean, and is still continued in reference to actions at Gallipoli in 1915 and Fromelles in 1916, as well as in the glorification of the Australian mounted units in Palestine. Bean's influence is explored in the essays of Ken Inglis as collected in John Lack (ed.), *Anzac Remembered: Selected Writings of K. S. Inglis* (1998); Alistair

---

56 See also Alex Watson and Patrick Porter, 'Bereaved and Aggrieved: Combat Motivation and the Ideology of Sacrifice in the First World War', *Historical Research* 83 (2010), 146–64; Edward Madigan, 'Sticking to a Hateful Task: Resilience, Humour and British Understanding of Combatant Courage, 1914–18', *WH* 20 (2013), 76–98; J. Brent Wilson, 'The Morale and Discipline of the BEF, 1914–18', MA dissertation, University of New Brunswick, 1978.

Thomson, *Anzac Memories: Living with a Legend* (1994); J. F. Williams, *Anzacs, the Media and the Great War* (1999); and Bruce Scates, *Return to Gallipoli: Walking the Battlefields of the Great War* (2006). Thomson in particular is a forensic examination of how the memories of the last surviving Anzac veterans became inextricably entangled with the myth, the latter forming part of the fabric of their own recollections.[57]

Further academic work can be found in slightly older publications such as Lloyd Robson, *The First AIF: A Study of its Recruitment* (1970); John Robertson, *Anzac and Empire: The Tragedy and Glory of Gallipoli* (1990); and, especially, E. M. Andrews, *The Anzac Illusion: Anglo-Australian Relations during the First World War* (1993). Suzanne Brugger, *Australians and Egypt, 1914–19* (1980), examines the indifferent disciplinary record of the Australians, who burned down the brothel district of Cairo in both world wars, while there are also some interesting articles on aspects of Australian attitudes.[58] As suggested earlier, work on the Canadian Expeditionary Force has tended to focus on its military development as a fighting formation but, in the light of the work on German atrocities by historians such as John Horne and Alan Kramer Tim Cook has also thrown light on some Canadian practices, while there is an unpublished thesis on the British experience.[59] Again, those general

---

57 See also Kevin Kent, 'The Anzac Book and the Anzac Legend: C. E. W. Bean as Editor and Image-Maker', *Historical Studies* 21 (1985), 376–90; Alistair Thomson, 'Steadfast unto Death? C. E. W. Bean and the Representation of Australian Military Manhood', *Australian Historical Studies* 23 (1989), 462–78; idem, 'The Anzac Legend: Exploring National Myth and Memory in Australia', in Raphael Samuel and Paul Thompson (eds), *The Myths We Live By* (London: Routledge, 1990), pp. 73–82.

58 R. White, 'The Soldier as Tourist: The Australian Experience of the Great War', *W&S* 5 (1987), 63–77; idem, 'Europe and the Six-Bob-a-Day Tourist: The Great War as Grand Tour, or Getting Civilised', *Australian Studies* 5 (1991), 122–39; Dale James Blair, 'The Miserable Tommies: Anti British Sentiment in the Australian Imperial Force, 1915–18', *W&S* 19 (2001), 71–91; Clare Roden, 'Another Perspective on Australian Discipline in the Great War: The Egalitarian Bargain', *WH* 19 (2012), 445–63; Amanda Laugesen, 'More than a Luxury: Australian Soldiers as Entertainers and Audience in the First World War', *Journal of War and Cultural Studies* 6 (2012), 226–38.

59 Tim Cook, 'The Politics of Surrender: Canadian Soldiers and the Killing of Prisoners in the Great War', *JMH* 70 (2006), 637–66; idem, 'Tokens of Fritz: Canadian Soldiers and the Art of Souveneering in the Great War', *W&S* 31 (2012), 211–26; idem, 'Fighting Words: Canadian Soldiers' Slang and Swearing in the Great War', *WH* 20 (2013), 323–44; Paul Hodges, 'The British Infantry and Atrocities on the Western Front, 1914–18', PhD dissertation, University of London 2007.

Canadian histories already mentioned have reference to wider journal literature on the controversies of Canadian involvement in the war such as the introduction of conscription, for which there is also J. L. Granatstein and J. M. Hitsman, *Broken Promises: A History of Conscription in Canada* (1977). In addition, however, there are Geoffrey Hayes, Andrew Iarocci and Mike Berchtold (eds), *In the Shadow of Vimy Ridge: The Canadian Corps, April and May 1917* (2007); and Tim Cook's recent two-volume study, *At the Sharp End: Canadians Fighting the Great War, 1914–16* (2007), and *Shock Troops: Canadians Fighting the Great War, 1917–18* (2008).

Some additional studies of morale include, perhaps surprisingly, several studies of the contribution of religion by Richard Schweitzer, *The Cross and the Trenches: Religious Faith and Doubt among British and American Great War Soldiers* (2003); Michael Snape, *God and the British Soldier: Religion and the British Army in the First and Second World Wars* (2005); and Michael Snape and Edward Madigan (eds), *The Clergy in Khaki: New Perspectives on British Army Chaplains in the First World War* (2013).[60] S. Paul Mackenzie, *Politics and Military Morale: Current Affairs and Citizenship Education in the British Army, 1918–50* (1992), looks at early attempts to bolster morale through a low-level programme of patriotic instruction. A particularly innovative approach is provided by Rachel Duffett, *The Stomach for Fighting: Food and the Soldiers of the Great War* (2012), which highlights the very real importance of maintaining ration scales in sustaining morale.[61]

A pioneering approach to soldiers' experience was by a sociologist, Tony Ashworth, *Trench Warfare, 1914–18: The Live and Let Live System* (1980), now supplemented by John Williams, *The Nursery Sector of the Western Front, 1914–18* (2008).[62] Craig Gibson, *Behind the Front: British Troops and French Civilians,*

---

60 See also Richard, Schweitzer, 'The Cross and the Trenches: Religious Faith and Doubt among Some British Soldiers on the Western Front', *W&S* 16 (1998), 33–58; Sarita Cargas, 'Christ in No Man's Land: Religion and the British Soldier, 1914–18', DPhil dissertation, University of Oxford, 2006; Patrick Porter, 'Slaughter or Sacrifice? The Religious Rhetoric of Blood Sacrifice in the British and German Armies, 1914–19', DPhil dissertation, University of Oxford, 2006.

61 See also Rachel Duffett, 'A War Unimagined: Food and the Rank and File Soldier of the First World War', in Jessica Meyer (ed.), *British Popular Culture and the First World War* (Leiden: Brill, 2008), pp. 47–70.

62 See also Gavin Brown, 'Dig for Bloody Victory: The British Soldier's Experience of Trench Warfare, 1939–45', DPhil dissertation, University of Oxford, 2012.

1914–18 (2014), is the long awaited published version of his thesis.[63] There is growing interest in the issue of prisoners of war, for which there is a useful comparative study, Heather Jones, *Violence Against Prisoners of War in the First World War: Britain, France and Germany, 1914–20* (2011).[64]

As in the case of the concentration on conscientious objection, much popular interest has centred on the small minority of capital courts martial that resulted in actual execution and the assumption that all must have been suffering from 'shell shock', a subject that has also resulted in a considerable body of work. Leaving aside the more emotive popular polemics, and impressionistic works on morale and discipline, rather more solid analysis is offered by Gerard Oram in *Death Sentences Passed by Military Courts of the British Army, 1914–24* (1998), and *Worthless Men: Race, Eugenics and the Death Penalty in the British Army during the First World War* (1998).[65] For shell shock, the many works include Peter Reese, *Homecoming Heroes* (1991) and *Shell Shock: Traumatic Neurosis and the British Soldier of the First World War* (2002); Jeffrey Reznick, *Healing the Nation: Soldiers and the Culture of Caregiving in Britain during the Great War* (2004); Peter Barham, *Forgotten Lunatics of the Great War* (2004); Fiona Reid, *Broken Men: Shellshock, Treatment and Recovery in Britain 1914–1930* (2011);

---

63 See also Craig Gibson, 'My Chief Source of Worry: An Assistant Provost Marshal's View of Relations between 2nd Canadian Division and Local Inhabitants on the Western Front, 1915–17', *WH* 7 (2000), 413–41; idem, 'Sex and Soldiering in France and Flanders: The BEF along the Western Front, 1914–19', *IHR* 23 (2001), 535–79; idem, 'The British Army, French Farmers and the War on the Western Front, 1914–18', *P&P* 180 (2002), 175–240; Christopher Kempshall, 'Unwilling Allies? Tommy-Poilu Relations on the Western Front, 1914–18', PhD dissertation, University of Sussex, 2013.

64 See also Heather Jones, 'The Final Logic of Sacrifice? Violence in German Prisoner of War Labour Companies in 1918', *The Historian* 68 (2006), 770–91; S. Paul Mackenzie, 'The Ethics of Escape: British Officer POWs in the First World War', *WH* 15 (2008), 1–16; Brian Feltman, 'Tolerance as a Crime? The British Treatment of German Prisoners of War on the Western Front, 1914–18', *WH* 17 (2010), 435–58.

65 See also David Englander and James Osborne, 'Jack, Tommy and Henry Dubb: The Armed Forces and the Working Class', *HJ* 21 (1978), 593–62; Gerald Oram, '"The Administration of Discipline by the English is very rigid": British Military Law and the Death Penalty, 1858–1918', *Crime, History and Societies* 5 (2001), 93–110; idem, 'Pious Perjury: Discipline and Morale in the British Forces in Italy, 1917–18', *WH* 9 (2002), 412–30.

and J. P. Anderson, *War, Disability and Rehabilitation in Britain: Soul of a Nation* (2011).[66]

The only real wartime difficulty experienced by the British army was the short-lived and often exaggerated events at Etaples in September 1917. Douglas Gill and Glodden Dallas, *The Unknown Army: Mutinies in the British Army in World War One* (1985), for example, is not altogether reliable.[67] The rigorous academic work of David Englander is to be preferred.[68] Significantly, larger-scale disruption occurred only once the war was over with the pressure for demobilisation. Again, there is a popular account that accords an entirely unlikely political element to the disturbances, Andrew Rothstein, *The Soldiers' Strikes of 1919* (1980). Englander is again a surer guide.[69]

These studies begin to touch upon post-war attitudes towards ex-servicemen, for which there is a large literature including Deborah Cohen, *The War Come Home: Disabled Veterans in Britain and Germany, 1914–39* (2001); and Niall Barr, *The Lion and the Poppy: British Veterans, Politics and Society, 1921–39* (2005).[70] One attempted solution to the problems being experienced by some

---

66 See also P. J. Lynch, 'The Exploitation of Courage: Psychiatric Care in the British Army, 1914–18', MPhil dissertation, University of London, 1977; E. W. Elsey, 'The Rehabilitation and Employment of Disabled Ex-Servicemen After Two World Wars', PhD dissertation, Teeside University, 1995.

67 See also D. Gill and G. Dallas, 'Mutiny at Etaples Base, 1917', *Past & Present* 69 (1975), 88–112; Julian Putkowski, 'Toplis, Etaples and the "Monocled Mutineer"', *Stand To* 18 (1986), 6–11.

68 David Englander, 'Discipline and Morale in the British Army, 1917–18', in John Horne (ed.), *State, Society and Mobilisation in Europe during the First World War* (Cambridge: Cambridge University Press, 1997), pp. 132–6.

69 David Englander, 'Die Demobilmachung in Grossbritannien nach dem Ersten Weltkrieg', *Geschichte und Gesellschaft* 9 (1983), 195–210; idem, 'Troops and Trade Unions, 1919', *History Today* 37: 3 (1987), 8–13; Ian Brown, 'The BEF and the Difficult Transition to Peace, 1918–19', *JSS* 19 (1996), 89–104.

70 See also David Englander, 'Military Intelligence and the Defence of the Realm: The Surveillance of Soldiers and Civilians in Britain during the First World War', *Bulletin of the Society for the Study of Labour History* 52 (1987), 24–32; idem, 'The National Union of Ex-Servicemen and the Labour Movement, 1918–20', *History* 76 (1991), 24–42; Stephen R. Ward, 'The British Veterans' Ticket of 1918', *Journal of British Studies* 8 (1968), 155–69; idem, 'Intelligence Surveillance of British Ex-Servicemen, 1918–20', *HJ* 16 (1973), 179–88; idem, 'Great Britain: Land Fit for Heroes Lost', in Stephan Ward (ed.), *The War Generation: Veterans of the First World War* (Port Washington, NY: Kennikat Press, 1975), pp. 10–37; C. C. Kimball, 'The Ex-Service Movement in England and Wales, 1916–30', PhD dissertation, Stanford University, 1990.

ex-servicemen was settlement schemes, on which there is a large literature in academic journals and an overall guide in Kent Fedorowich, *Unfit for Heroes: Reconstruction and Soldier Settlement in the Empire between the Wars* (1995). Pensions were not just an issue for veterans but also for bereaved dependents, a subject explored in theses.[71]

Commemoration - often contentious – has also attracted a great deal of attention, to the extent that only the principal monographs can be mentioned, namely Adrian Gregory, *The Silence of Memory: Armistice Day, 1919–46* (1994); Michael Gavaghan, *The Story of the Unknown Warrior, 11 November 1920* (1995); Alex King, *Memorials of the Great War in Britain: The Symbolism and Politics of Remembrance* (1998); Angela Gaffney, *Aftermath: Remembering the Great War in Wales* (1998); David Lloyd, *Battlefield Tourism: Pilgrimage and the Commemoration of the Great War in Britain, Australia and Canada, 1919–39* (1998), Mark Connelly, *The Great War, Memory and Ritual: Commemoration in the City and East London, 1916–39* (2002); and Catherine Switzer, *Unionists and Great War Commemoration in the North of Ireland, 1914–39: Peoples, Places and Politics* (2007).[72] The longer-term legacies extending to the present are the subject of two stimulating studies, Brian Bond, *The Unquiet Western Front: Britain's Role in Literature and History* (2002), and Dan Todman, *The Great War: Myth and Memory* (2005). The essays in Stephen Badsey, *The British Army in Battle and its Image, 1914–18* (2009), are also suggestive of how a misleading impression of the realities of the Western Front were perpetuated in popular memory.

The inter-war period was hardly devoid of conflict, even the immediate post-war period in Europe seeing considerable violence as suggested by Robert Gerwarth and John Horne (eds), *War in Peace: Paramilitary Violence in Europe after the Great War* (2012). The Russian Civil War continued until 1921, and there were also the Russo-Polish War of 1919–20, and the Greco-Turkish War

---

71 Janis Lomas, 'War Widows in British Society, 1914–90', PhD dissertation, University of Staffordshire 1997; I. H. James, 'To Keep Me all My Life: Policy, Provision and the Experience of War Widowhood, 1914–25', PhD dissertation, University of Cambridge, 2000.

72 See also Catherine Moriarty, 'Narratives of the Absent Body: Mechanics of Meaning in the First World War', DPhil dissertation, University of Sussex, 1995; Ross Wilson, 'The Burial of the Dead: The British Army on the Western Front, 1914–18', *W&S* 31 (2012), 22–41; Jackie Leach Scully and Rachel Woodward, 'Naming the Unknown of Fromelles: DNA Profiling, Ethics and the Identification of First World War Bodies', *Journal of War and Cultural Studies* 5 (2012), 59–72.

of 1919–22. For these there are respectively, Evan Mawdsley, *The Russian Civil War* (1987); Norman Davies, *White Eagle: Red Star: The Polish-Soviet War 1919–20 and the Miracle on the Vistula* (1972); and Michael Llewellyn Smith, *Ionian Vision: Greece in Asia Minor* (1998). For perspectives on the inter-war period as a whole, see Geoffrey Jensen, *Warfare in Europe, 1919–38* (2008), and Jeremy Black, *Avoiding Armageddon: From the Great War to the Fall of France, 1918–40* (2012). Studies of the Spanish Civil War include Paul Preston, *The Spanish Civil War, 1936–39* (1986); Paul Preston and A. L. Mackenzie (eds), *The Republic Besieged: Civil War in Spain, 1936–39* (1996); and Stanley Payne, *The Spanish Civil War* (2012). For the Chinese Civil War, which began in 1926, see Arthur Waldron, *The Chinese Civil Wars, 1911–49* (2004), and S. C. M. Paine, *The Wars for Asia, 1911–49* (2012). For the Sino-Japanese War from 1937 onwards, there are Lincoln Li, *The Japanese Army in North China, 1937–41: Problems of Political and Economic Control* (1975); Hsi-shang Ch'i, *Nationalist China at War: Military Defeats and Political Collapse, 1937–45* (1982); and Mark R. Peattie, Edward J. Drea and Hans J. Van De Ven (eds), *The Battle for China: Essays on the Military History of the Sino-Japanese War of 1937–1945* (2010).

Naturally enough there has been a great deal of attention paid to the French, Russian and, especially, the German armies between 1919 and 1939, for which the more general texts already cited must suffice. In the case of the British army, there are some older works that examine British military policy including Robin Higham, *The Armed Forces in Peacetime* (1962); D. C. Watt, *Too Serious a Business* (1975); and Peter Dennis, *Decision by Default* (1972), which looks at the re-introduction of conscription in April 1939.[73] Barry Posen, *The Sources of Military Doctrine: France, Britain and Germany between the World Wars* (1984), and Elizabeth Keir, *Imagining War: French and British Military Doctrine between the Wars* (1999), make comparisons, Posen from the perspective of events in 1940. Michael Howard, *The Continental Commitment: The Dilemma of British Defence Policy in the Era of Two World Wars* (1974), looks at the long running dilemma facing British policymakers in his usual incisive manner. However, by far the best overview of the army is Brian Bond, *British Military Policy between the Wars* (1980), which charts the uncertain course from its imperial concerns to the attempt to learn appropriate lessons from the Great War, against the background of a deteriorating international climate,

---

73 See also P. J. Wainwright, 'The National Service Debate: The Government, Conscription and the Peace Movement in Britain, 1936–42', PhD dissertation, Stanford University, 1993.

and the refusal by politicians and public to contemplate even a limited continental liability.[74] The essays in Martin S. Alexander and William Philpott (eds), *Anglo-French Defence Relations between the Wars* (2002), further illuminate the strategic aspects of British policy.[75] Increasingly, of course, it was apparent that Germany posed a renewed threat, as explored by Wesley Wark, *The Ultimate Enemy: British Intelligence and Nazi Germany* (1985), and by essays in Ernest May (ed.), *Knowing One's Enemies: Intelligence Assessment before the Two World Wars* (1984).

Wider strategic concerns are covered in W. Roger Louis, *British Strategy in the Far East, 1919–39* (1971), and Steve Morewood, *The British Defence of Egypt, 1935–40* (2013), as well as a number of theses.[76] An over-riding factor was financial retrenchment. The financial parameters such as the notorious Ten Year Rule in force from 1919 to 1934 are explored by R. P. Shay, *Rearmament in the Thirties: Politics and Profits* (1977); G. C. Peden, *British Rearmament and the Treasury, 1932–39* (1979); John Ferris, *Men, Money and Diplomacy: The Evolution of British Strategic Policy, 1919–26* (1989); and Dick Richardson, *The Evolution of British Disarmament Policy in the 1920s* (1989). Peden also provides a general overview of economic pressures on strategic choices in the first half of the twentieth century in *Arms, Economics and British Strategy: From Dreadnought to the Hydrogen Bomb* (2007).[77]

The popular perception of an army unwilling to fully embrace mechanisation and to take on board the armoured warfare theories of apparent prophets such as Basil Liddell Hart and J. F. C. Fuller has been a particular theme in the

---

74 See also J. Paul Harris, 'Two War Ministers: A Re-assessment of Duff Cooper and Hore-Belisha', *W&S* 6 (1998), 65–78; G. F. Spillman, 'Manpower Problems in the British Army, 1918–39', DPhil dissertation, University of Oxford, 1985.

75 See also J. N. Hickok, 'Anglo-French Military Co-operation, 1935–40', PhD dissertation, University of Wisconsin-Madison, 1991.

76 Karl A. Hack, 'British Strategy and South East Asia, 1914–57', DPhil dissertation, University of Oxford, 1995; D. Austin, 'The Place of Malta in British Strategic Policy, 1925–34', PhD dissertation, University of London, 2002; O. Babij, 'The Development of British Strategic Policy, 1929–33', DPhil dissertation, University of Oxford, 2003.

77 See also G. C. Peden, 'Sir Warren Fisher and British Rearmament Against Germany', *EHR* 94 (1979), pp. 29–47; Christopher Bell, 'Winston Churchill and the Ten Year Rule', *JMH* 74 (2010), 1097–1128; P. Bell, 'The British Government and the Menace from Germany and Japan: A Study of the First Defence Requirement Inquiry, 1933–34', PhD Leeds, 1989.

historiography.[78] Studies of Liddell Hart and Fuller have been mentioned in a previous section and can be set in the context of the wider debate outlined in two works by Azar Gat, *Fascist and Liberal Visions of War: Fuller, Liddell Hart, Douhet and Other Modernists* (1998), and *British Armour Theory and the Rise of the Panzer Arm: Revisiting the Revisionists* (2000). Gat generally is more sympathetic to the idea of Liddell Hart's influence than some other historians.[79] The cavalry is often seen as particularly resistant to mechanisation and has been the subject of several theses as well as important articles by David French.[80] The evolution of British armoured doctrine itself is covered in Robert H. Larson, *The British Army and Theory of Armored Warfare 1918–1940* (1984), and Harold R. Winton, *To Change an Army: General Sir John Burnett-Stuart and British Armoured Doctrine, 1927–38* (1988). Larson in particular suggests British armoured doctrine was at fault in equating the role of light and heavy tanks with the previous roles of light and heavy cavalry. The sometimes-fraught relationship with the RAF has also been studied, as well as progress on

---

78 See G. P. Armstrong, 'Resistance to Armoured Warfare in the 1920s and 1930s', PhD dissertation, University of London, 1976.
79 See also Azar Gat, 'The Hidden Sources of Liddell Hart's Strategic Ideas', *WH* 3 (1996), 293–308; Timo Baumann, 'Die Entgrenzung taktischer Szenarien: Der Krieg der Zukunft in britischen Militärzeitschriften', in Stig Förster (ed.), *An der Schwelle zum Totalen Krieg: Die Militarische Debatte uber Den Krieg der Zukunft, 1919–39* (2002), pp. 179–266; Brian Holden Reid, 'Young Turks or Not So Young Turks: The Frustrated Quest of Major General J. F. C. Fuller and Captain B. H. Liddell Hart', *JMH* 73 (2009), 147–75; Alaric Searle, 'Inter-Service Debate and the Origins of Strategic Culture: The Principles of War in the British Armed Forces, 1919–39', *WH* 21 (2014), 4–32; idem, 'Was there a "Boney" Fuller after the Second World War? Major General J. F. C. Fuller as Military Theorist and Commentator, 1945–66', *WH* 11 (2004), 327–57. See also Azar Gat, 'British Influence and the Evolution of the Panzer Arm: Myth or Reality?', *WH* 4 (1997), 150–73, 316–38.
80 David French, 'Doctrine and Organisation in the British Army, 1919–32', *HJ* 44 (2001), 477–515; idem, 'The Mechanisation of the British Cavalry between the World Wars', *WH* 10 (2003), 296–320; J. Paul Harris, 'British Armour and Rearmament in the 1930s', *JSS* 11 (1988), 220–44; Michael Waller, 'The Conservatism of the British Cavalry and its Effect on the British Army of World War II', PhD dissertation, Drew University, 2009; Gilman Barndollar, 'British Military Use of Armoured Cars, 1919–39', PhD dissertation, University of Cambridge, 2010; Gary Evans, 'The British Cavalry, 1920–40', PhD dissertation, University of Kent, 2012.

communications. Ben Coombs, *British Tank Production and the War Economy, 1934–45* (2013), is useful study of design and production issues.[81]

Whatever the future of warfare, immediate priorities were imperial though there were also crises in Britain itself, as indicated in Keith Jeffery and Peter Hennessy, *State of Emergency* (1983), which deals with military aid to the civil power in industrial disputes. The British Empire was at its greatest height in 1918 following the absorption of former German colonies and the division of the Ottoman Empire between Britain and France. As Keith Jeffery, *The British Army and the Crisis of Empire, 1918–1922* (1984) shows, however, nationalist disturbances stretched an army being rapidly demobilised. The best study of the British part in the Anglo-Irish War remains Charles Townshend, *The British Campaign in Ireland, 1919–21: The Development of Political and Military Policies* (1975), while the use of ex-servicemen to bolster the police is studied in D. M. Leeson, *The Black and Tans: British Police and Auxiliaries in the Irish War of Independence, 1920–21* (2012). Peter Hart, *The IRA and its Enemies: Violence and Community in Cork, 1916–23* (1998), and his *The IRA at War, 1916–23* (2003), are important correctives to persistent myths.[82]

Other inter-war experience of low-intensity campaigns is covered in Tom Mockaitis, *British Counter-Insurgency, 1919–60* (1990); and Charles Townshend, *Britain's Civil Wars: Counterinsurgency in the Twentieth Century* (1986). Immediate concerns in the Middle East are dealt with in Matthew Hughes's studies of Allenby, previously mentioned. The newly acquired mandate for Iraq also proved troublesome, Townshend's *When God Made Hell*, previously mentioned, extending to 1921.[83] The later Arab Revolt in Palestine is covered in Tom Bowden, *The Breakdown of Public Security: The Case of Ireland, 1916–21 and Palestine,*

---

81 A. D. Harvey, 'The RAF and Close Air Support, 1918–40', *WH*15 (2008), 462–86; D. J. P. Waldie, 'Relations between the Army and the RAF, 1918–39', PhD dissertation, University of London, 1980; Simon Godfrey, 'Command and Communications in the British Army, 1919–45', PhD dissertation, University of London 2009.

82 See also J. R. Linge, 'British Forces and Irish Freedom: Anglo-Irish Defence Relations, 1922–31', PhD dissertation, University of Stirling, 1995; F. J. Costello, 'The Anglo-Irish War, 1919–21: A Reassessment', PhD dissertation, Boston College, 1992; Benjamin Butler, 'The British Army in Ireland, 1916–21: A Social and Cultural History', PhD dissertation, University of Hull, 2007; William Sheehan, 'The British Army's Experience in Cork City and County, 1919–21', PhD dissertation, Mary Immaculate College, 2008.

83 See also Mark Jacobsen, 'Only by the Sword: British Counterinsurgency in Iraq, 1920', *SWI* 2 (1991), 323–63; R. V. J. Young, 'The History of the Iraq Levies, 1915–32', PhD dissertation, University of London, 1998.

1936–39 (1977), and in a series of journal articles that have contributed to the recent on-going debate on the use of 'minimum force' by the British army.[84] Palestine was also the first campaign in which Orde Wingate's ideas of irregular warfare were formulated, as suggested by Simon Anglim, *Orde Wingate and the British Army, 1922–44* (2010).[85]

The problem of post-1918 'Indianisation' within the Indian army is touched upon in an Army Records Society volume, Mark Jacobsen (ed.), *Rawlinson in India* (2002), Rawlinson being CinC in India from 1920 to 1925, and the subject of Jacobsen's earlier thesis. There is another unpublished thesis on the role of the colonial army in inter-war India and, similarly, another on provision for Indian army veterans.[86] Much of this particular area of study plays into a developing interest generally in the evolution of British counter-insurgency, and the contentious debate on whether or not post-1945 British campaigns adhered or not to an apparent doctrine of 'minimum force'. Inevitably, this raises the question of Amritsar in 1919, on which radically different views are offered by Nigel Collett, *The Butcher of Amritsar: General Reginald Dyer* (2006), and Nick Lloyd, *The Amritsar Massacre: The Untold Story of One Fateful Day* (2011), the latter the more convincing.[87] Imperial policing in India generally has also come under the spotlight from Srinath Raghaven, Gyanesh Kudaisya, and especially from

---

84 See Charles Townshend, 'The Defence of Palestine: Insurrection and Public Security, 1936–39', *EHR* 103 (1988), 917–49; Jacob Norris, 'Repression and Rebellion: Britain's Response to the Arab Revolt in Palestine, 1936–39', *JICH* 36 (2008), 26–46; Matthew Hughes, 'The Practice and Theory of British Counterinsurgency: The Histories of the Atrocities at the Palestinian Villages of al-Bassa and Halhul, 1938–39', *SWI* 20 (2009), 528–50; idem, 'The Banality of Brutality: British Armed Forces and the Repression of the Arab Revolt in Palestine, 1936–39', *EHR* 124 (2009), 313–54; idem, 'A Very British Affair? British Armed Forces and the Suppression of the Arab Revolt in Palestine, 1936–39', *JSAHR* 87 (2009), 234–55, 357–73.

85 See also Simon Anglim, 'The British Army, 1922–40: Military Thought and Practice Compared and Contrasted', PhD dissertation, University of Wales, 2007.

86 Mark Jacobsen, 'The Modernisation of the Indian Army, 1925–39', PhD dissertation, University of California, 1979; N. Narain, 'Co-option and Control: The Role of the Colonial Army in India, 1918–47', PhD dissertation, University of Cambridge, 1993; Susan VanKoski, 'The Indian Ex-Soldier from the Eve of the First World War to Independence and Partition: A Study of Provision for Ex-Soldiers and the Ex-Soldier's Role in Indian National Life', PhD dissertation, Colombia University, 1996.

87 See also Nick Lloyd, 'The Amritsar Massacre and the Minimum Force Debate', *SWI* 21 (2010), 382–403; idem, 'Sir Michael O'Dwyer and Imperial Terrorism in the Punjab, 1919', *South Asia: Journal of South Asian Studies* 33 (2010), 363–80.

Simeon Shoul, who died tragically young and before he could convert his 2006 thesis into a monograph, leaving just two journal articles.[88]

For continuing warfare on the frontier there are the later chapters of Moreman's monograph mentioned in the previous section as well as Alan Warren, *Waziristan: The Faqir of Ipi and the Indian Army: The North West Frontier Revolt* (2000); and Brian Robson, *Crisis on the Frontier: The Third Afghan War and the Campaign in Waziristan, 1919–20* (2004).[89] Edward Spiers covers the debates on the use of both explosive bullets and gas on the frontier.[90] David Omissi, *Air Power and Colonial Control: The Royal Air Force, 1919–39* (1990), examines aerial policing in India as well as elsewhere in the empire.

On inter-war strategic concerns relating to India, there are a number of unpublished theses as well as articles.[91] Some of those works on political pacification mentioned in an earlier section remain relevant since their date range extends into the twentieth century, while Robert Taylor has looked at the

---

88 Srinath Raghaven, 'Protecting the Raj: The Army in India and Internal Security, 1919–39', *SWI* 16 (2005), 253–79; Gyanesh Kudaisya, 'In Aid of Civil Power: The Colonial Army in Northern India, 1919–42', *JICH* 32 (2004), 41–68; Simeon Shoul, 'Soldiers, Riot Control and Aid to the Civil Power in India, Egypt and Palestine, 1919–39', *SWI* 36 (2008), 120–39; idem, 'British Tear Gas Doctrine between the World Wars', *WH* 15 (2008), 168–90; idem, 'Soldiers, Riot Control and Aid to the Civil Power in India, Egypt and Palestine, 1919–39', PhD dissertation, University of London, 2006.

89 See also Tim Moreman, 'Small Wars and Imperial Policing: The British Army and the Theory and Practice of Colonial Warfare in the British Empire, 1919–39', *JSS* 19 (1996), 105–31; idem, 'Watch and Ward: The Army in India and the North West Frontier', in David Killingray and David Omissi (eds), *Guardians of Empire* (Manchester: Manchester University Press, 1999), pp. 137–56; Alan Warren, 'Bullocks Treading Down Wasps? The British Army in Waziristan in the 1930s', *South Asia: Journal of South Asian Studies* 20 (1997), 35–56.

90 Edward Spiers, 'The Use of the Dum-Dum Bullet in Colonial Warfare', *JICH* 13 (1985), 157–84; idem, 'Gas and the North West Frontier', *JSS* 6 (1983), 94–112.

91 Lesley Jackman, 'Afghanistan in British Imperial Strategy and Diplomacy, 1919–41', PhD dissertation, University of Cambridge, 1978; J. C. Rawson, 'The Role of India in Imperial Defence Beyond her Frontiers and Home Waters, 1919–39', DPhil dissertation, University of Oxford, 1976; Brandon Marsh, 'Ramparts of Empire: India's North West Frontier and British Imperialism, 1919–47', PhD dissertation, University of Texas at Austin, 2009; Keith Jeffery, 'An English Barrack in the Oriental Seas? India in the Aftermath of the First World War', *MAS* 15 (1981), 369–86; Pradeep Barua, 'Strategies and Doctrine of Imperial Defence: Britain and India, 1919–45', *JICH* 25 (1997), 240–66.

organisation of local forces in Burma.[92] Other imperial forces have attracted relatively little attention.[93]

For the Dominions, the war had brought a new sense of national identity that differentiated their interests from those of Britain. Indeed, the assumption that the Dominions would simply fall into line with British military policy was disproved almost immediately by the Chanak crisis in 1922, when only New Zealand and Newfoundland were prepared to support a renewed war against Turkey. David Walder, *The Chanak Affair* (1969), is now somewhat dated and the events would repay a revisitation from the army's perspective.[94] Studies of inter-war military relations between the British army and its Dominion counterparts, moreover, are few and far between.[95] Apart from the more general histories of the Australian, Canadian and New Zealand armies, James Eayrs, *In Defence of Canada: From the Great War to the Great Depres*sion (1964); W. David McIntyre, *New Zealand Prepares for War: Defence Policy, 1919–39* (1988); and essays in Barry Hunt and Ronald Haycock (eds), *Canada's Defence: Perspectives on Policy in the Twentieth Century* (1993), provide some additional context.[96]

Turning to the Second World War, as might be supposed, there are again a plethora of general histories, many of a popular rather than an academic nature. Gordon Wright, *The Ordeal of Total War* (1968), and Peter Calvocoressi and Guy Wint, *Total War* (1972) still have much to recommend them, while

92 See also Christian Tripodi, 'Peace-Making Through Bribes or Cultural Empathy: The Political Officer and Britain's Strategy towards the North West Frontier, 1901–1945', *JSS* 31 (2008), 123–51; idem, 'Good for One But Not the Other: The Sandeman System of Pacification as Applied to Baluchistan and the North West Frontier, 1871–1947', *JMH* 73 (2009), 767–802. For Burma, see Robert Taylor, 'Colonial Forces in British Burma: A National Army Postponed', in Tobias Rettig and Karl Hack (eds), *Colonial Armies in Southeast Asia* (Abingdon: Routledge, 2009), pp. 195–210.

93 See N. Haron, 'The Malay Regiment: A Political and Social Study, 1933–47', PhD dissertation, University of Essex, 1988; K. R. Brown, 'The Military and Social Change in Colonial Tanganyika, 1919–64', PhD dissertation, Michigan State, 2001.

94 See also A. L. Macfie, 'The Chanak Affair (September-October 1922)', *Balkan Studies* 20 (1979), 309–41; J. G. Darwin, 'The Chanak Crisis and the British Cabinet', *History* 65 (1980), 32–48.

95 John Gooch, 'The Politics of Strategy: Great Britain, Australia and the War Against Japan, 1939–45', *WH* 10 (2003), 424–47.

96 See also Britton W. MacDonald, 'The Policy of Neglect: The Canadian Militia in the Inter-War Years, 1919–39', PhD dissertation, Temple University, 2009.

H. P. Willmott, *The Great Crusade* (1989) is idiosyncratic but insightful. Of the more recent academic works, Gerhard Weinberg, *A World at Arms: A Global History of World War II* (1994); S. Paul Mackenzie, *The Second World War in Europe* (1999); Williamson Murray and Allan Millett, *A War to be Won: Fighting the Second World War* (2000); Norman Davies, *Europe at War, 1939–45: No Simple Victory* (2008); and Evan Mawdsley, *World War II: A New History* (2009), all have their qualities. Richard Overy, *Why the Allies Won* (1995), seeks to explain ultimate allied victory over Germany and Japan in terms of materiel.

General histories of the British experience in the Second World War have a heavy concentration on the home front as in Angus Calder, *The People's War, Britain 1939–1945* (1969); Henry Pelling, *Britain and the Second World War* (1971); Mark Donnelly, *Britain in the Second World War* (1999); and Robert McKay, *The Test of War: Inside Britain, 1939–45* (1999). Even more explicitly about the home front are Arthur Marwick, *The Home Front: The British and the Second World War* (1976); Rayner Minns, *Bombers and Mash: The Domestic Front, 1939–45* (1980); Harold L. Smith (ed.), *War and Social Change: British Society in the Second World War* (1986); Harold L Smith (ed.), *Britain in the Second World War: A Social History* (1996); and Pat Kirkham and David Thoms (eds), *War Culture: Social Change and Changing Experience in World War Two* (1995). Two recent monographs, David Edgerton, *Britain's War Machine: Weapons, Resources and Experts in the Second World War* (2012), and Andrew Stewart, *A Very British Experience: Coalition, Defence and Strategy in the Second World War* (2012), have a more strategic focus, Edgerton suggesting that the underlying resilience of the British economy and its wealth of technological expertise sustained the war effort even in the face of German invasion to a greater extent than usually realised. As in the case of the Great War, all these general texts provide a guide to further reading on such aspects as political and social change, identity and citizenship, leisure and morals, women and children, and myth and memory. Indeed, there is a wealth of literature on all these aspects.

For the empire generally, see Ashley Jackson, *The British Empire and the Second World War* (2006). There are also general texts on the contribution of the empire to British and imperial defence. For Canada there are Terry Copp and Richard Neilsen, *No Price Too High: Canadians and the Second World War* (1995); David Bercuson, *Maple Leaf Against the Axis: Canada's Second World War* (1995); and Brereton Greenhous, *Out of the Shadows: Canada in the Second World War* (1996). For Canada, one particular controversy was the loss in December 1941 of two battalions sent to Hong Kong and another the losses in the Dieppe raid in April

1942.[97] Bill McAndrew, *Canadians and the Italian Campaign, 1943–45* (1996) is a scholarly account. John English, *The Canadian Army and the Normandy Campaign: A Study of Failure in High Command* (1991), critically examines the Canadian efforts to close the Falaise gap but, in two important revisionist studies, *Fields of Fire: The Canadians in Normandy* (2003), and *Cinderella Army: The Canadians in North West Europe, 1944–45* (2006), Terry Copp argues that the Canadian 1st Army has been greatly underrated in the Normandy and North West Europe campaigns of 1944–5.[98] Copp and McAndrew together also contribute *Battle Exhaustion: Soldiers and Psychiatrists in the Canadian Army, 1939–45* (1990).

For New Zealand, there is the outstanding John Crawford, *Kia Kaha: New Zealand in the Second World War* (2002), to which can be added the earlier John McLeod, *Myth and Reality: The New Zealand Soldier in World War II* (1986), and Gerald Hensley, *Beyond the Battlefield: New Zealand and its Allies, 1939–45* (2009). A new study, albeit somewhat marred by being strangely written in the present tense, is Christopher Pugsley, *A Bloody Road Home: World War II and New Zealand's Heroic Second Division* (2014). For Australia, a starting point is Joan Beaumont (ed), *Australia's War, 1939–45* (1996), but its essays can be supplemented with the more comprehensive John Robertson, *Australia at War, 1939–45* (1981), while Michael McKernan, *All In! Australia during the Second World War* (1983), is good for the home front. Australia in particular felt its vulnerability to the Japanese threat, not least after the collapse of the British position in Malaya and Singapore. Inevitably, Australia looked more to the United States for its salvation, as explored in Roger John Bell, *Unequal Allies: Australian-American Relations and*

---

97 Christopher Bell, 'Our Most Exposed Outpost: Hong Kong and British Far Eastern Strategy, 1921–41', *JMH* 60 (1996), 61–88; Kent Fedorowich, 'Cocked Hats and Swords and Small Little Garrisons: Britain, Canada and the Fall of Hong Kong, 1941', *MAS* 37 (2003), 111–57; Franco Macri, 'C Force and Hong Kong: The Price of Collective Security in China, 1941', *JMH* 77 (2013), 141–72; Peter Henshaw, 'The British Chiefs of Staff Committee and the Preparation of the Dieppe Raid, March-August 1942: Did Mountbatten Really Evade the Committee's Authority?', *WH* 1 (1994), 197–214; H. G. Henry, 'The Planning, Intelligence, Execution and Aftermath of the Dieppe Raid, 19 August 1942', PhD dissertation, University of Cambridge, 1996.

98 See also Marc Milner, 'Stopping the Panzers: Reassessing the Role of 3rd Canadian Infantry Division in Normandy, 7–10 June 1944', *JMH* 74 (2010), 491–522; Alex Souchen, 'The Culture of Morale: Battalion Newspapers in the 3rd Canadian Infantry Division, June-August 1944', *JMH* 77 (2013), 543–68; R. J. Jarymowycz, 'The Quest for Operational Manoeuvre in the Normandy Campaign: Simmonds and Montgomery Attempt the Armoured Breakout', PhD dissertation, McGill University, 1997.

the Pacific War (1977); David Horner's two studies, *High Command: Australia and Allied Strategy, 1939–45* (1982); and *Inside the War Cabinet: Directing Australia's War Effort, 1939–45* (1996); and David Day's two volumes, *The Great Betrayal: Britain, Australia and the Onset of the Pacific War, 1939–42* (1988), and *Reluctant Nation: Australia and the Allied Defeat of Japan, 1942–45* (1992). Horner's work is altogether more measured than Day's nationalist polemic against what he regards as British betrayal of Australia's interests. Horner also analyses Australia's own war in the Pacific in *Crisis of Command: Australian Generalship and the Japanese Threat, 1941–43* (1978). Part of the difficulties in Anglo-Australian relations resulted from the continued deployment of the Australians in the Middle East and Mediterranean when Australia itself was under threat, the campaigns in Greece, on Crete and in North Africa all arousing controversy. Mark Johnston is somewhat more reliant upon personal testimonies than upon official archives in *At the Front Line: The Experiences of Australian Soldiers in World War II* (1996), and *Australian Soldiers and Their Adversaries in World War Two* (2000). Johnston's *Anzacs in the Middle East: Australian Soldiers, their Allies and the Local People* (2012) is better for the use of more official sources, and Peter Stanley and Mark Johnston, *Alamein: The Australian Story* (2002) is also a valuable operational narrative based upon primary sources.[99] Another fine analysis is Gareth Pratten, *Australian Battalion Commanders in the Second World War* (2009).

In the case of South Africa, there is only a chronological narrative for the general reader by a journalist, Jennifer Crwys-Williams, *A Country at War, 1939–45: The Mood of a Nation* (1992), although the impact of the war on Black South African servicemen has been examined.[100] The role of African servicemen has been covered by David Killingray and Richard Rathbone (eds), *Africa and the Second World War* (1986), and David Killingray, *Fighting for Britain: African Soldiers in the Second World War* (2010).[101] In addition to his general study mentioned previously, Ashley

99 See also Craig Stockings, 'The Anzac Legend and the Battle of Bardia', *WH* 17 (2010), 86–112.

100 Louis W. F. Grundlingh, 'The Participation of South African Blacks in the Second World War', PhD dissertation, Rand Afrikaans University, 1986; idem, 'Aspects of the Impact of the Second World War on the Lives of Black South African and British Colonial Soldiers', *Transafrica Journal of History* 21 (1992), 19–35.

101 See also David Killingray, 'Soldiers, Ex-Servicemen and Politics in the Gold Coast, 1939–50', *Journal of Modern African Studies* 21 (1983), 523–34; Jennifer Warner, 'Recruitment and Service in the King's African Rifles in the Second World War', MPhil dissertation, University of Bristol, 1983; Adrienne Manns, 'The Role of Ex-Servicemen in Ghana's Independence Movement', PhD dissertation, John Hopkins University, 1984; Owino Meshack, 'For Your Tomorrow We Gave Our Today: A History of Kenya African Soldiers in the Second World War', PhD dissertation, Rice University, 2004.

Jackson has also contributed specific studies of *Bostwana, 1939–45: An African Country at War* (1999) and *War and Empire in Mauritius and the Indian Ocean* (2001).[102] The contribution of West Indian servicemen and women has attracted only popular works and would benefit from the kind of academic work done on the Caribbean in the Great War. Johannes Voight, *India in the Second World War* (1987) provides a general overview of wartime developments in the sub-continent.

Unlike that for the Great War, the British Official History of the Second World War has a series devoted to grand strategy but most of the strategy volumes were published at an early stage in the 1950s or early 1960s. The two notable exceptions were Michael Howard, *Grand Strategy:* volume 4, *September 1942–August 1943* (1970), and Norman Gibbs, *Grand Strategy:* volume 1, *Rearmament Policy* (1976). Equally, also contrasting to the Official History of the Great War, there are the immensely valuable five volumes of *British Intelligence in the Second World War*, overseen by F. H. Hinsley between 1979 and 1990, with an abridged summary published in 1993, all of which made full use of the Ultra material that had only become known to historians in 1975. Much of Howard's strategy volume deals with the fractious relationship between Britain and the United States over the British desire to exploit fully strategic opportunities in the Mediterranean, already illustrated by Howard's own, *The Mediterranean Strategy in the Second World War* (1968).[103] British strategy generally is also greatly illuminated by Alex Danchev and Dan Todman (eds), *War Diaries, 1939–45: Field Marshal Lord Alanbrooke* (2001), and also by Danchev's *Very Special Relationship: Field Marshal Sir John Dill and the Anglo-American Alliance* (1986).[104] As successive Chiefs of the Imperial General Staff, Dill and Brooke

---

102 See also Ashley Jackson, 'Motivation and Mobilisation for War: Recruitment for the British Army in the Bechuanaland Protectorate, 1941–42', *African Affairs* 96 (1997), 399–417; idem, 'African Soldiers and Imperial Authorities: Tensions and Unrest during the Service of High Commission Territories' Soldiers in the British Army, 1941–46', *Journal of Southern African Studies* 25 (1999), 645–65; idem, 'Supplying War: The High Commission Territories' Military Logistical Contribution to the Second World War', *JMH* 66 (2002), 719–60.

103 See also M. C. Jones, 'The Politics of Command: Britain, the United States and the War in the Mediterranean, 1942–44', DPhil dissertation, University of Oxford, 1992.

104 See also Sally Parker, 'Attendant Lords: A Study of the British Joint Staff Mission to Washington, 1941–45', PhD dissertation, University of Maryland 1984; W. T. Johnsen, 'Forging the Foundations of the Grand Alliance: Anglo-American Military Collaboration, 1938–41', PhD dissertation, Duke University, 1986; B. P. Farrell, 'War by Consensus: Power Perceptions and British Grand Strategy, 1940–43', PhD dissertation, McGill University, 1992; D. J. Rigby, 'The Combined Chiefs of Staff and Anglo-American Strategic Co-ordination in World War II', PhD dissertation, Brandeis University, 1996.

had to contend with the dominating figure of Churchill, for whose manipulation of the wartime record, David Reynolds, *In Command of History: Churchill Fighting and Writing the Second World War* (2004), is essential reading.[105]

As suggested previously, academic study of the British army in the Second World War has lagged well behind that of the Great War, the field being dominated by the more popular accounts intended for the general reader. This is changing, however, with a welcome new interest on the part of scholars, although much of the work remains buried in unpublished theses. The essential starting point is David French, *Raising Churchill's Army: The British Army and the War against Germany, 1919–45* (2000), an outstanding analysis of the problems that had to be overcome, including poor understanding of combined-arms operations, and a preference for mobility over firepower conditioned by fears of casualties that also made British commanders averse to risk taking.[106] Improved training led to more effective operational performance, as shown by Timothy Harrison-Place, *Military Training in the British Army, 1940–1944* (2000), which suggests that realistic battle training under live firing conditions improved morale as well as tactical skills.[107] John Buckley, *British Armour in Normandy* (2004), addresses the heavily criticised British handling of tanks in the North African desert and in Normandy, arguing that the usually under-gunned British armour undertook a steep learning process. Buckley has taken his revisionist view of British

---

105 See also Alex Danchev, 'Waltzing with Winston: Civil-Military Relations in Britain in the Second World War', *WH* 2 (1995), 202–30.

106 See also David French, 'Colonel Blimp and the British Army: British Divisional Commanders in the War Against Germany, 1939–1945', *EHR* 111 (1996), 1182–1201; idem, 'Discipline and the Death Penalty in the British Army in the Second World War', *JCH* 33 (1998), 531–45; idem, '"Tommy is no Soldier": The Morale of the Second British Army in Normandy, June-August 1944', *JSS* 19 (1996), 154–78; '"You cannot hate the bastard who is trying to kill you": Combat Ideology in the British Army in the War Against Germany, 1939–1945', *Twentieth Century British History* 11 (2000), 1–22; idem, 'Invading Europe: The British Army and its Preparations for the Normandy Campaign, 1942–44', *Diplomacy and Statecraft* 14 (2003), 271–94; Matthew Ford, 'Operational Research, Military Judgement and the Politics of Technical Change in the British Army, 1943–53', *JSS* 32 (2009), 871–97; Patrick Rose, 'Command Culture in the British Army, 1939–45', PhD dissertation, University of London, 2009.

107 See also Tim Harrison-Place, 'Lionel Wigram, Battle Drill and the British Army in the Second World War', *WH* 7 (2000), 442–62; Hew Strachan, 'Training, Morale and Modern War', *JCH* 41 (2006), 211–27.

operational effectiveness further in *Monty's Men: The British Army and the Liberation of Europe* (2013).

As with the Great War, there are plenty of studies of commanders, campaigns and battles but only academic texts will be considered here. Generally, there are some useful essays in Paul Addison and Angus Calder (eds), *Time to Kill: The Soldier's Experience of War in the West, 1939–45* (1997). For 1940 there is Brian Bond, *France and Belgium, 1939–40* (1975); and Brian Bond and Michael Taylor (eds), *The Battle of France and Flanders 1940: Sixty Years On* (2001).[108] *Against All Odds: The British Army of 1939–40* (1990) is a short book that accompanied a National Army Museum exhibition.

For North Africa, general works include Douglas Porch, *Hitler's Mediterranean Gamble: The North African and Mediterranean Campaigns in World War II* (2004), and Martin Kitchen, *Rommel's Desert War: Waging World War II in North Africa, 1941–43* (2009), both of which set the British operations in the wider context.[109] The contrasting generalship of figures such as Wavell, O'Connor, Ritchie, Auchinleck and Montgomery have long been the staple fare of popular accounts.[110] Morale, however, has become very much the focus of academic work, as in Jonathan Fennell, *Combat and Morale in the North African Campaign: The Eighth Army and the Path to El Alamein* (2011), and Allan Converse, *Armies of Empire: The 9th Australian and 50th British Divisions in Battle, 1939–45* (2011).[111] Using a very wide range of archival sources, Fennell in particular argues persuasively that Montgomery did have a substantial impact when succeeding Auchinleck in command of 8th Army in August 1942. By far the best account of the battles around Alamein in the summer and autumn of 1942 is provided

---

108 See also Mark Connelly and Walter Miller, 'The BEF and the Issue of Surrender on the Western Front, 1940', *WH* 11 (2004), 424–41; Glyn Prysor, 'The "Fifth Column" and the British Experience of Retreat, 1940', *WH* 12 (2005), 418–47.

109 See also Nicholas Tamkin, 'Britain, the Middle East and the Northern Front, 1941–42', *WH* 15 (2008), 314–36.

110 See, however, Harold E. Raugh, 'Wavell in the Middle East, 1939–41', PhD dissertation, University of California, Los Angeles, 1991.

111 See also Mark Connelly and Walter Miller, 'British Courts Martial in North Africa, 1940–43', *Twentieth Century British History* 15 (2004), 217–42; Jonathan Fennell, 'Courage and Cowardice in the North African Campaign: The Eighth Army and Defeat in the Summer of 1942', *WH* 20 (2013), 99–122; Ashley Arensdorf, 'The Influence of Operational and Tactical Doctrine, Leadership and Training on the North African Campaign, 1941–42', DPhil dissertation, University of Oxford, 2008.

by Niall Barr, *Pendulum of War: The Three Battles of El Alamein* (2004), while there is also the Army Records Society edition of Montgomery's papers in Stephen Brooks (ed.), *Montgomery and the Eighth Army* (1991). Some specialist aspects of the campaign such as logistics, intelligence and communications in the desert have also been studied.[112] The landings in Tunisia and Algeria in November 1942 were the first effective Anglo-American operations, the decision for which is examined in Keith Sainsbury, *The North African Landings, 1942: A Strategic Decision* (1976).[113]

The initial successful advance of the Western Desert Force against the Italians in Libya in 1940–1 was halted by the decision to assist the Greeks, a campaign that has attracted less academic than popular attention although one article argues that it says much about continued failures in British appreciation of the use of armour.[114] The battle for Crete, however, has a good academic account in Callum Macdonald, *The Last Battle: Crete 1941* (1973). As suggested earlier, British strategic preference was for continued exploitation of opportunities in the Mediterranean and the Italian campaign has attracted considerable attention. The best overview is Dominick Graham and Shelford Bidwell, *Tug of War: The Battle for Italy, 1943–45* (1986); while Kevin Jones, *Intelligence, Command and Military Operations: The 8th Army Campaign in Italy* (2013), based on his dissertation, is also revealing although a study of British morale in Italy remains unpublished.[115] The brief and unsuccessful attempt to seize the Dodecanese in 1943 has also been covered, together with British activities in supporting partisan warfare in the Balkans.[116]

---

112 P. H. Collier, 'The Logistics of the North African Campaign, 1940–43', DPhil dissertation, University of Oxford, 2001; Adam Shelley, 'British Intelligence in the Middle East, 1939–46', PhD dissertation. University of Cambridge, 2008.

113 See also A. Harouni, 'The Anglo-American Invasion of North Africa in 1942', PhD dissertation, University of Reading, 1987.

114 Peter Ewer, 'The British Campaign in Greece, 1941: Assumptions about the Operational Art and Their Influence on Strategy', *JMH* 76 (2010), 727–46.

115 See Brian Holden Reid, 'The Italian Campaign, 1943–45: A Reappraisal of Allied Generalship', *JSS* 13 (1990), 128–61; Patrick Rose, 'Allies at War: British and US Army Command and Culture in the Italian Campaign, 1943–44', *JSS* 36 (2013), 42–74; Christine Bielecki, 'British Infantry Morale in the Italian Campaign, 1943–45', PhD dissertation, University of London, 2006.

116 Ian Gooderson, 'Shoestring Strategy: The British Campaign in the Aegean, 1943', *JSS* 25 (2002), 1–36; N. C. A. Bradshaw, 'A Study of the British Personnel Involved with the Yugoslavian Resistance, 1941–45', PhD dissertation, University of Southampton, 2002.

In Britain itself, in addition to the rebuilding of the army after Dunkirk, there was the initial fear of invasion, resulting in the raising of the Home Guard. S. Paul Mackenzie, *The Home Guard: A Military and Political History* (1995) provides a good overview, although he misses the projection of the force as a people's militia. Brian Osborne, *The People's Army: The Home Guard in Scotland* (2009), is a useful regional study. Some aspects of the Home Guard's effectiveness are explored in articles.[117] Penny Summerfield and Corinna Peniston-Bird, *Contesting Home Defence: Men, Women and the Home Guard in the Second World War* (2007) use the force as a means of examining gender relations and attitudes both at the time, and in the way in which the Home Guard is remembered in popular culture.[118] Curiously, mixed anti-aircraft units have attracted arguably disproportionate interest.[119] Sex, however, remained a concern for the military authorities as in the Great War, Emma Vickers, *Queen and Country: Same-Sex Desire in the British Armed Forces, 1939–45* (2013), suggesting a flexibility so far as military discipline was applied to at least one aspect of sexuality. Emma Newlands, *Civilians into Soldiers: War, the Body and British Army Recruits, 1939–45* (2014) also concerns itself with issues of manliness.[120]

---

117 See S. Paul Mackenzie, 'Citizens in Arms: The Home Guard and the Internal Security of the United Kingdom, 1940–41', *INS* 6 (1991), pp. 548–72; D. K. Yelton, 'British Public Opinion, the Home Guard and the Defence of Great Britain, 1940–46', *JMH* 58 (1994), pp. 461–80; Craig Armstrong, 'Tyneside's Home Guard Units: An Able Body of Men?', *Contemporary British History* 22 (2008), 257–78; D. J. Newbould, 'British Planning and Preparations to Resist Invasion on Land, September 1939 to September 1940', PhD dissertation, University of London, 1988; D. M. Clarke, 'Arming the Home Guard, 1940–44', PhD dissertation, Cranfield University, 2011.

118 See also Juliette Pattinson, 'Passing Performances: The Gendering of Military Identity in the SOE', PhD dissertation, University of Lancaster 2003.

119 Gerard De Groot, 'I Love the Scent of Cordite in Your Hair: Gender Dynamics in Mixed Anti-Aircraft Batteries during the Second World War', *History* 82: 265 (1997), 73–92; idem, 'Whose Finger on the Trigger? Mixed Anti-Aircraft Batteries and the Female Combat Taboo', *WH* 4 (1997), 434–53; idem, 'Lipstick on Her Nipples, Cordite in Her Hair: Sex and Romance among British Servicewomen during the Second World War', in Gerard de Groot and Corinna Peniston-Bird (eds), *A Soldier and a Woman: Sexual Integration in the Military* (Harlow: Pearson/Longman, 2000); Jutta Schwarzkopf, 'Combatant or Non Combatant? The Ambiguous Status of Women in British Anti Aircraft Batteries during the Second World War', *W&S* 28 (2009), 105–31.

120 See also Andrea Harris, 'Venereal Disease in the Military in Britain through Conflict and Reconstruction, 1939–50', PhD dissertation, University of Southampton, 2009.

There was the same concern, too, for morale, which has been explored beyond particular campaigns.[121] Alan Robinson, *Chaplains at War: The Role of Clergymen during World War II* (2012), contributes to the understanding of morale.[122] So, too, does the important study, Mark Harrison, *Medicine and Victory: British Military Medicine in the Second World War* (2004), which shows that developments like penicillin and mepacrim were just as crucial to allied victory as men and guns in campaigns such as those in Italy and Burma.[123] S. Paul Mackenzie deals with one aspect of British POWs in *The Colditz Myth: British and Commonwealth Prisoners of War in Nazi Germany* (2004) but, generally, accounts of POWs tend to be popular in nature.[124]

Wartime cinema has been covered in a previous section and mention made of S. Paul Mackenzie, *British War Films, 1939–45: The Cinema and the Services* (2001), but the projection of the army's image to the public is also examined in Fred McGlade, *The History of the British Army Film and Photographic Unit in the Second World War* (2010). Jeremy Crang, *The British Army and the People's War, 1939–1945* (2000), demonstrates that the radically minded Adjutant General, Sir Ronald Adam, came to terms with a citizen army very different from that which its regular officers had previously experienced, his impact shown in officer selection and maintenance of morale.[125] A crucial figure, Adam now has a well-deserved biography in Roger Broad, *The Radical General: Sir Ronald Adam and Britain's New Model Army, 1941–46* (2013). In particular, there was the understanding that British manpower was finite and a citizen army must be

---

121 David Reynolds, 'The GI and Tommy in Wartime Britain: The Army "Inter-Attachment" Scheme of 1943–044', JSS 7 (1984), 406–22; S. Paul Mackenzie, 'Vox Populi: British Army Newspapers in the Second World War', *JCH* 24 (1989), 665–81.

122 See also Alan Robinson, 'Lighten Our Darkness? Army Chaplains of the British Empire in Two World Wars', *WH* 6 (1999), 479–85; D. G. Coulter, 'The Church of Scotland Chaplains in the Second World War', PhD dissertation, University of Edinburgh, 1998.

123 See also Emma Newlands, 'They Even Gave Us Oranges on One Occasion: Human Experimentation in the British Army during the Second World War', *W&S* 32 (2013), 19–63.

124 See also Barbara Hately-Broad, 'Prisoner of War Families and the British Government during the Second World War', PhD dissertation, University of Sheffield, 2003.

125 See also J. A. Crang, 'The British Army as a Social Institution, 1939–45', in Hew Strachan (ed.), *The British Army, Manpower and Society: Towards 2000* (London: Frank Cass, 2000), pp. 16–35.

conserved.[126] Interestingly, there has not been the same focus on studying units below army level as with the Great War but this would be beneficial.[127] One interesting aspect examined in an unpublished dissertation is the recruitment of German and Austrian Jews.[128]

Irrespective of when the army might be re-introduced to North West Europe, there were attempts to create new kinds of forces to take the battle to occupied Europe. Commandos and airborne forces again tend to attract popular accounts but there are also academic analyses, albeit mostly unpublished.[129] Commandos were utilised against targets in Norway, although early British amphibious operations were not a great success.[130] Military support for resistance activities in occupied Europe was also sometimes problematic.[131]

There has been a great deal of criticism of the British operational methods in Normandy by popular historians. Academic work now largely refutes this, particularly the work of John Buckley, referred to previously, and Russell and Stephen Hart. Solid work on the North-West Europe campaign includes Stephen

---

126 E. Y. Whittle, 'British Casualties on the Western Front, 1914–18 and their Influence on the Military Conduct of the Second World War', PhD dissertation, University of Leicester, 1991; John R. Peaty, 'Problems of British Military Manpower, 1944–45', PhD dissertation, University of London, 2000.

127 See Tracy Craggs, 'An Unspectacular War? Reconstructing the History of the 2nd Battalion, The East Yorkshire Regiment during the Second World War', PhD dissertation, University of Sheffield, 2007.

128 B. Kern, 'Jewish Refugees from Germany and Austria in the British Army, 1939–45', PhD dissertation, University of Nottingham, 2004.

129 R. W. F. Buckingham, 'The Establishment and Development of a British Airborne Force, June 1940 to January 1942', PhD dissertation, University of Glasgow, 2001; Andrew Hargreaves, 'An Analysis of the Rise, Use, Evolution and Value of Anglo-American Commando and Special Forces Formations, 1939–45', PhD dissertation, University of London, 2008; John Greenacre, 'The Development of Britain's Airborne Forces during the Second World War', PhD dissertation, University of Leeds, 2008; Peter Brock, 'Excellent in Battle: British Conscientious Objectors as Medical Paratroopers, 1943–46', *W&S* 22 (2004), 41–57.

130 M. Christopher Mann, 'British Policy and Strategy towards Norway, 1941–45', PhD dissertation, University of London, 1999; idem, 'Combined Operations, the Commandos and Norway, 1941–44', *JMH* 73 (2009), 471–96; Tim Benbow, '"Menace" to "Ironclad": The British Operations against Dakar (1940) and Madagascar (1942)', *JMH* 75 (2011), 769–810.

131 Thomas Keene, 'Beset by Secrecy and Beleaguered by Rivals: The SOE and Military Operations in Western Europe, 1940–42, with Special Reference to Operation Frankton', PhD dissertation, University of Plymouth, 2011.

Hart, *Montgomery and Colossal Cracks: The 21st Army Group in North-West Europe, 1944–1945* (2000); Russell A. Hart, *Clash of Arms: How the Allies Won in Normandy, 1944* (2001); John Buckley (ed.), *The Normandy Campaign 1944: Sixty Years On* (2006); and another useful Army Records Society edition of Montgomery's papers in Stephen Brooks (ed.), *Montgomery and the Battle for Normandy* (2008).[132] A specialist study is Simon Godfrey, *British Army Communications in the Second World War: Lifting the Fog of Battle* (2013).

For the war in the Far East, there are two recent studies looking at how the 'forgotten' Fourteenth Army in Burma was transformed into one confident of operating in the jungle, namely Daniel Marston, *Phoenix from the Ashes: The Indian Army in the Burma Campaign* (2003), and Tim Moreman, *The Jungle, the Japanese and the British Commonwealth Armies at War, 1941–1945: Fighting Methods, Doctrine and Training for Jungle Warfare* (2005). Marston's focus is on the Indian rather than the British soldier, and the Indian army is also well covered in Alan Jeffreys and Patrick Rose (eds), *The Indian Army, 1939–47: Experience and Development* (2012).[133]

---

132 See also Stephen Hart, 'Montgomery, Morale, Casualty Conservatism and "Colossal Cracks": 21st Army Group's Operational Technique in North West Europe, 1944–45', *JSS* 19 (1996), 132–53; John Buckley, 'Tackling the Tiger: The Development of British Armoured Doctrine for Normandy, 1944', *JMH* 74 (2010), 1161–83; idem, 'Victory and Defeat? Perceptions of the British Army in North West Europe, 1944–435', *Global War Studies* 10 (2013), 76–97; E. R. Flint, 'The Development of British Civil Affairs and its Employment in the British Sector of Allied Military Operations during the Battle of Normandy, June to August 1944', PhD dissertation, Cranfield University, 2008; Charles Forrester, 'Montgomery and His Legions: A Study of Operational Development, Innovation and Command in 21st Army Group, North West Europe, 1944–45', PhD dissertation, University of Leeds, 2011; idem, 'Field Marshal Montgomery's Role in the Creation of the British 21st Army Group's Combined Arms Doctrine for the Final Assault on Germany', *JMH* 78 (2014), 1295–1320..

133 See also Sanjay Bhattacharya, 'British Military Information Management Techniques and the South Asian Soldier: Eastern India during the Second World War', *MAS* 34 (2000), 483–510; Pradeep Barua, 'Culture and Combat in the Colonies: The Indian Army in the Second World War', *Journal of Contemporary History* 41 (2006), 325–55; idem, 'Discipline and Morale of the African, British and Indian Army Units in Burma and India during World War II, July 1943–August 1945', *MAS* 44 (2010), 1256–82; Kaushik Roy, 'Military Loyalty in the Colonial Context: A Case Study of the Indian Army during World War Two', *JMH* 73 (2009), 497–530; Tarak Barkawi, 'Culture and Combat in the Colonies: The Indian Army in the Second World War', *JCH* 41 (2006), 325–55; idem, 'Battle and Culture: British Imperial Forces in South-East Asia in the Second World War', PhD dissertation, University of Minnesota, 2001.

David Smurthwaite (ed.), *The Forgotten War: The British Army in the Far East, 1941–45* (1992), accompanying a National Army Museum exhibition, has some useful essays. Gujendra Singh, *The Testimonies of Indian Soldiers and the Two World Wars: Between Self and Sepoy* (2014), betrays aspects of impenetrable post-modernism.

The fall of Singapore in February 1942 was a particularly low point, as discussed in Raymond Callahan, *The Worse Disaster: The Fall of Singapore* (1977); Alan Warren, *Singapore 1942: Britain's Greatest Defeat* (2002); and Brian Farrell and Sally Hunter (eds), *Sixty Years On: The Fall of Singapore Revisited* (2003). There had been a persistent underestimation of Japanese capabilities.[134] The fate of allied prisoners of war in Japanese hands contributed to the racial antagonisms apparent in the war in the Far East.[135]

Defeat in Malaya and Singapore exposed Burma and India to the Japanese. Like the campaign in North Africa, that in Burma has attracted a great deal of coverage. An early academic study of strategic aspects was Raymond Callahan, *Burma, 1943–45* (1978), but the outstanding account, drawing on Japanese as well as British sources, is Louis Allen, *Burma: The Longest War, 1941–45* (1984). There have been many accounts of the battles around Kohima and Imphal in 1944 and of the generalship of 'Bill' Slim, an altogether more attractive figure than Montgomery, not least for his essential modesty and humanity. While Robert Lyman has tended to write for the general reader in such titles as *The Generals: From Defeat to Victory, Leadership in Asia, 1941–45* (2000) and *Japan's Last Bid for Victory: The Invasion of India* (2011), his *Slim, Master of War: Burma and the Birth of Modern Warfare* (2004) is solidly based and Lyman has gone on to gain a doctorate on Slim.[136] There is also now Russell Miller, *Uncle*

---

134 Douglas Ford, 'British Intelligence on Japanese Army Morale during the Pacific War: Logical Analysis or Racial Stereotyping?' *JMH* 69 (2005), 439–74; idem, 'Strategic Culture, Intelligence Assessment and the Conduct of the Pacific War: The British-Indian and Imperial Japanese Armies in Comparison, 1941–45', *WH* 14 (2007), 63–95; idem, 'British Intelligence on Japanese Expansionism and Military Capabilities during the Second World War in Asia and the Pacific', PhD dissertation, University of London, 2002; Brian Farrell, 'High Command, Irregular Forces and Defending Malaya, 1941–42', *Global War Studies* 8 (2011), 32–65; O. C. Chung, 'Operation Matador and the Outbreak of War in the Far East: The British Plan to Forestall the Japanese, 1940–41', PhD dissertation, University of London, 1985.

135 Tatjana Kraljic, 'Forgotten Armies: British and American Troops in South-East Asia and the Brutalisation of Warfare, 1942–45', PhD dissertation, University of London, 2005

136 Robert Lyman, 'A Discussion of Field Marshal Bill Slim as Military Commander', PhD dissertation, University of East Anglia, 2012.

Bill: The Authorised Biography of Field Marshal Viscount Slim (2011). Logistics was an immensely important aspect of the war in the Far East and unpublished work looks at the RAF's co-operation with the army and the issue of rations.[137]

The fate of Singapore contributed to the creation of the Indian National Army, which is among the subjects dealt with in Christopher Bayly and Tim Harper, *Forgotten Armies: The Fall of British Asia, 1941–45* (2006). Bayly and Harper have continued the story of the re-assertion of colonial rule in *Forgotten Wars: Freedom and Revolution in Southeast Asia* (2007), a period also partly covered by Peter Dennis, *Troubled Days of Peace: Mountbatten and South East Asia Command, 1945–46* (1987).[138] An older work on the INA is Peter Fay, *The Forgotten Army: India's Armed Struggle for Independence, 1942–45* (1993). Indian perspectives on the INA are found in K. K. Ghosh, *The Indian National Army: The Second Front of the Indian Freedom Movement* (1969).[139] Another consequence of the Japanese threat to India was the wartime promise of post-war independence, the unhappy consequence being partition of the former Indian army, the subject of the outstanding Daniel Marston, *The Indian Army and the End of the Raj* (2014).[140]

Demobilisation after the Second World War is the subject of a somewhat anecdotal Alan Allport, *Demobbed: Coming Home After the Second World War* (2009).[141] But, of course, wartime conscription remained in the form of national service until the last conscript left the army in 1963, the latter a consequence of the Sandys White Paper of 1957. L. V. Scott, *Conscription and the Attlee Governments: The Politics and*

---

137   A. C. Williamson, 'Co-operation between the British Army and the RAF in South-East Asia, 1941–45', PhD dissertation, University of Cambridge, 2002; Rachel Johnstone, 'Operational Rations and Anglo-American Long-Range Infantry in Burma, 1942–44: A Sub-Cultural Study of Combat Feeding', DPhil dissertation, University of Oxford, 2007.

138   See also R. Macmillan, 'The British Occupation of Indonesia, 1945–46', PhD dissertation, University of London, 2002.

139   See also Chandar Sundaram, 'A Paper Tiger: The Indian National Army in Battle, 1944–45', *W&S* 13 (1995), 35–59.

140   See R. B. Osborn, 'Field Marshal Sir Claude Auchinleck: The Indian Army and the Partition of India', PhD dissertation, University of Texas at Austin, 1994; Robin Jeffrey, 'The Punjab Boundary Force and the Problem of Order, August 1947', *MAS* 8 (1974), 491–520; Daniel Marston, 'The Indian Army, Partition and the Punjab Boundary Force, 1945–47', *WH* 16 (2009), 469–505.

141   See also Rex Pope, 'British Demobilisation after the Second World War', *JCH* 30 (1995), 65–81; idem, 'Demobilisation Planning and Achievement during and after the Second World War', PhD dissertation, Open University, 1986; Jeremy Crang, 'Welcome to Chivvy Street: The Demobilisation of the British Armed Forces after the Second World War', *The Historian* 46 (1995), 18–21.

Policy of National Service, 1945–51 (1993), deals with the initial decision to retain conscription while it is set in the longer context in Roger Broad, *Conscription in Britain, 1939–60: The Militarisation of a Generation* (2005), and the overly anecdotal Richard Vinen, *National Service: Conscription in Britain, 1945–63* (2014).[142]

The background, of course, was the onset of the Cold War and the necessity to situate the army within broader strategic policy in an age of nuclear weapons. The Cold War itself is the subject of an extensive literature that has embraced so-called 'traditionalist', 'revisionist' and 'post-revisionist' interpretations, the latter acknowledging the ultimate success of the West in achieving the collapse of communism in Europe between 1989 and 1991. A leading 'post-revisionist', John Gaddis has produced an excellent overview in *The Cold War* (2005), while the most recent research can be found in Melvyn Leffler and Odd Arne Westad (eds), *The Cambridge History of the Cold War*, 3 vols. (2010). John Young, *Cold War Europe, 1945–89* (1991) is a useful guide to the European dimension.

Colin McInnes, *Hot War, Cold War: The British Army's Way in Warfare, 1945–95* (1996), provides a useful general survey of British military operations in the post-war world in the context of changing British defence policy priorities, including the end of national service in 1963, the strategic choices at the close of the Cold War, and financial pressures. Another detailed study by David French, *Army, Empire and Cold War: The British Army and Military Policy, 1945–71* (2012), is a groundbreaking contribution to the still relatively sparse historiography of British army policy after 1945, although it is not an easy read. It is the first time that the British Army of the Rhine has received any real attention in published form.[143] Immediate concerns included occupation policy and the defence of Western Germany against the new Soviet threat, as examined

---

142 See also Wyn Rees, 'The 1957 Sandys White Paper: New Priorities in British Defence Policy', *JSS* 12 (1989), 215–29; Martin Navias, 'Terminating Conscription? The British National Service Controversy, 1955–56', *JCH* 24 (1989), 195–208; idem, 'The Sandys White Paper of 1957 and the Move to the British New Look: An Analysis of Nuclear Weapons, Conventional Force and Strategic Planning, 1955–57', PhD dissertation, University of London, 1989; Steven Martin, 'Does Your Country Need You? An Oral History of the National Service Experience in Britain, 1945–63', PhD dissertation, University of Lampeter, 1997; J. T. Fensome, 'The Administrative History of National Service in Britain, 1950–63', PhD dissertation, University of Cambridge, 2001.

143 See also Richard Aldrich, 'Intelligence within BAOR and NATO's Northern Army Group', *JSS* 31 (2008), 89–112; and especially Peter Speiser, 'The British Army of the Rhine and the Germans, 1948–57', PhD dissertation, University of Westminster, 2013.

in Paul Cornish, *British Military Planning for the Defence of Germany, 1945–50* (1995).[144] Slightly oddly, the post-war occupation of Libya has attracted particular attention.[145] Other specific areas are covered in works such as David Devereux, *The Formation of British Defence Policy towards the Middle East, 1948–56* (1990).[146]

There is no shortage of studies of post-1945 British defence policy *per se* such as David Brown, *The Development of British Defence Policy* (2010), and Robert Self, *British Foreign and Defence Policy since 1945: Challenges and Dilemmas in a Changing World* (2010).[147] Ian Speller, *The Role of Amphibious Warfare in British Defence Policy, 1945–56* (2001), covers one specific part of evolving policy.[148] Nuclear policy is analysed by Laurence Freedman, *Britain and Nuclear Weapons* (1980), and S. Twigge and L. V. Scott, *Planning Armageddon: Britain, the US and the Command of Western Nuclear Forces, 1945–64* (2000).[149]

The most painful aspect of post-war retrenchment was arguably the end of the role in South East Asia as covered in J. Pickering, *Britain's Withdrawal*

---

144   See also M. A. Longden, 'Britain and Europe: Quests for Security – An Examination of Military and Political Relations between the United Kingdom and the European Powers, with Special Reference to France, 1944–63', PhD dissertation, University of Leeds, 2000.

145   L. A. Appleton, 'Education Development in Western Libya: A Critical Assessment of the Aims, Policies and Methods of British Military Administration, 1942–52', PhD dissertation, University of London, 1993; Richard Worrall, 'Britain and Libya: A Study of Military Bases and State Creation, 1945–56', DPhil dissertation, University of Oxford, 2008; Sean Straw, 'Anglo-Libyan Relations and the British Military Facilities, 1964–70', PhD dissertation, University of Nottingham, 2011.

146   See also O. Zametica, 'British Strategic Planning for the Eastern Mediterranean and Middle East, 1944–47', PhD dissertation, University of Cambridge 1986; J. G. Albert, 'Attlee, the Chiefs of Staff and the Restructuring of Commonwealth Defence between VJ Day and the Outbreak of the Korean War', DPhil dissertation, University of Oxford, 1986; N. J. Ashton, 'British Strategy and Anglo-American Relations in the Middle East, January 1955 to March 1959', PhD dissertation, University of Cambridge, 1992; D. Varble, 'The Atlantic Partnership and Middle Eastern Strategy in the Early Cold War', DPhil dissertation, University of Oxford, 2000.

147   See also C. D. Murray, 'The Anglo-American Defence Relationship during the Kennedy Presidency', PhD dissertation, University of Ulster, 1997.

148   See also Christian Liles, 'The Development of Amphibious Warfare Doctrine and Practice in the UK and US, 1945–67', PhD dissertation, University of London, 2010.

149   See also N. J. Wheeler, 'The Role Played by the British Chiefs of Staff Committee in the Evolution of Britain's Nuclear Weapons Planning and Policy-Making, 1945–55', PhD dissertation, University of Southampton, 1988.

from East of Suez: The Politics of Retrenchment (1998).[150] In the face of its changing role, the army has had to adapt its doctrine as analysed in Julian Lider, *British Military Thought After World War II* (1985), J. J. G. Mackenzie and Brian Holden Reid (eds), *The British Army and the Operational Level of War* (1989), and Markus Mäder, *In Pursuit of Conceptual Excellence: The Evolution of British Military Doctrine in the Post-Cold War Era, 1989–2002* (2004).[151] Hew Strachan (ed.), *The British Army, Manpower and Society into the Twenty First Century* (2000), looks at general aspects of the army's relationship with society.[152]

The post-1945 world may have been one of 'cold war' between the major powers but it was hardly devoid of either conventional or unconventional conflict. The Korean War (1950–3), the Arab-Israeli Wars and the Gulf Wars were primarily conventional while the Vietnam War had a significant conventional element alongside the 'other war' being waged against communist insurgents. All of these conflicts have resulted in an extensive literature, as have the varying forms of insurgency and terrorism that have been even more prevalent. Consequently, only some selected more recent titles can be offered as a guide to the wider body of work. Moreover, the more recent the conflict, the more uncertain the historiography in terms of access to archival sources. For the Korean War, there are Callum MacDonald, *Korea: The War before Vietnam* (1986); Peter Lowe, *The Korean War* (2000); William Stueck, *Rethinking the Korean War: A New Diplomatic and Strategic History* (2002), and Allan Millett, *The War for Korea, 1945–1950: A House Burning* (2005). Overviews are provided by Callum MacDonald, *Britain and the Korean War* (1990); Jeffrey Grey, *The Commonwealth Armies and the Korean War* (1988); and the two-volume official history, Anthony Farrar-Hockley, *The British Part in the*

---

150 See also P. L. Pham, 'The End to East of Suez: Britain's Decision to Withdraw from Malaysia and Singapore, 1964–68', DPhil dissertation, University of Oxford, 2001; Susan Thompson, 'The British Military Withdrawal from Southeast Asia, 1964–69: Rhetoric and Reinterpretation', PhD dissertation, University of London, 2006.

151 See also John Kizely, 'The British Army and Approaches to Warfare since 1945', *JSS* 19 (1996), 179–206; Matthew Ford, 'Operational Research, Military Judgment and the Politics of Technical Change in the British Infantry, 1943–53', *JSS* 32 (2009), 871–97.

152 See also Marianna Dudley, 'Traces of Conflict: Environment and Eviction in British Military Training Areas, 1943 to the Present', *Journal of War and Cultural Studies* 6 (2013), 112–26; Jon Lamonte, 'Attitudes in Britain towards its Armed Forces and War, 1960–2000', PhD dissertation, University of Birmingham, 2011.

Korean War (1990 and 1995).[153] A specialised study is S. Paul Mackenzie, *British Prisoners of the Korean War* (2012).[154]

The other British conventional operations prior to the 1990s were the diplomatic disaster of Suez in 1956 and the military success in the Falklands in 1982. The best accounts for Suez are Keith Kyle, *Suez* (1991); W. Scott Lucas, *Britain and Suez: The Lion's Last Roar* (1996); and Anthony Gorst and Lewis Johnman, *The Suez Crisis* (1996).[155] The Falklands has generated an extraordinary amount of popular literature and memoirs given its short duration. Overviews are provided by Lawrence Freedman, *Britain and the Falklands War* (1988), and G. D. Boyce, *The Falklands War* (2005), while Freedman also contributed the two-volume *The Official History of the Falklands Campaign* (2005). The Falklands, of course, was fought against a backdrop of further defence retrenchment, as explored by Andrew Dorman, *Defence under Thatcher* (2002), and in the medium term the termination of the Cold War would bring yet more. It is instructive to compare the media coverage of the Falklands with the First Gulf War, for which the best guides are Valerie Adams, *The Media and the Falklands Campaign* (1986), and Philip Taylor, *War and the Media: Propaganda and Persuasion in the Gulf War* (1992).[156] Robert Scales, *Certain Victory: The US Army in the Gulf* (1994) and Anthony Cordesman and Abraham Wagner, *The Gulf War* (1996) deal with

---

153 See also C. P. Alcock, 'Great Britain and the Korean War, 1950–53', PhD dissertation, University of Manchester 1986; Julie Cocks, 'Allied Military Co-operation in the Korean War: Issues of Command and Integration in Lead-Nation Coalitions', DPhil dissertation, University of Oxford, 2004; James Goulty, 'Training Preparations and Combat Experience of the British Army during the Korean War, 1950–53', PhD dissertation, University of Leeds, 2009.

154 See also S. Paul Mackenzie, 'Progressives and Reactionaries among British POWs at Pyoktang and Chongson, North Korea, 1951–53', *JMH* 77 (2013), 203–28.

155 See also A. Al-Solami, 'British Preparations for the Suez War, 1956', PhD dissertation, University of Exeter, 1988; Jonathan Riley, 'Instinctive Leadership, Intuitive Decision-Making: A Command Study of General Sir Hugh Stockwell', PhD dissertation, Cranfield University, 2006.

156 See also Nora Femenia, 'National Self Images, Enemy Images and Conflict Strategies in the 1982 Falklands/Malvinas War', PhD dissertation, Syracuse University, 1992; David Wilcox, 'Propaganda, the British Press and Contemporary War: A Comparative Study of the Gulf War, 1990–91, and the Kosovo Conflict, 1999', PhD dissertation, University of Kent, 2005; Rachel Woodward, Trish Winter and K. Neil Jenkings, 'Heroic Anxieties: The Figure of the British Soldier in Contemporary Print Media', *Journal of War and Cultural Studies* 2 (2009), 211–23.

the First Gulf War, while the Second Gulf War is covered in Paul Cornish (ed.), *The Conflict in Iraq, 2003* (2004) and a comprehensive study. Michael Gordon and Bernard Trainor, *Cobra II: The Inside Story of the Invasion and Occupation of Iraq* (2007).

For those conventional conflicts in which Britain did not participate, Ahron Bregman, *Israel's Wars: A History since 1947* (2000) is the most up to date general account. On Vietnam, where there is again a contrast between revisionist and post-revisionist accounts (that now claim the United Sates was deprived of victory by Congress cutting financial aid to South Vietnam in 1972), the many general works include George Herring, *America's Longest War: The United States and Vietnam, 1950–1975* (1986); Gerard DeGroot, *A Noble Cause? America and the Vietnam War* (2000); Andrew Wiest (ed.), *Rolling Thunder in a Gentle Land: The Vietnam War Revisited* (2006); Mark Lawrence, *The Vietnam War: A Concise International History* (2008); Mark Bradley, *Vietnam at War* (2009); and Gary Hess, *Vietnam: Explaining America's Lost War* (2009).

The fact that a British serviceman has been killed on active service in every year since 1945 except 1968 when conventional experience has been so lacking demonstrates how far the services have been forced to confront the particular problems of low-intensity conflicts of one kind or another. As in other areas, British conduct of counter-insurgency has been regarded in the past as markedly different in terms of the adherence to the principle of 'minimum force'. However, there is increasing academic questioning of British exceptionalism in this area. The more traditional view is represented by Tom Mockaitis, who added to his work on the period between 1919 and 1960 mentioned previously, in *British Counter-Insurgency in the Post-Imperial Era* (1995), which takes the story up to the Dhofar campaign of 1965–75, and to Northern Ireland. Other general accounts include Robert Holland (ed.), *Emergencies and Disorder in the European Empires After 1945* (1994); John Newsinger, *British Counter-Insurgency: From Palestine to Northern Ireland* (2002), which is generally critical of the army; and Paul Dixon (ed.), *The British Approach to Counterinsurgency: From Malaya and Northern Ireland to Iraq and Afghanistan* (2012). Susan Carruthers, *Winning Hearts and Minds: British Governments, the Media and Colonial Counter-Insurgency, 1944–60* (1995) is more specialised.[157] Intelligence has also attracted a number of general articles as well as those on specific campaigns,

---

157 See also P. D. J. T. Jennings, 'British Mass Media Coverage of the Late Colonial Wars in Cyprus and Kenya in the 1950s', PhD dissertation, University of Wales, 1996.

as will be seen below.[158] David French, *The British Way in Counter-Insurgency, 1945–67* (2012) is in the forefront of revisionist studies, substituting the notion of 'exemplary force' for 'minimum force'.[159] Pseudo operations have been a particular development and can court controversy.[160]

Early experiences with combating the new politicised insurgency in the Greek Civil War are covered in two works by Tim Jones, *Post-War Counter-Insurgency and the SAS, 1945–52* (2001), and *SAS: The First Secret Wars* (2010). For Palestine, there are Bruce Hoffman, *The Failure of Britain's Military Strategy in Palestine, 1939–47* (1983); David Charters, *The British Army and Jewish Insurgency in Palestine, 1945–47* (1989); and David Cesarani, *Major Farran's Hat: Scandal and Britain's War against Jewish Terrorism* (2009).[161] British operations in the Canal Zone prior to 1955 have received less attention although the background can be traced in M. J. Cohen and M. Kolinsky (eds), *Demise of the British Empire in the Middle East: Britain's Response to Nationalist Movements, 1943–55* (1998)[162]

The Malayan Emergency was long regarded as the model of post-war counter-insurgency and has attracted a substantial literature including Anthony Short, *The Communist Insurrection in Malaya, 1948–60* (1975); Richard Stubbs, *Hearts and Minds in Guerrilla Warfare: The Malayan Emergency, 1948–60* (1988); John Coates, *Suppressing Insurgency: An Analysis of the Malayan Emergency, 1948–60* (1992); Karl Hack, *Defence and Decolonisation in Southeast Asia: Britain, Malaya*

---

158 See Keith Jeffery, 'Intelligence and Counter-insurgency Operations: Some Reflections on the British Experience', *INS* 2 (1987), 118–49; Richard Popplewell, 'Lacking Intelligence: Some Reflections on Recent Approaches to British Counter-insurgency', *INS* 10 (1995), 336–52; Rory Cormac, 'Finding a Role: The Joint Intelligence Committee and Counterinsurgency at the End of Empire', PhD dissertation, University of London, 2011.

159 See also David French, 'Nasty Not Nice: British Counterinsurgency Doctrine and Practice, 1945–67', *SWI* 23 (2012), 744–61.

160 See P. Melshen, 'Pseudo Operations: The Use by British and American Armed Forces of Deception in Counter-Insurgencies, 1945–73', PhD dissertation, University of Cambridge, 1996.

161 See also Tim Jones, 'The British Army and Counter-Guerrilla Warfare in Greece, 1945–49', *SWI* 8 (1997), 88–106; idem, 'The British Army and Counter-Guerrilla Warfare in Transition, 1944–52', *SWI* 7 (1996), 265–307; David Charters, 'British Intelligence in the Palestine Campaign', *INS* 6 (1991), 115–40; C. M. Smith, 'Two Revolts in Palestine: An Examination of the British Response to Arab and Jewish Rebellion, 1936–48', PhD dissertation, University of Cambridge, 1990.

162 Michael Mason, 'Killing Time: The British Army and its Antagonists in Egypt, 1945–54', *W&S* 12 (1997), 103–26.

and Singapore, 1941–68 (2001); and Kumar Ramakrishna, *Emergency Propaganda: The Wining of Malayan Hearts and Minds, 1948–58* (2002). Direct comparison, indeed, has been made between the lessons of Malayan and of Vietnam, as in Sam Sarkesian, *Unconventional Conflicts in a New Security Era: Lessons from Malaya and Vietnam* (1993), and John Nagl, *Learning to Eat Soup with a Knife: Counterinsurgency Lessons from Vietnam and Malaya* (2005). Malaya, however, has also come under the revisionist spotlight.[163]

For Cyprus, there is Robert Holland, *Britain and the Revolt in Cyprus, 1954–59* (1998), and for Aden, Jonathan Walker, *Aden Insurgency: The Savage War in South Arabia, 1964–67* (2004).[164] The 'Confrontation' between Malaysia and Indonesia is covered in Raffi Gregorian, *The British Army, The Gurkhas and Cold War Strategy in the Far East, 1947–54* (2002); David Easter, *Britain and the Confrontation with*

---

163 See also Anthony Stockwell, 'Insurgency and Decolonisation during the Malayan Emergency', *Journal of Commonwealth and Comparative Politics* 25 (1987), 71–81; Raffi Gregorian, 'Jungle Bashing in Malaya: Towards a Formal Tactical Doctrine', *SWI* 5 (1994), 338–59; Karl Hack, 'Iron Claws on Malaya: The Historiography of the Malayan Emergency', *Journal of Southeast Asia Studies* 30 (1999), 99–125; idem, 'Corpses, Prisoners of War and Captured Documents: British and Communist Narratives of the Malayan Emergency and the Dynamics of Intelligence Transformation', *INS* 14 (1999), 211–48; idem, 'The Malayan Emergency as Counterinsurgency Paradigm', *JSS* 32 (2009), 383–414; idem, 'Screwing Down the People: The Malayan Emergency, Decolonisation and Ethnicity', in Hans Antlöv and Stein Tønnesson (eds), *Imperial Policy and Southeast Asian Nationalism. 1930–57* (Richmond: Curzon, 1994), pp. 83–109; idem, 'Everyone Lived in Fear: Malaya and the British Way of Counter-Insurgency', *SWI* 23 (2012), 671–99; Simon Smith, 'General Templer and Counter-Insurgency in Malaya: Hearts and Minds, Intelligence and Propaganda', *INS* 16 (2001), 60–78; Kumar Ramakrishna, 'Transmogrifying Malaya: The Impact of Sir Gerald Templer', *Journal of Southeast Asian Studies* 32 (2001), 79–92; idem, 'Bribing the Reds to Give Up: Rewards Policy in the Malayan Emergency', *WH* 9 (2002), 332–53; Huw Bennett, 'A Very Salutary Effect: The Counter-Terror Strategy in the Early Malayan Emergency', *JSS* 32 (2009), 415–44; M. Zarougui, 'Propaganda and Psychological Warfare in Guerrilla and Counter-Guerrilla Warfare: The Malayan Emergency, 1948–60', PhD dissertation, University of Reading 1992.

164 See also Dimitrakis Panagiotis, 'British Intelligence and the Cyprus Insurgency, 1955–59', *International Journal of Intelligence and Counter-Intelligence* 21 (2008), 375–94; Simon Robbins, 'The British Counter-Insurgency in Cyprus', *SWI* 23 (2012), 720–43; K. A. Kyriakides, 'British Cold War Strategy and the Struggle to Maintain Military Bases in Cyprus, 1951–60', PhD dissertation, University of Cambridge, 1997.

Indonesia, 1960–66 (2004), and Christopher Tuck, *Confrontation, Strategy and War Termination: Britain's Conflict with Indonesia* (2012).[165] The other 'model' campaign in the Dhofar is covered in J. E. Petersen, *Oman's Insurgencies* (2007).[166]

It is the Mau Mau insurgency in Kenya, however, that has attracted most attention in terms of the minimum force debate. An early and still useful account is Anthony Clayton, *Counter-insurgency in Kenya, 1952–60* (1976). John Newsinger was one of the first to question the concept of minimum force in Kenya and debated the issue with Mockaitis in 1995.[167] Subsequently, David Anderson, *Histories of the Hanged: Britain's Dirty War in Kenya and the End of Empire* (2005), and Caroline Elkins, *Imperial Reckoning: The Untold Story of Britain's Gulag in Kenya* (2005), revived the controversy. David Percox, *Britain, Kenya and the Cold War* (2004), and Daniel Branch, *Defeating Mau Mau, and Creating Kenya: Counter-Insurgency, Civil War and Decolonisation* (2009) are somewhat less emotive texts than Anderson and, especially, Elkins, who has taken a particularly extremist position.[168] The most recent analysis is by Huw Bennett,

---

165 See also Raffi Gregorian, 'Claret Operations and Confrontation, 1964–66', *Conflict Quarterly* 11 (1991), 46–72; Christopher Tuck, 'Cut the Bonds Which Bind our Hands: Deniable Operations during the Confrontation with Indonesia, 1963–66', *JMH* 77 (2013), 599–624; J. A. Subritzky, 'Great Britain, the United States, Australia, New Zealand and the Malaysian/Indonesian Confrontation, 1961–65', PhD dissertation, University of Cambridge, 1997.

166 See also Geraint Hughes, 'A Model Campaign Reappraised: The Counterinsurgency War in Dhofar, Oman, 1965–76', *JSS* 32 (2009), 271–305; Marc DeVore, 'A More Complex and Conventional Victory: Revisiting the Dhofar Counterinsurgency, 1963–75', *SWI* 23 (2012), 144–73.

167 John Newsinger, 'Minimum Force: British Counter-Insurgency and the Mau Mau Rebellion', *SWI* 6 (1995), 47–57; Tom Mockaitis, 'Minimum Force, British Counterinsurgency and the Mau Mau Rebellion: A Reply', *SWI* 3 (1992), 87–89. See also John Newsinger, 'Revolt and Repression in Kenya: The Mau Mau Rebellion, 1952–60', *Science and Society* 45 (1981), 159–85; idem, 'A Counter-Insurgency Tale: Kitson in Kenya', *Race and Class* 31 (1990), 61–72.

168 See also David Percox, 'British Counter-Insurgency (COIN) Policy in Kenya, 1952–56: Extension of Internal Security (IS) Policy or Prelude to Decolonisation?', *SWI* 9 (1998), 46–101; idem, 'Internal Security and Decolonisation in Kenya, 1956–63', *JICH* 29 (2001), 92–116; Caroline Elkins, 'Alchemy of Evidence: Mau Mau, the British Empire and the High Court of Justice', *JICH* 39 (2011), 731–48; David Anderson, 'Mau Mau in the High Court and the "Lost" British Empire Archives: Colonial Conspiracy or Bureaucratic Bungle?', *JICH* 39 (2011), 699–716; idem, 'British Abuse and Torture in Kenya's Counter-Insurgency, 1952–60', *SWI* 23 (2012), 700–19; R. W. Heather, 'Intelligence and Counter-Insurgency in Kenya, 1952–56', *INS* 5 (1990), 57–83; idem, 'Counterinsurgency and Intelligence in Kenya, 1952–56', PhD dissertation, University of Cambridge, 1993.

Fighting the Mau Mau: The British Army and Counter-Insurgency in the Kenya Emergency (2012), who has become the leading revisionist. In an Army Records Society volume, Huw Bennett and David French (eds), *The Kenya Papers of General Sir George Erskine, 1953–55* (2013) adds materially to the debate by including material from the hitherto restricted 'Hanslope archive', which featured in the recent court case.[169] His interpretation, however, has been challenged while others including Bennett himself have also contributed to the on-going general debate.[170]

Perhaps surprisingly, the Northern Ireland campaign lacks an academic study though there is now an overview in a non-academic book, Nick van der Bijl, *Operation Banner: The British Army in Northern Ireland, 1969–2007* (2009). It should be supplemented by a number of academic journal articles.[171]

Involvement in Iraq and Afghanistan since 2001 has proved highly controversial, raising significant issues as to the culpability of the Blair government in deceiving the British public in the aftermath of the 9/11 terrorist attack on the

---

169 See also Huw Bennett, 'The Other Side of the COIN: Minimum and Exemplary Force in British Army Counterinsurgency in Kenya', *SWI* 18 (2007), 638–64; idem, 'The Mau Mau Emergency as Part of the British Army's Post-War Counterinsurgency Experience', *Defence and Security Analysis* 23 (2007), 143–63'; idem, 'Soldiers in the Court Room: The British Army's Part in the Kenya Emergency under the Legal Spotlight', *JICH* 39 (2011), 717–30.

170 See Rod Thornton, ' The British Army and the Origins of its Minimum Force Philosophy', *SWI* 15 (2004), 83–106; idem, 'Minimum Force: A Reply to Huw Bennett', *SWI* 20 (2009), 215–26; Huw Bennett, 'Minimum Force in British Counterinsurgency', *SWI* 18 (2007), 459–75; Paul Dixon, 'Hearts and Minds: British Counter-Insurgency from Malaya to Iraq', *JSS* 32 (2009), 353–81; Tom Mockaitis, 'The Minimum Force Debate: Contemporary Sensibilities Meet Imperial Practice', *SWI* 23 (2012), 762–80; and Bruno Reis, 'The Myth of British Minimum Force in Counterinsurgency Campaigns during Decolonisation, 1945–70', *JSS* 34 (2011), 245–79.

171 See Caroline Kennedy-Pipe and Colin McInnes, 'The British Army in Northern Ireland, 1969–72: From Policing to Counter-Terror', *JSS* 20 (1997), 1–24; Christopher Bass and M. L. R. Smith, 'The Dynamics of Irwin's Army: A Strategic Understanding of the British Army's Role in Northern Ireland after 1998', *SWI* 15 (2004), 1–27; Rod Thornton, 'Getting it Wrong: The Crucial Mistakes in the Early Stages of the British Army's Deployment to Northern Ireland, 1969–72', *JSS* 30 (2007), 73–107; Paul Dixon, 'Hearts and Minds? British Counter-Insurgency Strategy in Northern Ireland', *JSS* 32 (2009), 445–74; Aaron Edwards, 'Misapplying Lessons Learned? Analysing the Utility of British Counterinsurgency Strategy in Northern Ireland, 1971–76', *SWI* 21 (2010), 303–30; and Huw Bennett, 'From Direct Rule to Motorman: Adjusting British Military Strategy for Northern Ireland in 1972', *Studies in Conflict and Terrorism* 33 (2010), 511–32; David Charters, 'Have a Go? British Army/MI5 Agent-Running in Northern Ireland, 1970–72', *INS* 28 (2013), 181–201.

United States. Jason Burke, *The 9/11 Wars* (2012) is a reasonable overview while John Kampfner, *Blair's Wars* (2003), and Warren Chin, *Britain and the War on Terror* (2013) provide the specific British context. Jonathan Bailey, Richard Iron and Hew Strachan (eds), *British Generals in Blair's Wars* (2013), is an important work, covering Northern Ireland, Kosovo, Sierra Leone, Iraq and Afghanistan.[172] The earlier limited intervention of the Blair government in Sierra Leone is the subject of Andrew Dorman, *Blair's Successful War: British Military Intervention in Sierra Leon*e (2009).[173]

Iraq and Afghanistan, however, have raised much criticism of British counter-insurgency, suggesting complacency from past successes and a failure to adapt. There is the highly polemical Frank Ledwidge, *Losing Small Wars: British Military Failure in Iraq and Afghanistan* (2011), but articles can again supplement this.[174] Perceived failures in Iraq have also been highlighted in accounts by a political 'blogger', Richard North, *The Ministry of Defeat: The British War in Iraq, 2003–09* (2009), and a journalist, Jack Fairweather, *A War of Choice: The British in Iraq, 2003–09* (2011).

Clearly, the historiography of the most recent of the army's campaigns is still evolving for historians and, especially, postgraduates have always responded to the moving frontier of the 30 Year Rule for the release of government archives, now to be reduced to a 20 Year Rule. As suggested by earlier sections, however, there remains considerable scope for further examination of so many aspects of the British army's past.

---

172 See also Paul Cornish and Andrew Dorman, 'Blair's Wars and Brown's Budgets: From Strategic Defence Review to Strategic Decay in Less than a Decade', *International Affairs* 85 (2009), 247–61.

173 See also Richard Connaughton, 'The Mechanics and Nature of British Intervention into Sierra Leone (2000) and Afghanistan (2001–2)', *Civil Wars* 5 (2002), 77–95.

174 See Alice Hills, 'Basra and the Referent Points of Twofold War', *SWI* 14 (2003), 23–44; Warren Chin, 'British Counter-Insurgency in Afghanistan', *Defence and Security Analysis* 23 (2007), 201–25; idem, 'Colonial Warfare in a Post-Colonial State: British Military Operations in Helmand Province', *Defence Studies* 10 (2010), 215–47; and James Wither, 'Basra's Not Belfast: The British Army, Small Wars and Iraq', *SWI* 20 (2009), 611–35; Theo Farrell, 'Improving in War: Military Adaptation and the British in Helmand Province, Afghanistan, 2006–09', *JSS* 33 (2010), 567–94; Daniel Branch, 'Footprints in the Sand: British Colonial Counter-insurgency and the War in Iraq', *Politics & Society* 38 (2010), 15–34; Alex Alderson, 'The Validity of British Counterinsurgency Doctrine After the War in Iraq, 2003–09', PhD dissertation, Cranfield University, 2010; Sergio Catignari, 'Getting COIN at the Tactical Level in Afghanistan: Reassessing Counter-insurgency Adaptation in the British Army', *JSS* 35 (2012), 513–39.

PART III
Resources

Chapter 8

Teaching and Research Centres

From a position in the 1970s when military history was barely offered outside of the Department of War Studies at King's College, London, the department being established in 1962 – though the Chichele Chair in the History of War at Oxford dates from 1909, and was known as the Chichele Chair in Military History until 1946 – there has been an extraordinary growth in the academic profile of the subject in Britain.

Currently, undergraduate degree programmes in aspects of military history or war studies are available in Britain at Aberystwyth, Birmingham, Hull, Kent, King's College, Reading, Salford, Swansea and Wolverhampton. Of course, there will be individual courses in these areas taught as part of wider history programmes at several other institutions, notably where Masters programmes are on offer.

Masters programmes in aspects of military history or war studies are available currently in Britain at Birmingham, Buckingham, Cardiff, Chester, Edinburgh, Exeter, Glasgow, Hull, Kent, King's College, Leeds, Portsmouth, Reading, Swansea, and Wolverhampton. Other institutions offering more contemporary courses such as security studies and strategic studies (often taught by political scientists rather than historians) are Aberdeen, Aberystwyth, Birkbeck, Bristol, Brunel, Dundee, Kingston, Lancaster, Leicester, Nottingham, St Andrews, and Sussex.

In a number of institutions, academic staff are also grouped in research centres, these including Birmingham (Centre for War Studies), Buckingham (Centre for Security and Intelligence Studies), Exeter (Centre for the Study of War, State and Society), Glasgow (Scottish Centre for War Studies), Hull (Centre for Security Studies), Kent (Centre for the Study of War, Propaganda and Society), Reading (Centre for Strategic Studies), Sussex (Centre for the History of War and Society), and Swansea (Callaghan Centre for the Study of Conflict, Power and Empire). Others may have academic staff who come together through mutual interests as at King's College, London (Imperial, Diplomatic and Military History Research Group) or Leeds (War and Peace Research Group).

Many British institutions will be able to offer supervision at doctoral level. The Institute of Historical Research, part of the School of Advanced Study at the University of London, produces an annual list of *Teachers of History in the Universities of the United Kingdom* (also available online at http://www.history. ac.uk/history-online/teachers), which includes broad research areas. In addition, the Institute publishes annually *Historical Research for Higher Degrees in the United Kingdom: Theses Completed* (also available online at http://www.history. ac.uk/history-online/theses/completed), and *Historical Research for Higher Degrees in the United Kingdom: Theses in Progress* (also available online at http:// www.history.ac.uk/history-online/theses/in-progress). Together, these offer an overview of the areas of doctoral research in military history extending back to 1970, as well as current projects. The IHR lists have included Irish institutions since 2009. Theses are steadily being put online by the British Library EThOS Project at http://ethos.bl.uk/Home.do It does not cover all British universities.

In the United States, masters programmes in aspects of military history or war studies are available currently at Austin Peay State (Tennessee), Colombia College (Missouri), East Tennessee State, Georgia Southern, Hawaii Pacific, High Point (North Carolina), Indianapolis, Norwich (Vermont), Sam Houston State (Texas), South Dakota, West Georgia, Western Illinois, Texas at El Paso, and Wright State (Ohio). Masters programmes and postgraduate supervision is available at Alabama, George Mason (Virginia), George Washington, Duke (North Carolina), Houston, Kansas, Nebraska-Lincoln, New Mexico, North Carolina at Chapel Hill, North Texas, Ohio State, Penn State, Southern Mississippi, Tennessee, Temple (Philadelphia), Texas A & M, Texas Christian, and Texas Tech. In Canada, masters programmes and postgraduate supervision is available at Calgary, New Brunswick, and Royal Military College, Canada (Ontario). In Australia, such programmes are available at Australian National University (Canberra).

In the United States, research centres include Duke and North Carolina at Chapel Hill (Triangle Institute for Security Studies), Florida State (Institute of World War Two and the Human Experience), Massachusetts Boston (William Joiner Institute for the Study of War and Social Consequences), North Texas (Military History Center), Norwich (Center for the Study of War and Peace), Ohio State (Mershon Center for International Security Studies), Shepherd (George Tyler Moore Center for the Study of the Civil War), Southern Mississippi (Dale Center for the Study of War and Society), Tennessee (Center for the Study of War and Society), Texas at Austin (Military History Institute), Texas Tech (Vietnam Center and Archive), and Virginia Military Institute (Adams Center for Military History). In Canada research centres include Calgary (Centre for Military and Strategic Studies), New Brunswick (Gregg Centre for the Study of War and Society), and Wilfrid Laurier (Laurier Centre for Military,

Strategic and Disarmament Studies). Elsewhere there are research centres at the Australian National University (Strategic and Defence Studies Centre), University of Ireland Maynooth (Centre for Military History and Strategic Studies), and University College Dublin (Centre for War Studies).

Many US theses can be located through ProQuest at http://www.proquest.com/en-US/catalogs/databases/detail/pqdt.shtml

In its July issue each year the *Journal of Military History* produces a list of recently completed theses on military subjects. It is generally good for US and Canadian institutions but is often less comprehensive so far as Britain is concerned. However, the *Journal of the Society for Army Historical Research* also produces an annual list of theses completed on British military history worldwide in its spring issue. Mention should also be made of André Wessels, *A Century of Postgraduate Anglo-Boer (1899–1902) Studies: Masters' and Doctoral Studies Completed at Universities in South Africa, in English-Speaking Countries and on the European Continent* (2010), which has the great merit of including theses in Afrikaans.

Often postgraduates are attached to particular research projects for which support has been obtained from funding councils or similar organisations. Additionally, like-minded groups also form research networks. Publications invariably result, and projects also often involve conferences at which research papers are presented. Accompanying websites may be particularly useful as additional research tools when they include databases or similar material. Examples include:

Changing Character of War Programme [University of Oxford]
http://www.history.ox.ac.uk/ccw/

Legacies of War [University of Leeds First World War centenary project]
http://arts.leeds.ac.uk/legaciesofwar/

Nations, Borders and Identities: The Revolutionary and Napoleonic Wars in European Experiences and Memories [Joint British and German Project of Free University of Berlin and University of York, but website hosted by University of North Carolina]
http://www.unc.edu/nbi/

The British Empire at War Research Group [Based at University of London]
http://britishempireatwar.org/

The Soldier in Later Mediaeval England [Database of soldiers, 1369–1453, from project at University of Southampton]
http://www.icmacentre.ac.uk/soldier/database/

Soldiers and Soldiering in Britain, 1750–1815 [Based at University of Leeds]
http://redcoats.ning.com/

Second World War Military Operations Research Group [A UK-wide academic group but convened from University of Birmingham]
https://secondworldwaroperationsresearchgroup.wordpress.com/

Mutiny on the Margins: New Perspectives on the Indian Uprising of 1857 project [Based at the University of Edinburgh]
http//www.csas.ed.ac.uk/mutiny/

The Centenary of the First World War has resulted in the Arts and Humanities Research Council funding five 'engagement centres' to promote work on the war in co-operation with local and community groups. Each centre is something of a consortium and has a different point of interest. They are:

Centre for Hidden Histories [University of Nottingham]
www.hiddenhistories.ac.uk

Gateways to the First World War [University of Kent]
www.gatewaysfww.org.uk

Everyday Lives in War [University of Hertfordshire]
www.everydaylivesinwar.herts.ac.uk

Living Legacies 1914–18 [Queen's Belfast]
www.livinglegacies1914-18.ac.uk

Voices of War and Peace [University of Birmingham]
www.voicesofwarandpeace.org

Chapter 9

Reference Works

Good examples of the contemporary approach to military history over the whole period of the history of warfare are Charles Townshend (ed.), *The Oxford History of Modern War* (2000), and Geoffrey Parker (ed.), *The Cambridge History of Warfare* (2005). Useful as general reference works, too, are André Corvisier (ed.), *A Dictionary of Military History and the Art of War* in the English edn revised, expanded and edited by John Childs (1994); R. Ernest and Trevor N. Dupuy (eds), *The Collins Encyclopedia of Military History: From 3500 BC to the Present* 4th edn. (1993); Richard Holmes (ed.), *The Oxford Companion to Military History* (2001); and Tony Jacques (ed.), *Dictionary of Battles and Sieges: A Guide to 8,500 Battles from Antiquity to the 21st Century*, 3 vols. (2006). While there is no 'companion' for the history of the British army, there are Ian McGibbon, *The Oxford Companion to New Zealand Military History* (2000); Peter Dennis and Jeffrey Grey, *The Oxford Companion to Australian Military History* (2008); J. L. Granatstein and Dean Oliver, *The Oxford Companion to Canadian Military History* (2010); and Kaushik Roy, *The Oxford Companion to Modern Warfare in India* (2009). For the First World War, Robin Higham and Dennis Showalter (eds), *Researching World War I: A Handbook* (2003), and John Horne (ed.), *A Companion to World War One* (2010) are also useful guides to current research. For the Second World War, there is I. C. B. Dear and M.R. D. Foot (eds), *The Oxford Companion to the Second World War* (1995).

While primarily interested in subjects of American interest, ABC Clio has produced a number of encyclopedias that include David and Jeanne Heidler (eds), *Encyclopedia of the War of 1812* (1997); Harold Raugh, *The Victorians at War, 1815–1914: An Encyclopedia of British Military History* (2004); and Spencer Tucker (ed.), *Encyclopedia of North American Colonial Conflicts to 1775: A Political, Social and Military History* (2008). For the Indian Mutiny, there is P. J. O. Taylor (ed.), *A Companion to the Indian Mutiny of 1857* (1996), and for the Anglo-Boer War there is Daniel Hall, Franzjohan Pretorius and Gilbert Torlage (eds), *The Hall Handbook of the Anglo-Boer War* (1999).

The overall state of the subject has been reviewed by Jeremy Black, *Rethinking Military History* (2004), and Matthew Hughes and William Philpott (eds), *Modern Military History* (2006). Stephen Morillo and Michael Pavkovic, *What is Military History?* (2006) will strike many readers as excessively theoretical and philosophical in its approach.

Not unexpectedly, general reference works tend to become outdated. This is certainly true of Robin Higham (ed.), *A Guide to the Sources of British Military History* (1972); Anthony Bruce, *An Annotated Bibliography of the British Army, 1660–1914* (1975); and Gerry Jordan (ed.), *British Military History: A Supplement to Robin Higham's Guide to the Sources* (1988); though they do retain their utility in listing older works. Higham, for example, includes lists of all official histories for Britain and the Dominions from both world wars, and of the inter-war Carnegie Endowment for International Peace 'Preliminary Economic Studies of the World War' series. Higham's original 1972 edition is also available online at http://books.google.co.uk/books/about/A_guide_to_the_sources_of_British_milita.html?id=7n09AAAAIAAJ&redir_esc=y

Charles Messenger (ed.), *Reader's Guide to Military History* (2001), is a very substantial volume running to over 900 pages, with an extensive coverage of all armies and periods. While contributed by leading specialists, however, the individual entries are sometimes relatively limited in extent, typically listing perhaps a dozen or so monographs with a short linking analytical commentary although some have 20 or more listed.

Arthur S. White, *A Bibliography of Regimental Histories of the British Army* (1965) was last updated in 1988, and has been supplemented by Roger Perkins, *Regiments and Corps of the British Empire and Commonwealth, 1758–1993: A Critical Bibliography of Their Published Histories* (1994). Both White and Perkins have now been combined on one CD-Rom by Naval and Military Press as *Armies of the Crown*. Victor Sutcliffe, however, is undertaking an online bibliography of regimental histories for the Army Museums Ogilby Trust, which can be found at http//www.armymuseums.org.uk/

For British history generally, there is the annually updated *Bibliography of British and Irish History* (BBIH) by the Royal Historical Society, which contains over 518,000 references to monographs, edited collections, and journal articles from 1900 onwards. Since 2010 it has become a subscription service in association with the Institute of Historical Research and Brepols, a Belgian publisher, details of which can be found at http://www.history.ac.uk/projects/bbih

The International Bibliography of Military History, which reviews a selection of new monographs, has appeared annually since 1978 from the International Commission of Military History in association with the Dutch publisher, Brill and is again available by subscription, details of which can be found at http://www.brill.com/publications/journals/international-bibliography-military-history

Other more specialised bibliographies are Robin Higham (ed.), *Official Histories: Essays and Bibliographies from All Over the World*, 2 vols. (1970); Ronald Hackett (ed.), *South African War Books: Illustrated Bibliography of English Language Publications Relating to the Boer War, 1899–1902* (1994); Harold Raugh (ed.), *British Military Operations in Egypt and the Sudan: A Select Bibliography* (2008); and Donal Seaton, *The Western European and Mediterranean Theatres in World War II: An Annotated Bibliography of English Language Sources* (2008).

Oxford Bibliographies is a new online venture with a growing number of military history subjects surveyed. They can be located at http://www.oxford bibliographies.com/

Chapter 10

Journals

The principal academic journal for articles on British military history is:

Journal of the Society for Army Historical Research (Published in Britain by the Society for Army Historical Research since 1921). Initially only quasi-academic with an unhealthy emphasis on uniforms, badges and buttons, the Society has now become increasingly respectable and its journal increasingly academic.

Three other academic military history journals of particular importance often carrying articles of British military historical interest are:

British Journal for Military History (Published online by the British Commission for Military History at www.bjmh.org.uk)
Journal of Military History (Published by the Society of Military History in the United States since 1941, but known as *Military Affairs* until 1988)
War and Society (Published in Australia since 1983)
War in History (Published in Britain since 1994)

Other academic journals with a wider remit that have some articles of British military historical interest (with starting date in parentheses) are:

Armed Forces and Society (1974)
Canadian Military History (1992)
First World War Studies (2010)
Global War Studies (2004)
Journal of the Centre for First World War Studies (2004)
Journal of Conflict Archaeology (2005)
Journal of Conflict Studies (1980, but known as *Conflict Quarterly* until 1994)
Journal of Mediaeval Military History (2003)
Journal of Political and Military Sociology (1973)
Journal of the South African Military History Society (1967)
Journal of Strategic Studies (1978)
Journal of War and Cultural Studies (2008)
Small Wars and Insurgencies (1990)
Journal of the Royal United Services Institute for Defence Studies (1857)
Journal of the United Service Institution of India (1871)

General academic historical journals with occasional articles of British military historical interest (with starting date in parentheses) are:

Albion (1969–2005)
Contemporary European History (1992)
English Historical Review (1886)
French History (1987)
German History (1984)
Historical Journal (1958)
Historical Research (1923, but known as *Bulletin of the Institute of Historical Research* until 1987)
History (1916)
History Workshop Journal (1976)
International History Review (1979)
Intelligence and National Security (1986)
Journal of African History (1960)
Journal of Asian Studies (1941, but known as *Far Eastern Quarterly* until 1956)
Journal of British Studies (1961)
Journal of Contemporary History (1966)
Journal of Imperial and Commonwealth History (1972)
Journal of Modern History (1927)
Modern Asian Studies (1966)
Past and Present (1952)
Transactions of the Royal Historical Society (1872)
Twentieth Century British History (1990)
Victorian Studies (1974)

The German military history journal, *Militärgeschichtliche Mitteilungen*, produced an annual summary of journal literature, *War and Society Newsletter*, between 1973 and 1998. Sadly, there has been no successor but Ashgate have produced their 'International Library of Essays on Military History' series under the general editorship of Jeremy Black, each volume reprinting key journal articles. Thus far 22 volumes have appeared from a projected 34, the only purely British title as yet being Harold Raugh (ed.), *The British Army, 1815–1914* (2006), though others are relevant. In addition Ashgate have published separately Jeremy Black (ed.), *The Second World War,* 7 vols. (2007), which also bring together key journal articles.

Most academic journals are now accessible through a number of search engines such as Academic Search Complete, CUP Journals, EBSCOhost, InformaWorld, IngentaConnect, OUP Journals, JISC, JSTOR and SAGE Journals. *Historical Abstracts* (EBSCOhost) is a general tool for accessing articles in historical journals.

The *Journal of the Royal United Services Institute for Defence Studies* and the *Journal of the United Service Institution of India* are not included on these search engines. There is an online index, however, to the *Journal of the Royal United Services Institute for Defence Studies* at http://www.rusi.org/publications/journal/

There is also Robin Higham and Karen Cox Wing (eds), *The Consolidated Author and Subject Index to the JRUSI, 1857–1963* (1965).

There is an online index for the *Journal of the United Service Institution of India* at http://www.usiofindia.org/Publications/Journal/

Specialist journals published by societies with particular interests with articles by both academics and enthusiasts:

Bulletin of the Military Historical Society (1948)
Fort, journal of the Fortress Study Group (1976)
Irish Sword, journal of the Military History Society of Ireland (1949)
Soldiers of the Queen, journal of the Victorian Military Society (1974)
Stand To, journal of the Western Front Association (1980)

These journals are also not accessible through the search engines outlined above as all are by subscription to the society in question.

Indices of contents are online for
Bulletin of the Military Historical Society http://www.themilitaryhistorical society.co.uk/
Fort at http://www.fsgfort.com/publications/fort-journal/fort-contents. html
Irish Sword at http://www.mhsi.ie/thesword.htm
Soldiers of the Queen at http://www.victorianmilitarysociety.org.uk/
There is a partial index to contents of *Stand To* at http://www.westernfront association.com/wfa-publications.html
There is an online index to the issues of *Journal of the Society for Army Historical Research* since 2007 at http://www.sahr.co.uk/JSAHR.html
There are published indices for 1921–62, 1953–90 and 1991–2006

There are also other similar groups of often very knowledgeable enthusiasts, which publish journals. Examples include:

The Napoleonic Association Research Group:
http://www.napoleonicassociation.org/research.htm
The Anglo-Zulu War Historical Society
http://www.anglozuluwar.com/home/
The Crimean War Research Society
http://cwrs.russianwar.co.uk/cwrsentry.html

Attention should also be drawn to the British Commission for Military History, which embraces both academic and non-academic members. It arranges conferences and study days, including one at which papers are encouraged from postgraduates, and has a Newsletter with short articles as well as the online journal already referred to. The BCMH website is at http://www.bcmh.org.uk/

Issues of older professional military journals such as *United Service Magazine* (1829–1920), *Army and Navy Gazette* (1860–1921), *Broad Arrow* (1868–1917) and *Naval and Military Record* (1886–1936) are also available online from services such as the Internet Archive of the University of Toronto Libraries, Project Gutenberg, and the Families in British India Society (FIBIS), for which see http://wiki.fibis.org/index.php?title=Military_periodicals_online

Some are also available at the Internet Archive Text Archive at http://archive.org/

Chapter 11

Publishers' Academic Series

Former academic series were:

'British Battles' (Batsford, 1961–8)
'History of European War and Society' (Fontana, 1982–8)
'Origins of Modern Wars' (Longman, 1984–97)
'War, Armed Forces and Society' (Manchester University Press, 1987–95)

Current series are:

'Australian Army History' (Cambridge University Press)
'Birmingham Studies in First World War History' (Ashgate)
'Birmingham War Studies' (Bloomsbury)
'Bloomsbury Studies in Military History' (Bloomsbury)
'Cambridge Military Histories' (Cambridge University Press)
'Campaigns and Commanders' (University of Oklahoma Press)
'History of Warfare' (Cassell/Smithsonian)
'Contributions in Military Studies' (Greenwood/Praeger)
'Cultural History of Modern War' (Manchester University Press)
'History of Military Occupation' (University of Illinois Press)
'History of Warfare' (Brill)
'Laurier Military History' (Wilfrid Laurier University Press)
'Military History and Policy' (formerly Frank Cass, now Taylor & Francis)
'Military History' (Texas A&M University Press)
'Military Strategy and Operational Art' (Ashgate)
 'Modern Wars' (Edward Arnold)
'Modern Wars in Perspective' (Longman/Pearson)
'Modern War Studies' (Kansas University Press)
'Studies in Canadian Military History' (University of British Columbia Press)
'Studies in Military and Strategic History' (Palgrave)
'Studies in War, Society and the Military' (University of Nebraska Press)
'Twentieth Century Battles' (Indiana University Press)
'War and Culture' (New York University Press)
'War and Leadership' (University Press of North Georgia)

'War and Society in North America' (Ohio University Press)
'War and the Southwest' (University of North Texas Press)
'War, Culture and Society' (Continuum, now Bloomsbury)
'War, Culture and Society, 1750–1850' (Palgrave)
'Warfare and History' (formerly Routledge, now Taylor & Francis)
'Warfare in History' (Boydell & Brewer)
'Warfare, Society and Culture' (Pickering & Chatto)
'Wolverhampton Military Studies' (Helion)

Other university presses such as Oxford University Press and Yale University Press also publish military history without having a dedicated series.

Many long out of print books can be accessed online through JISC Historic Books, which combines Early English Books Online (EEBO), Eighteenth Century Collections Online (ECCO) and the 19th Century Books from the British Library Collection. Others have been digitised by Project Gutenberg, which can be found at www.gutenberg.org/

Equally, many older memoirs are being reprinted, usually in paperback editions, by commercial firms such as Helion, and Naval and Military Press. The latter has also reprinted the volumes of the Official Histories, and made these and other sources also available on CD-Rom.

Chapter 12

Archives

The internet has transformed the way in which archives can be located and assessed. In the 1970s, it was often the case of visiting archive repositories to consult catalogues on site, guided occasionally by the card indices of the National Register of Archives. More often than not, county record offices would supply a copy of their own index cards by way of reply. Now an extraordinary amount of information is available just by the click of the mouse.

The locations of all archive repositories in England, Wales, Scotland, Northern Ireland, the Channel Islands, the Isle of Man and Eire are listed by the ARCHON Directory maintained by the National Archives (formerly the Public Record Office) at Kew. at http://www.nationalarchives.gov.uk/archon/default.htm

The National Register and the Royal Commission on Historic Manuscripts have been located at the National Archives since 2003. Moreover, over 400 archive repositories in England and Wales have now placed many of their catalogues on the Access to Archives (A2A) database at http://www.nationalarchives.gov.uk/a2a/ This can be searched by keyword, reference or repository as well as by date. The National Register of Archives can also be searched by corporate name, family name, personal name, and place name at http://www.nationalarchives.gov.uk/nra/default.asp

These databases are regularly updated, and the National Archives issues annual thematic digests of its 'Accessions to Repositories' survey that are made available online at http://www.nationalarchives.gov.uk/accessions/ It is also distributed for publication in suitable journals and newsletters, the first being issued in 1994. The digest of military records is published annually in the winter issue of the *Journal of the Society for Army Historical Research*.

For Scotland, similar services are offered by the National Archives of Scotland. The National Register of Archives for Scotland can be searched online at http://www.nas.gov.uk/onlineRegister/ This does not include, however, records in local authority archives or universities, for which information is available from the Scottish Archive Network (SCAN), which covers 52 Scottish archives, at www.scan.org.uk/aboutus/indexonline.htm and the Archives Hub, which covers all of the UK, at www.archiveshub.ac.uk

The Public Record Office of Northern Ireland does not maintain a similar register for those private papers not already deposited with it, but those online catalogues available from archive repositories in Northern Ireland can be accessed through their websites as listed in the ARCHON Directory noted above.

For the papers of leading military personnel, there is an additional finding aid through the *Survey of the Papers of Senior UK Defence Personnel, 1793 to 1975,* compiled jointly by the Liddell Hart Centre for Military Archives (LHCMA) at King's College, London and the Hartley Library at the University of Southampton, Southampton compiling that for those holding senior posts prior to 1900, and LHCMA being responsible for those holding senior posts after 1900. For those serving prior to 1900 the list may be consulted at http://www.archives.soton.ac.uk/defence/ For those serving after 1900, see http://www.kcl.ac.uk/lhcma/searchlocreg.cgi For those soldiers who became politicians and for those politicians who served in the War Office, there are a number of published guides including Cameron Hazelhurst and Christine Woodland (eds), *A Guide to the Papers of British Cabinet Ministers, 1900–51* (1974), and the Royal Commission on Historical Manuscripts *Guides to the Sources for British History: Papers of British Politicians, 1782–1900* (1989).

AIM25 is an increasing online resource listing the archives of 100 higher education institutions, learned societies, cultural organisations and livery companies within the greater London area. It is managed through the University of London. Its military listing can be found at http://www.aim25.ac.uk/cgi-bin/vcdf/search?keyword=Military%20history

The principal repository for public military records (and many privately deposited records) is as follows.

The National Archives, Kew, Richmond, Surrey, TW9 4DU. The National Archives has a comprehensive online catalogue at http://discovery.nationalarchives.gov.uk/SearchUI/

It also has a range of finding aids online. In addition, as well as readers' guides and leaflets, it has published a number of catalogues including Michael Roper, *The Records of the War Office and Related Departments, 1660–1964* (1998); Ian F. W. Beckett, *The First World War: The Essential Guide to Sources in the UK National Archives* (2002); and J. D. Cantwell, *The Second World War: A Guide to Documents in the Public Record Office* (1993). A very much older publication, *Alphabetical Guide to WO and Other Military Records Preserved in the Public Record Office* (1931), is still useful, especially where records were lost to bombing during the Second World War. A number of collections have been digitised, including War Diaries from the First World War; Service Records of the Women's Army Auxiliary; 1917–20; Service Records of British Army Nurses, 1914–18;

British POW Interview Records for the First World War; and Durham Home Guard Records from the Second World War. These can be consulted at http://www.nationalarchives.gov.uk/records/army.htm

The website also offers a range of other online resources. The National Archives have co-operated with the commercial firm, ancestry.co.uk, to put online a number of military sources including the surviving personnel records from the First World War (WO 363 and WO 364). Equally another commercial enterprise, findmypast.co.uk, has put online other sources such as service records from 1806–1915 (WO 96) and the enlistment forms of the Imperial Yeomanry (WO 128). While these are primarily intended for genealogical research, they also allow databases to be compiled, for example, on the social composition of particular units. The cadet registers of the Royal Military College, Sandhurst (WO 151) and of the Royal Military Academy, Woolwich (WO 149) can also be searched online at http://archive.sandhurstcollection.org.uk/ All these require a subscription.

The National Archives of Scotland, H M General Register House, 2 Princes Street, Edinburgh, EH1 3YY. The online catalogue can be consulted at http://www.nas.gov.uk/onlineCatalogue/

There is an online guide to the military holdings at http://www.nas.gov.uk/guides/military.asp

A selection of images from the First World War military service tribunals for Peebles is online at http://www.nas.gov.uk/about/081103.asp

There are two published catalogues, *A Military Source List Part One: A Guide to Sources for Military History in Private Records held by the Scottish Record Office* (1996), and *A Military Source List: Part Two: A Guide to Sources on Military History from the National Archives for Scotland's Holdings of Government Records*

The Public Record Office of Northern Ireland, 2 Titanic Boulevard, Belfast, BT3 9HQ. The online catalogue can be consulted at http://www.proni.gov.uk/index/search_the_archives/ecatalogue.htm A range of leaflets are available.

The British Library, 96 Euston Road, London, NW1 2DB holds many manuscript collections of private papers but also the public archives of the India Office and East India Company, which are held in the Asia and Africa Collection. The British Library catalogue, which also includes its wider manuscript holdings, can be consulted at http://searcharchives.bl.uk/primo_library/libweb/action/search.do?dscnt=1&dstmp=1364489960359&vid=IAMS_VU2&fromLogin=true

A limited range of archives have been digitised including the Reports of the Censor for Indian Mails in France, 1914–15. The search facility for those records digitised can be found at http://www.bl.uk/manuscripts/Default.aspx

For the India Office records, there is a published *Select List of Private Collections in the European Manuscripts* (1985), and A. J. Farrington, *Guide to the Records of the India Office Military Department* (1982). In addition, there is also the more specialised Rosemary Seton, *The Indian Mutiny, 1857–58: A Guide to Source Material in the India Office Library and Records* (1986).

The principal repositories for private military records are as follows.

The Bodleian Library, Department of Special Collections and Western Manuscripts, Broad Street, Oxford, OX1 3BG. The online catalogue is at http://www.bodleian.ox.ac.uk/bodley/finding-resources/special/catalogues/ Twentieth-century international history and politics archives held within the University of Oxford as a whole have a separate online catalogue at http://ox.libguides.com/content.php?pid=134353

The Churchill Archives Centre, Churchill College, Cambridge, CB3 ODS. See the *Select Classified Guide to the Holdings of the Churchill Archives Centre* (1992), which can be supplemented by its online catalogue at http://www.chu.cam.ac.uk/archives/collections/ Records relating to the army can be found at http://www.chu.cam.ac.uk/archives/collections/subject/army.php/ The archives of Sir Winston Churchill are also available online http://www.churchillarchive.com/index/ They can be consulted online at the Centre itself free, or elsewhere by subscription

The Hartley Library, University of Southampton, Highfield, Southampton, SO17 1BJ. The online catalogue is at http://www.archives.soton.ac.uk/guide/ There are separate databases for the Mountbatten, Palmerston and Wellington collections as well as thematic guides online. There is also See C. M. Woolgar and K. Robson, *A Guide to the Archive and Manuscript Collections of the Hartley Library* (1992)

The Imperial War Museum Department of Documents, Lambeth Road, London, SE1 6HZ. There is a fully searchable online catalogue at http://www.iwm.org.uk/collections-research/ The website offers a range of online resources

The Liddell Hart Centre for Military Archives, King's College, University of London, Strand, London, WC2R 2LS. The online catalogue is at http://www.kcl.ac.uk/library/collections/archivespec/collections/lhcma.aspx/ So, too, are research guides such as Africa, South Asia and Special Forces at http://www.kcl.ac.uk/library/collections/archivespec/catalogues/researchguides.aspx

These research guides are available in printed form at the Centre and the online catalogue generally has superseded the published Consolidated *List of Accessions* (1986) and *Supplement, 1985–90* (1990).

The Liddle Collection, Brotherton Library, University of Leeds, Leeds, LS2 9JT. The summary guide to this collection relating to the two world wars is at http://library.leeds.ac.uk/liddle-collection

The National Army Museum, Dept of Archives, Photographs, Film and Sound, Royal Hospital Road, Chelsea, London, SW3 4HT. The online catalogue, which is still being developed, is at http://www.nam.ac.uk/inventory/objects/ Some material is available online at http://www.nam.ac.uk/online-collection/

The National Library of Scotland, Department of Manuscripts, George IV Bridge, Edinburgh, EH1 1EW. The online catalogues can be found at http:// www.nls.uk/catalogues/manuscripts
   The National Library is also in the process of digitising the *Army Lists*, details of which can be found at http://archive.org/details/nlsarmylists

The National Library of Wales, Aberystwyth, Ceredigion, Wales, SY23 3BU. The online catalogue is at http://www.llgc.org.uk/?id=117

   For amphibious or other joint operations with the army, there are additional records in the following.

The National Maritime Museum, Manuscripts Section, Centre for Research, Romney Road, Greenwich, London, SE10 9NF. The archive catalogue is available online at http://collections.rmg.co.uk/archive.html#!asearch

The Royal Air Force Museum, London, Grahame Park Way, Hendon, London, NW9 5LL. The online catalogue is available at http://www.rafmuseum.org.uk/research/default.aspx

The Royal Marines Museum, Eastney Esplanade, Southsea, Portsmouth, PO4 9PX. There is no online catalogue and enquires should be directed to archive@royalmarinesmuseum.co.uk

   Among the many other archive repositories that may be relevant, regimental archives should be mentioned. In many cases, regimental archives have passed to county record offices but others remain with the regiments and may or may not be catalogued. A full list of regimental museums compiled by the Army

Museums Ogilby Trust, which indicates the whereabouts of the archives, can be found at http://www.armymuseums.org.uk/ There is also *The Army Museums Ogilby Trust Guide to Military Museums in the UK* (2010), which contains the same information in printed form. An important archive of regional interest is the Sudan Archive of the University of Durham, Palace Green Library, Palace Green, Durham, DH1 3RN. The online guide can be found at https://www.dur.ac.uk/library/asc/collection_information/cldload/?collno=135

Chapter 13

Printed Primary and Digital Resources

As with archives, volumes of printed material such as *Hansard* and *Parliamentary Papers* that were once only available in the larger libraries can now be easily accessed online, though some collections are also available on the older technologies of microfilm and microfiche. Some sources are unlikely to be available online in the foreseeable future such as the reports on archives in private collections produced by the Historical Manuscripts Commission as listed by the Royal Historical Society at http://www.royalhistoricalsociety.org/histmanscommission.pdf

Online resources are increasing all the time although, of course, care will be needed in assessing the reliability of some sites.

In addition to those digital resources already mentioned, the following are the principal resources for historians of the British army.

Some of the early *Journals of the House of Commons* and the early *Journals of the House of Lords*, *Calendars of State Papers Domestic, 1537–1714*, and volumes of the *Victoria County Histories* are among a range of sources available through British History Online, a joint venture of the Institute of Historical Research and the History of Parliament Trust at http://www.british-history.ac.uk/Default.aspx

House of Commons Parliamentary Papers (including *Hansard* and House of Lords papers) are available online from 1688 onwards (*Hansard* from 1803) through ProQuest. *Hansard* is also available at http://hansard.millbanksystems.com/

British and Foreign State Papers, 1812–1960 are available online through HeinOnline

For newspapers and periodicals, a variety of online sources are now available, including:

Connected Histories: British History Sources, 1500–1900 (JISC funded)
British Newspapers, 1600–1900 (Gale)
British Periodicals (ProQuest)
17th-18th Century Burney Collection Newspapers (Gale)
18th Century Journals Portal (Adam Matthew)
19th Century Newspapers from the British Library (Gale)

19th Century Periodicals (Gale)
The Times Digital Archive from 1785 onwards
The Financial Times Historical Archive from 1888 onwards
The Economist Historical Archive from 1843 onwards
The Illustrated London News from 1842 onwards
UK Press Online (*Daily Mirror*) from 1903 onwards

A useful source for the Second World War is the Mass Observation archive at the University of Sussex, available online as Mass Observation Online, 1937–72 (Adam Matthew)

For the Northern Ireland 'Troubles' since 1968 there is the University of Ulster's Conflict and Politics in Northern Ireland (CAIN) website with a variety of resources at http://cain.ulst.ac.uk/

For material relating to UK battlefields, an invaluable source is the UK Battlefields Resource Centre of the Battlefields Trust at http://www.battlefieldstrust.com/resource-centre/index.asp

For war memorials and commemoration, there are the sites of the Commonwealth War Graves Commission at http://www.cwgc.org/ together with the UK National Inventory of War Memorials maintained by the Imperial War Museum at http://www.ukniwm.org.uk/

Film sources are available at:

News Film Online (Reuters and ITN) from 1910 onwards
Pathé News Archive
British Universities Newsreel Project (British Universities Film and Video Council)

The Dictionary of National Biography and *Who Was Who* are both available online through Oxford Online

It will be noted that Adam Matthew Publications and Chadwyck-Healey(ProQuest) have produced a number of online sources as well as microfilm and microfiche collections in the past. Thus, apart from those collections already noted, Adam Matthew Publications (http://www.ampltd.co.uk) have produced a range of Cabinet, Foreign Office and Confidential Print documents such as the Macmillan Cabinet Papers, as well as thematic collections. The back catalogues of Chadwyck-Healey (http://www.proquest.co.uk/en-UK/default.shtml) include microfilm versions of the papers of Jeffrey Amherst, the Dukes of Cambridge and Cumberland, and Garnet Wolseley.

Mention should also be made of the journals and series produced by local record and historical societies, which exist in every county. They are included in the Royal Historical Society's *Bibliography of British and Irish History* (BBIH). A full list of national, English, Irish, Scottish and Welsh history and record societies can be found at http://www.royalhistoricalsociety.org/textandcalendars.php

Moreover, since 1985, the Army Records Society has published an annual volume (and, occasionally two in three years) of historical documents related to the history of the British army. Its publications are listed at http://www.army recordssociety.org.uk/

Rather similarly, the Society for Army Historical Research occasionally issues special publications in addition to its journal, which are usually editions of unpublished papers. On occasion the Camden Miscellany Volumes series of the Royal Historical Society (available through Cambridge Journals Online) have included military-related sources.

Chapter 14

Practicalities

Basic training for history postgraduates in such aspects as compiling and using databases is available through History Spot, a sub-site of the Institute of Historical Research, which offers a range of other online and taught short courses. Details can be found at http://historyspot.org.uk/

There are a number of published guides to historical study and research. One of the best is Larry Butler and Anthony Gorst (eds), *Modern British History: A Guide to Study and Research* (1997), which includes sections on historical theory, using archives and libraries, computing techniques, managing and funding research, and the internet. Other useful guides include W. H. McDowell, *Historical Research: A Guide* (2002) and, albeit with an American perspective, Anthony Brundage, *Going to the Sources: A Guide to Historical Research and Writing*, 5th edn. (2013).

Index of Authors